IMAGES
of America

NORTHLAKE

On the Cover: Northlake Baseball celebrated its 60th anniversary in summer 2012. A long-standing tradition involves baseball players participating in a parade that proceeds through town. This baseball team is part of a tradition that has lasted for decades, handed down from parents to children.

IMAGES
of America

NORTHLAKE

Edgar Gamboa Návar

ARCADIA
PUBLISHING

ISBN 978-0-7385-9073-8

Published by Arcadia Publishing
Charleston, South Carolina

Printed in the United States of America

Library of Congress Control Number: 2012942215

For all general information, please contact Arcadia Publishing:
Telephone 843-853-2070
Fax 843-853-0044
E-mail sales@arcadiapublishing.com
For customer service and orders:
Toll-Free 1-888-313-2665

Visit us on the Internet at www.arcadiapublishing.com

To the younger Gamboas, Kalie and Xander:
enjoy all this area has to offer.

Contents

ACKNOWLEDGMENTS

After spending the first 10 years of my life in Chicago, I was more than a little apprehensive about moving to an unknown suburb named Northlake. Friends, school, and baseball played an important role in my life. That suburb would surely not have all those amenities that seemed vital to my life at that moment in time. The only link between these two places was a long stretch of North Avenue.

Little did I know that Northlake had more to offer than I could ever imagine. Baseball was more important here than back home. Friends began forging memorable moments in my life. And school? St. John Vianney and West Leyden High School provided an excellent education that has carried me this far. Along that route on North Avenue, the heart of this city remains. Businesses have come and gone, but many landmarks remain in a town that is truly "A City of Friendly People."

There are many people to thank for this project. First and foremost, Northlake mayor Jeff Sherwin has provided great insight and photographs that are unparalleled in this town. As longtime residents, we continue to be thankful for his leadership. Providing a place for my laptop, scanner, and myself has proven invaluable.

The staff members of the Northlake Public Library have shared photographs of their history that help tell the story of our community as well. People such as Pam Crowe, Norm Nissen, and Nancy Morris have shared some of their photographs, which will be treasured for years to come. The Northlake Fire Department has provided some of their photographs as well. And to the countless others who have contributed in some way or another, whether sharing stories or simply answering my questions, thanks!

Most important, though, are my mom and dad, who continue to be my heroes in so many ways. And to the Lord, for giving me every breath I take.

Introduction

The story of Northlake shows how patience, practicality, hard work, and determination will lead to success. The community, named for the intersection of North Avenue and Lake Street, was started in 1941 but was primarily built during the post–World War II housing boom. Incorporated in 1949, it was a town that in many respects was built backwards. The houses were built as "shells," with the interiors left for the new homeowners to finish after they moved in.

There were no curbs, sidewalks, streetlights, or storm or sanitary sewers, only gravel roads that fell apart after every winter or frequent flood plagued the area. Each home was served by its own septic system and water was provided by a central well.

Yet somehow the determination and sacrifice of the residents, with no master plan or guidance, transformed the town into the solid community we enjoy today. Those returning World War II veterans were determined to make our community a success, finishing their homes, installing sanitary sewers, providing a Lake Michigan water supply, installing curbs, sidewalks, and storm sewers, building the library, schools, parks, and churches, solving the recurrent flooding problems, and ensuring a strong economic base with large commercial and industrial areas.

Northlake is still a work in progress as we continue to build on the strong foundation laid by those early residents, who could have just as easily moved to another community rather than putting in the hard work to make our community the success it is today. Our thanks go to these early pioneers of the postwar Chicago suburban movement.

—Jeff Sherwin
Mayor of Northlake

One

Farmland, Shell Homes, and a Golf Course

Prior to incorporation, there was nothing but farmland in this unincorporated area of western Cook County. The major landowner was the Amling family, the renowned Chicago florists. In 1922, Westward Ho Golf Club purchased 200 acres to move their club and course to the quiet western suburbs in an attempt to avoid the urban sprawl of River Forest near Harlem Avenue and Lake Street, a place where Westward Ho had merged with River Forest Country Club in 1905. As much a social organization as a golf club, its members treasured privacy and exclusivity.

By fall 1923, the golf course was opened for play and former landowner Albert Amling was the first person to drive off the tee. This golf course enjoyed its location for the next several decades until 1957, when its land was sold to Automated Electric and to Villa Scalabrini Home for the Aged.

With the country at war, the defense plant in Melrose Park needed workers. Many of these workers desired to have their homes near their place of employment. The only sensible option was to build homes in nearby suburbs, such as North Lake City, further west of Melrose Park. Hundreds of "shell homes" went up in the early 1940s with owners who were willing to put in the weekend labor hours doing their own carpentry, plumbing, and electrical work.

Soon thereafter, commerce started emerging with taverns, stores, and markets. With plenty of new residents, challenges presented themselves as well. Fires ended some of the early businesses. City planning and street grids began to form, giving the town its structure. Eventually, a decision had to be made on whether to incorporate or merge with another town.

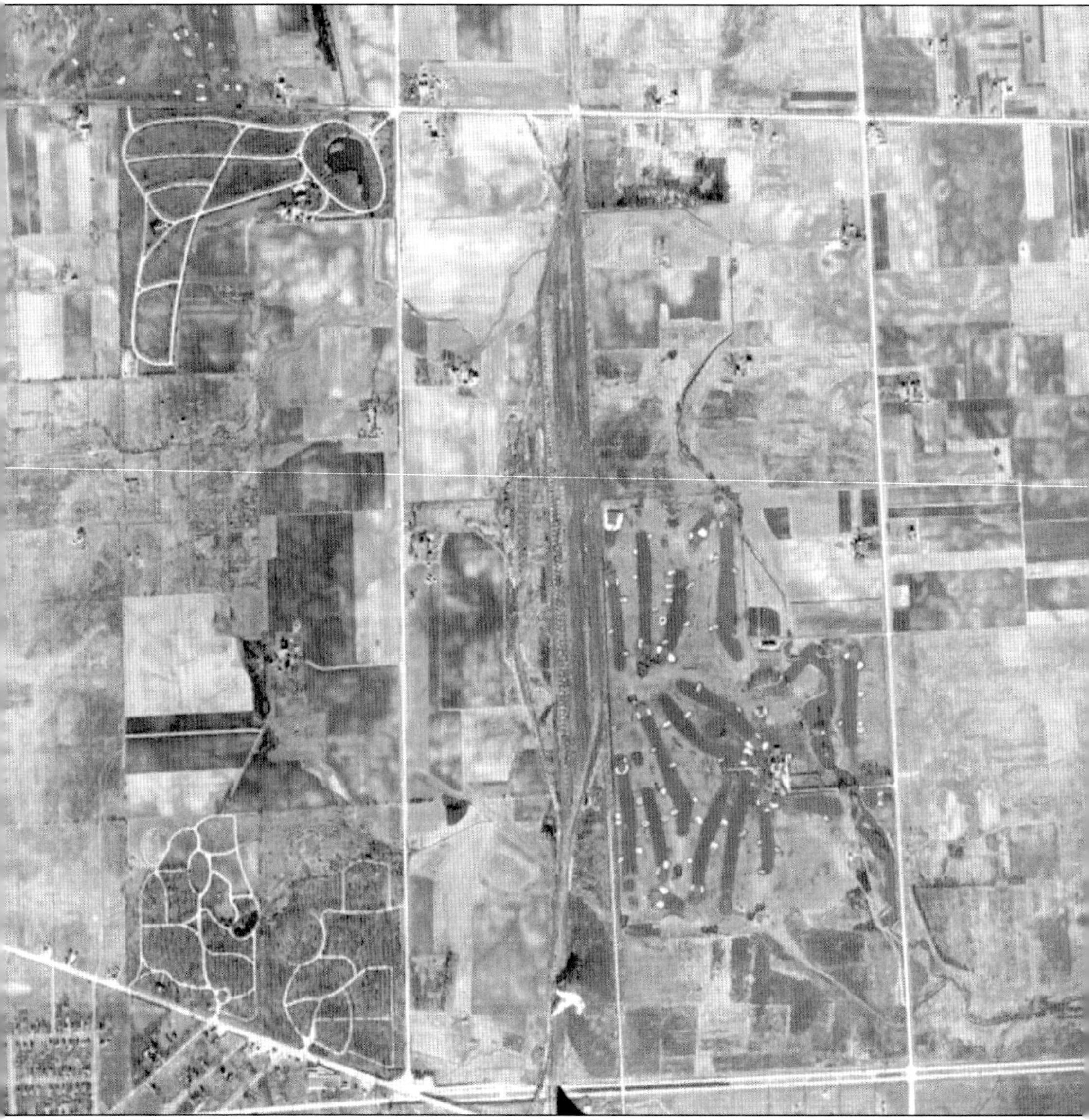

AERIAL MAP OF NORTHLAKE. This 1938 aerial view of Northlake shows the Westward Ho Golf Club west of Wolf Road and north of North Avenue. Rail lines ran along the course's western edge amidst the farmland. In the neighboring town, the cemetery was the only developed piece of property. The main thoroughfare is North Avenue, towards the bottom of the photograph. The diagonal street just south of North Avenue is Lake Street. Their intersection marks the western boundary of Northlake. Today, the city of Northlake is 4.4 square miles. (Courtesy of Bill Trudeau.)

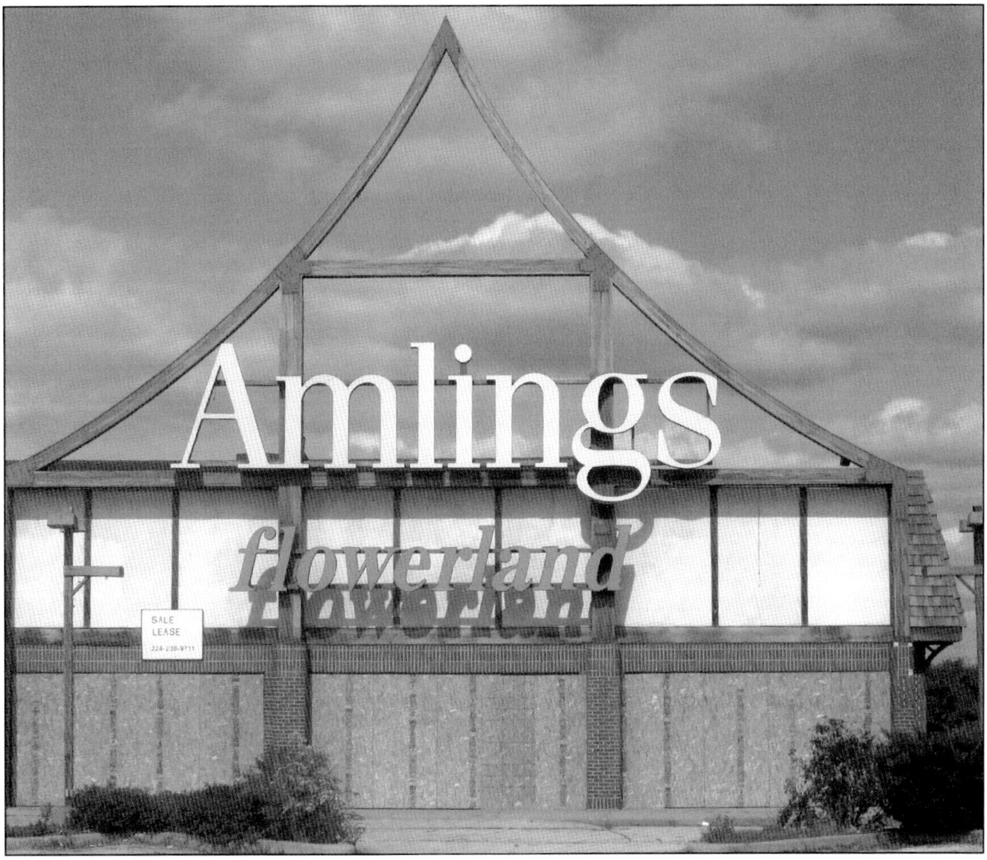

ALBERT FRIEDRICH AMLING. The land that eventually became the Westward Ho Golf Club was owned by Albert Friedrich Amling, the best-known florist in Chicagoland. He was a charter member of St. Paul's Lutheran Church in nearby Melrose Park and president of Melrose Park State Bank. (Both, author's collection.)

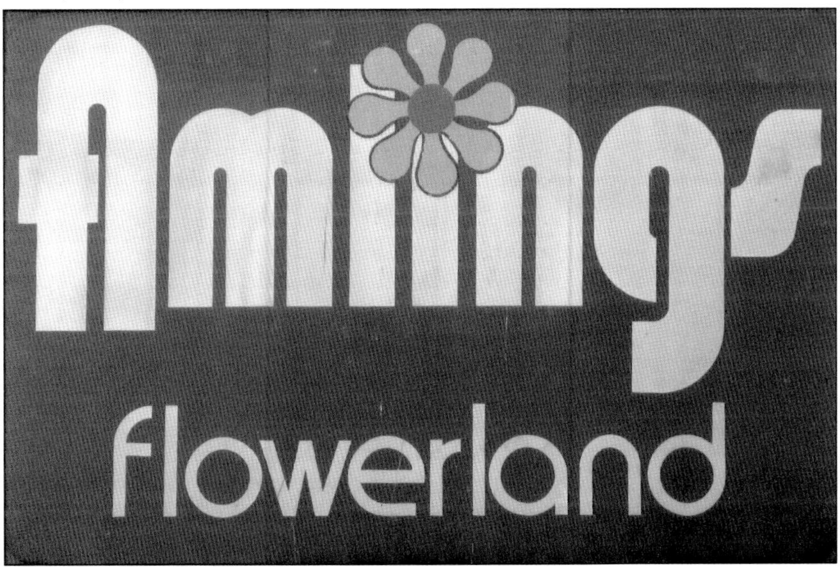

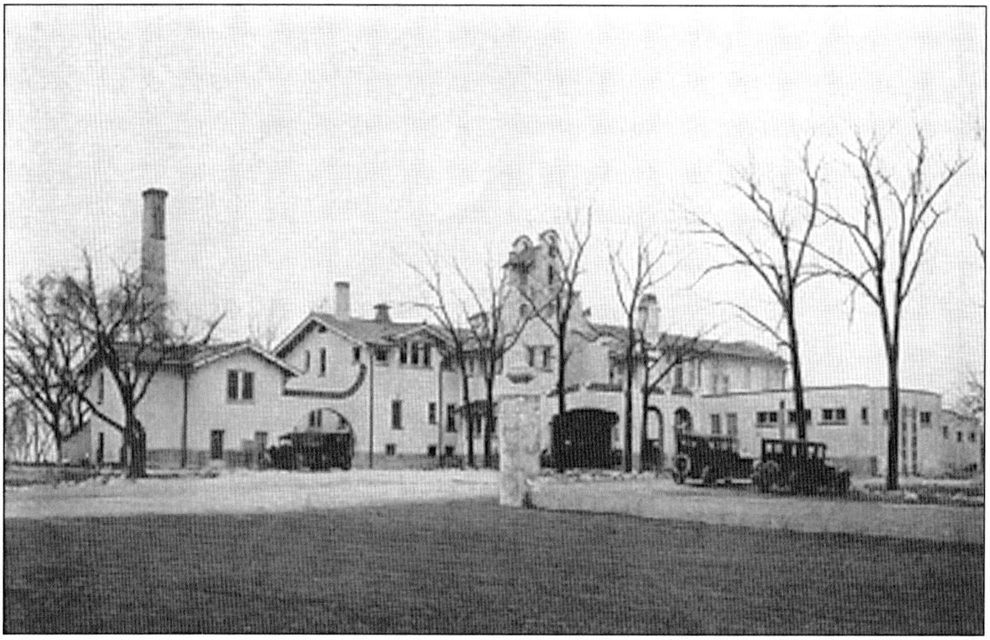

Westward Ho Golf Club. Before residents started living in Northlake, a large portion of its land belonged to the Westward Ho Golf Club. Members from the Oak Park Golf Club opened this club in 1923, where well-known golfers such as William Boyce Langford from Yale's national championship team played often, referring to it as their home course. Langford, who hailed from Austin, Illinois, became a prolific golf course designer. (Both, courtesy of Northlake City Hall.)

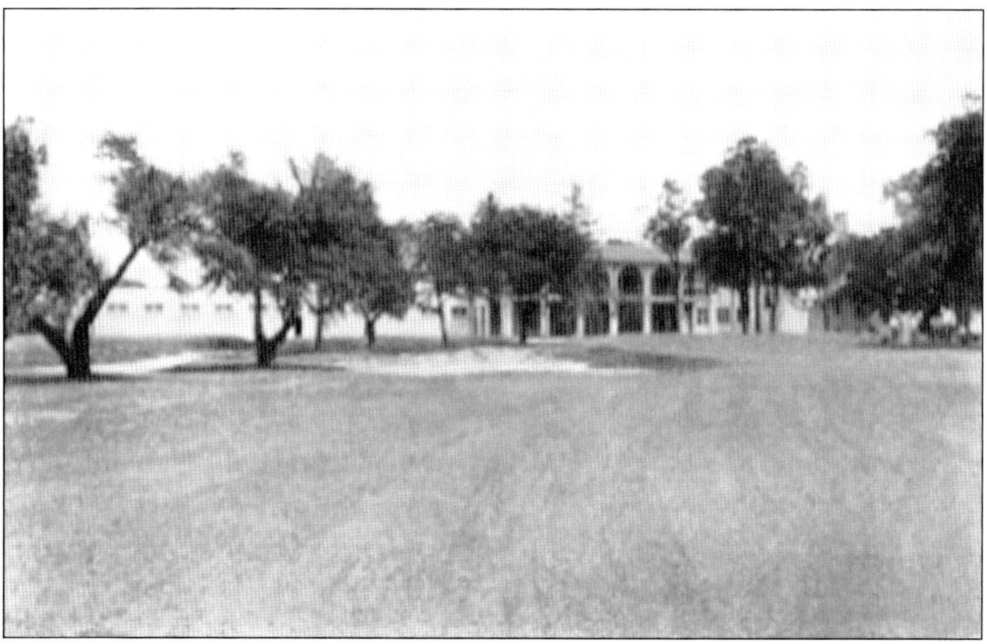

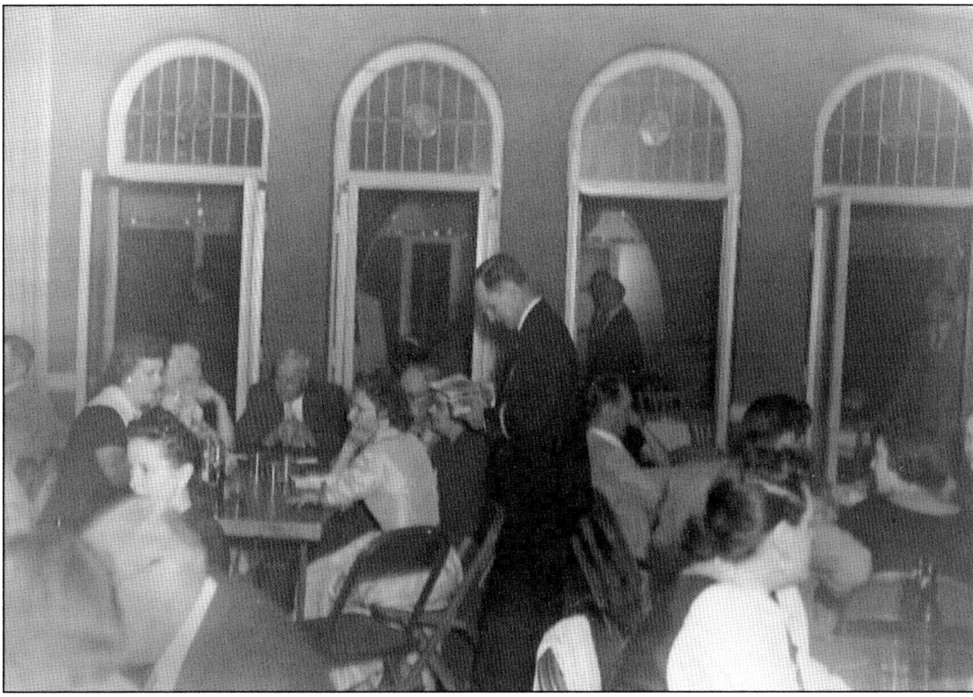

FIREMAN'S DANCE AT WESTWARD HO GOLF CLUB AND DISMANTLING. On October 9, 1954, the Northlake Fire Department held its Fireman's Dance (above) at the popular Westward Ho Country Club. The club, on Wolf Road and Armitage Avenue, was demolished in 1957 after the property was sold. Notice the opened doorways creating a ventilation system prior to the modern-day air conditioning system. The golf course was purchased by Automated Electric. The golf club's chimney, along with the rest of the building (right), was eventually dismantled in 1957, paving the way for the new development. (Both, courtesy of Northlake City Hall.)

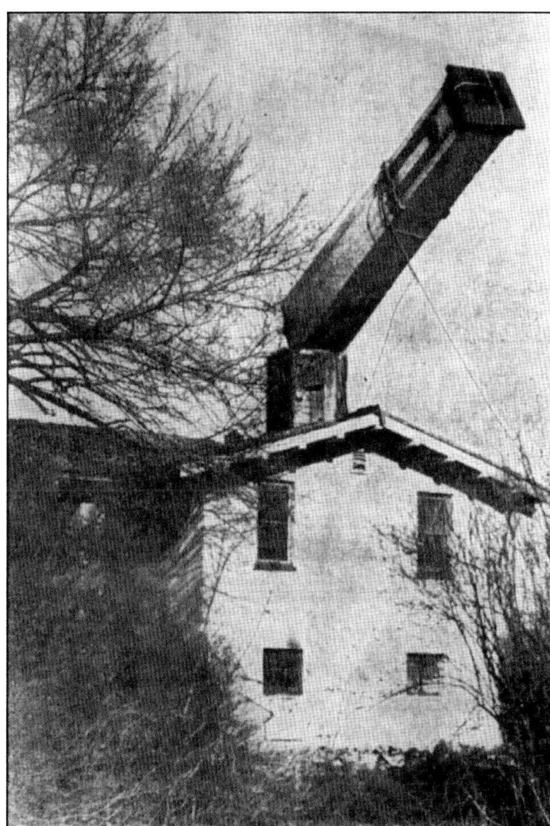

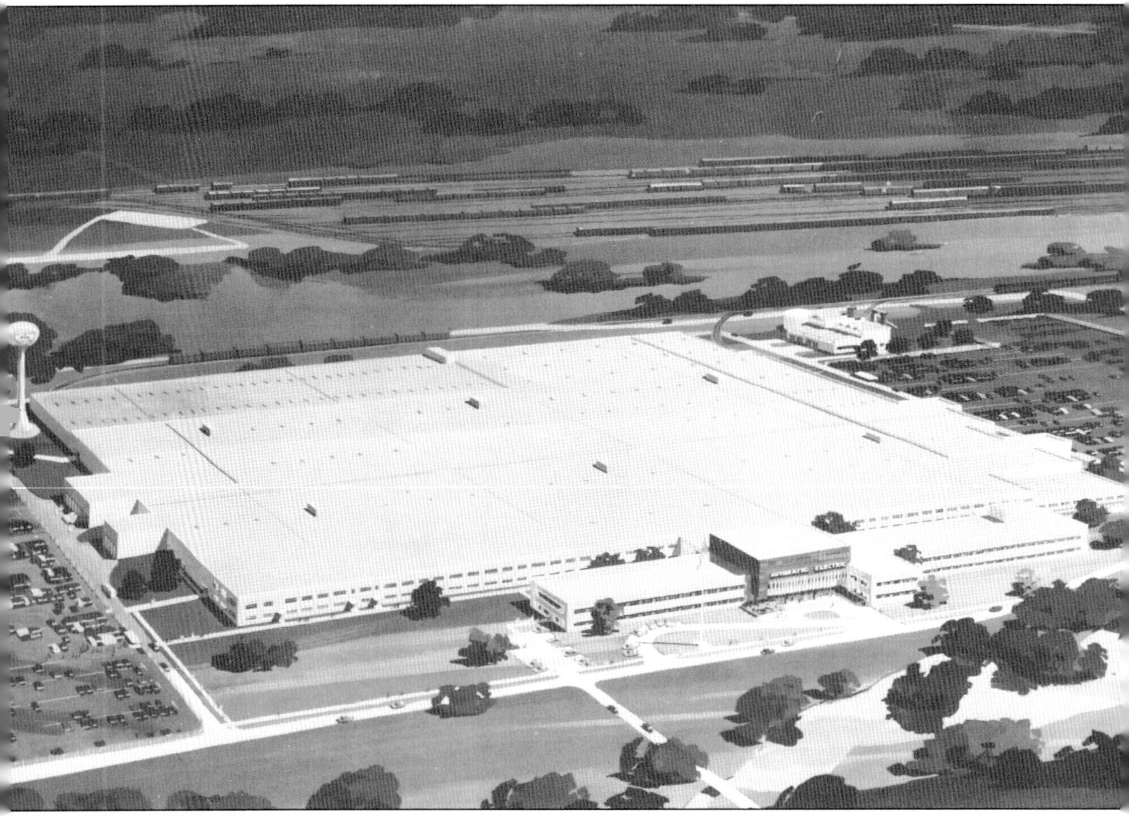

AUTOMATIC ELECTRIC. In 1956, the land was sold to Automatic Electric, a manufacturer of automatic stepping switches, which allowed customers to connect their own calls without operator assistance. The company employed more than 11,000 workers. Part of the land was also developed for Villa Scalabrini Home for the Aged, exactly where the fourth hole used to sit on the golf course. (Courtesy of Northlake Public Library.)

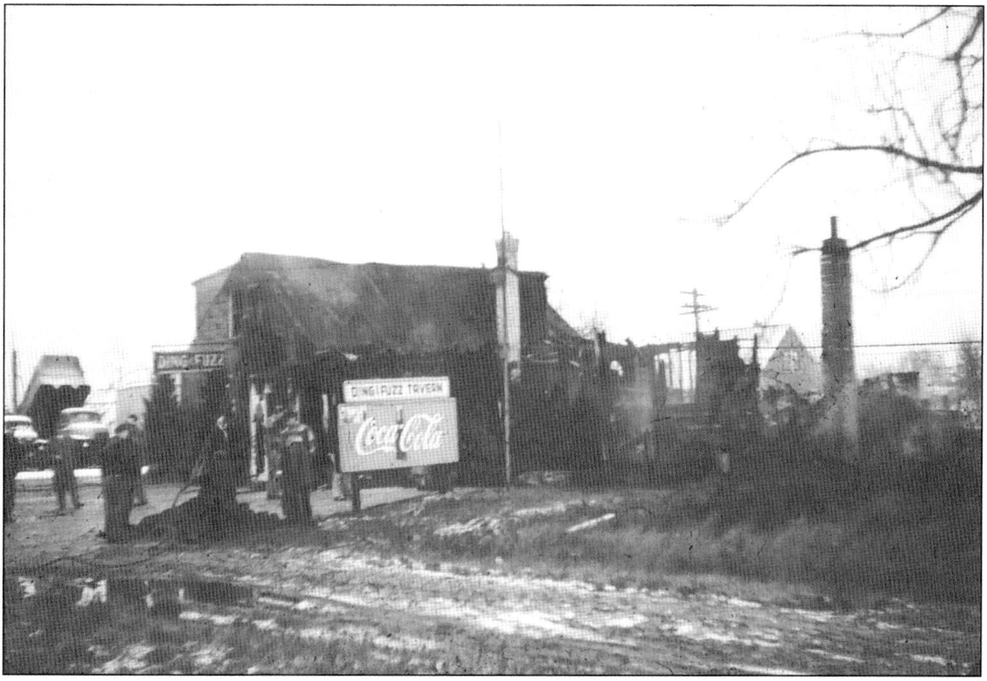

Ding and Fuzz Tavern. Soon after residents began moving into town, many businesses started opening up, such as the Ding and Fuzz Tavern (above). Unfortunately, the tavern burned to the ground in December 1954 and the owner died in the fire. At right, notice the open fields still around town behind this man, who stands in front of the Coca-Cola sign of another early local tavern. (Both, courtesy of Northlake Fire Department.)

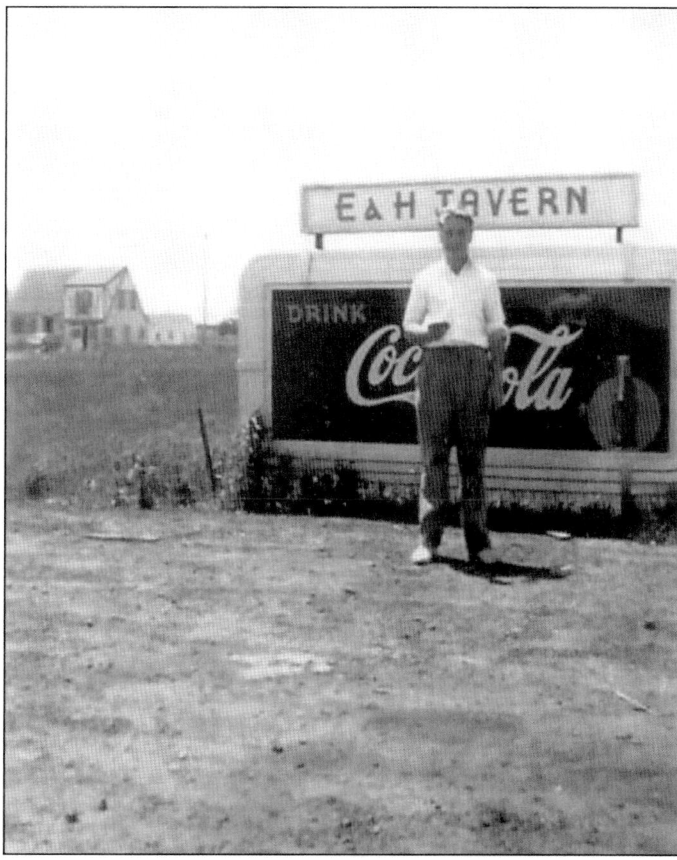

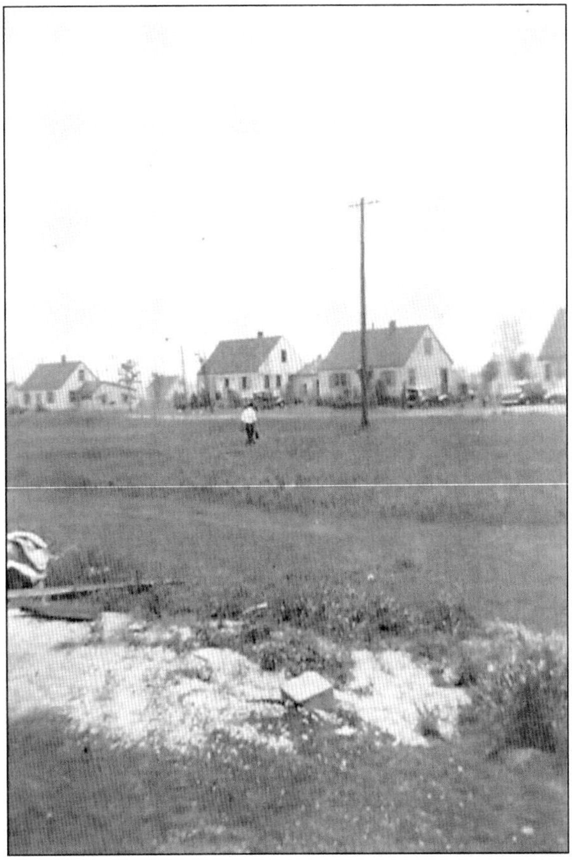

Open Northlake Field. That same open field still existed—as seen in the foreground of this photograph—when shell homes began to shape the street. The lone utility pole stands prominently, ready for further development. (Courtesy of Northlake City Hall.)

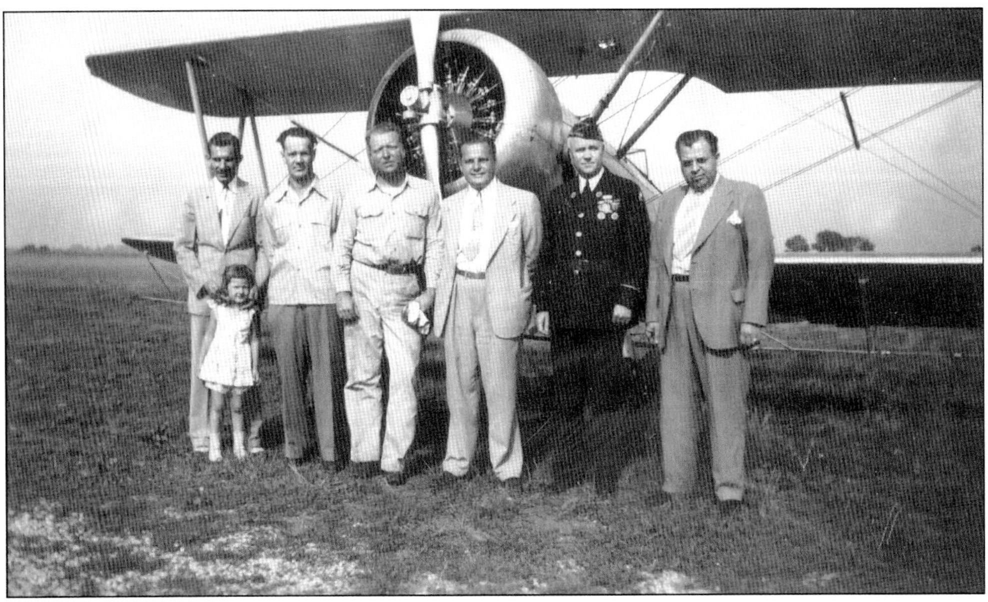

Mayor Eldon Hayes. Northlake's first mayor, Eldon Hayes, stands at the far right in an open field, which was likely Skyhaven Airport, near Wolf Road and Belmont Avenue. Other planes also landed on the Westward Ho Golf Course. (Courtesy of Northlake City Hall.)

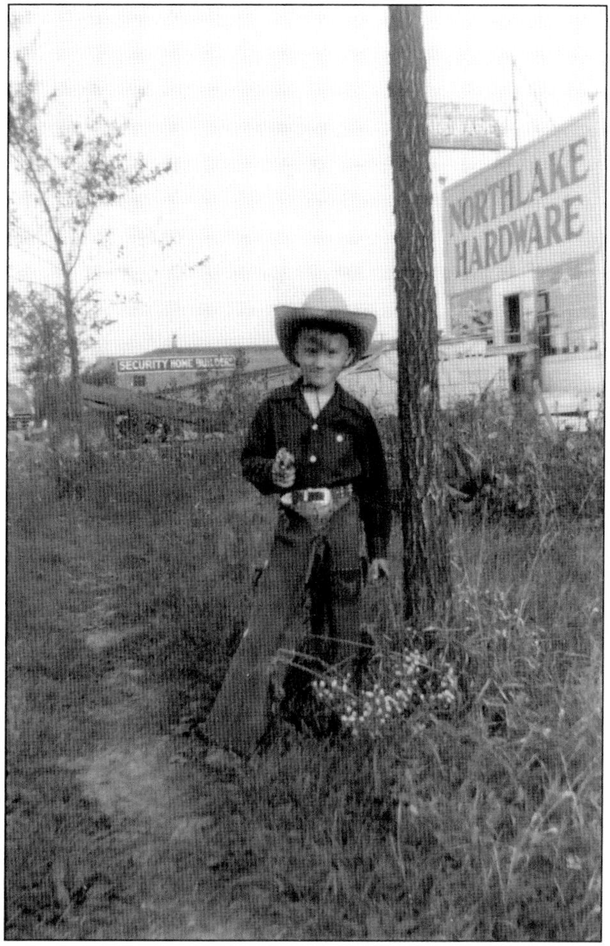

Northlake Hardware. With so many shell homes ready to be customized by new homeowners, businesses such as Tom McGrath's Northlake Hardware played a significant role. The young boy at right, likely part of one of the young families new to town, plays cowboy in front of the store. Years later, the same single-story building was remodeled and additions were made, as Danklefson's Bakery and a dentist's office were added on. However, the two-story building at 47 East North Avenue (below) was torn down in 1970, making way for the police department. In 1995, the original Northlake Hardware building at 45 East North Avenue was razed to provide needed parking spaces for the police station. (Both, courtesy of Northlake City Hall.)

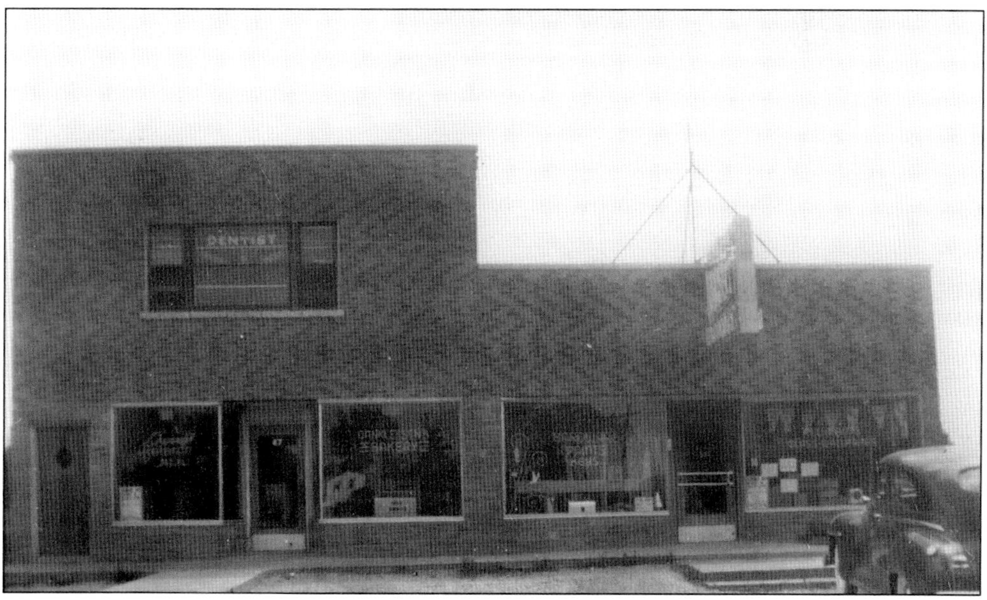

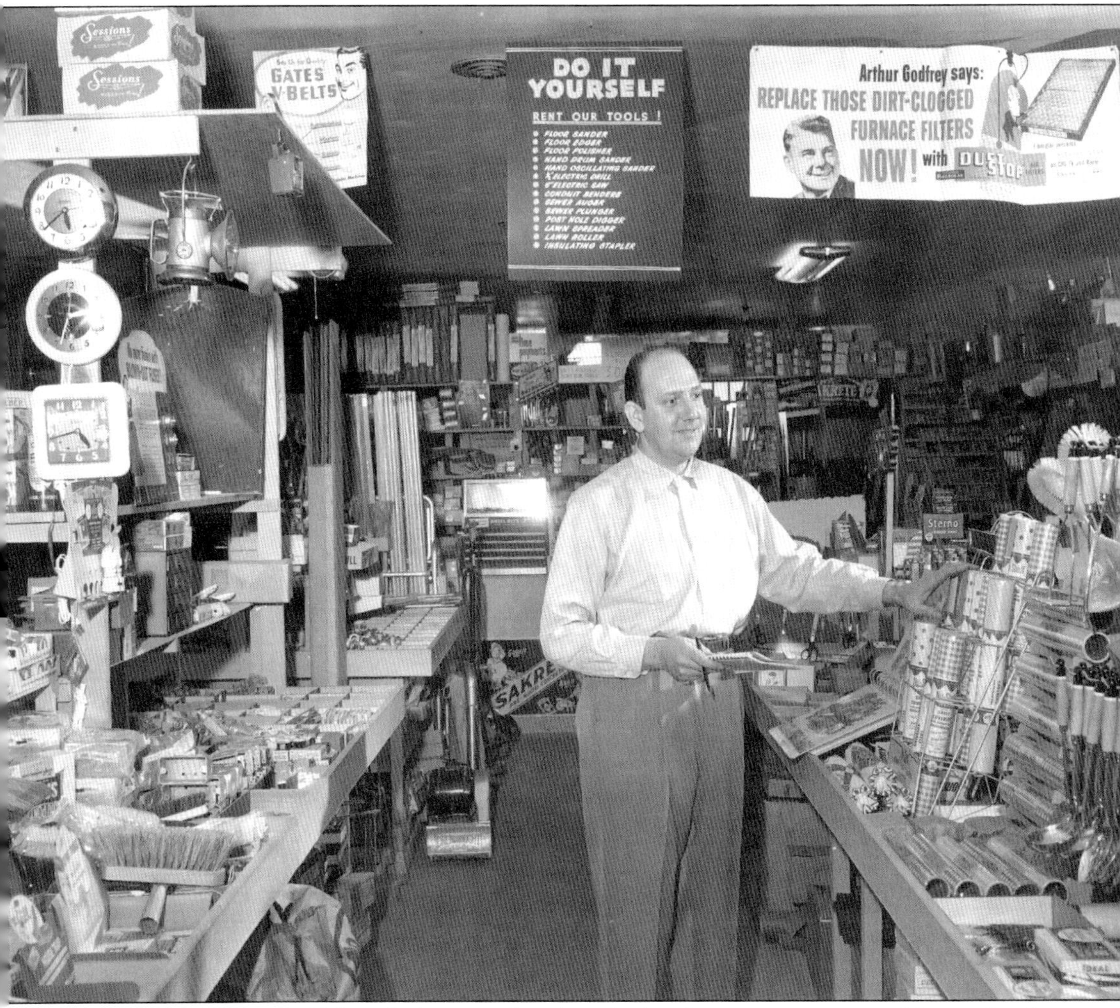

HARDWARE STORE. Although the items found in this hardware store are typical for any hardware store, it is important to note the abundance of electrical boxes, electrical outlets, and fuses. Since the Northlake shell homes allowed great flexibility to owners, having to do your own carpentry and plumbing created a need for many of these items. The owner takes inventory of his stock; the sign above him says he rents tools for "Do it Yourself" projects. (Courtesy of Northlake City Hall.)

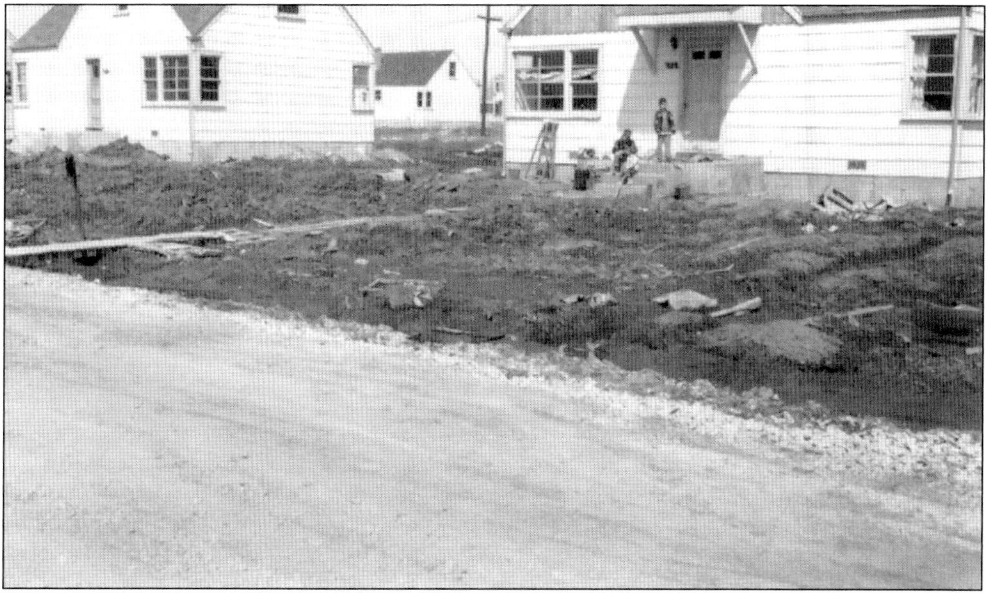

Shell Homes. Many of the shell homes were similar to the one pictured here at 248 Wagner Drive. The homes typically had a second floor, a crawl space, and not much else. The owner was responsible for doing the carpentry and installing the necessary electrical wiring and plumbing. There were no lawns and no paved roads; only dirt, mud, and gravel. By the 1940s, about 600 of these shell homes were available for customization. (Both, courtesy of Dickson Petzold.)

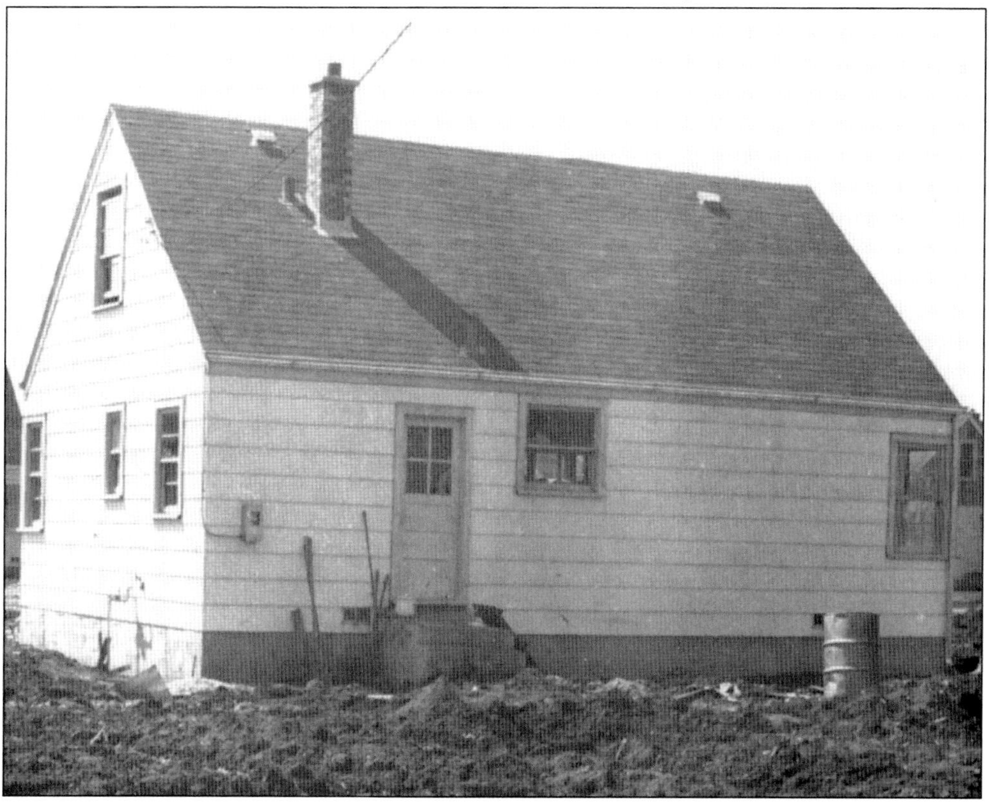

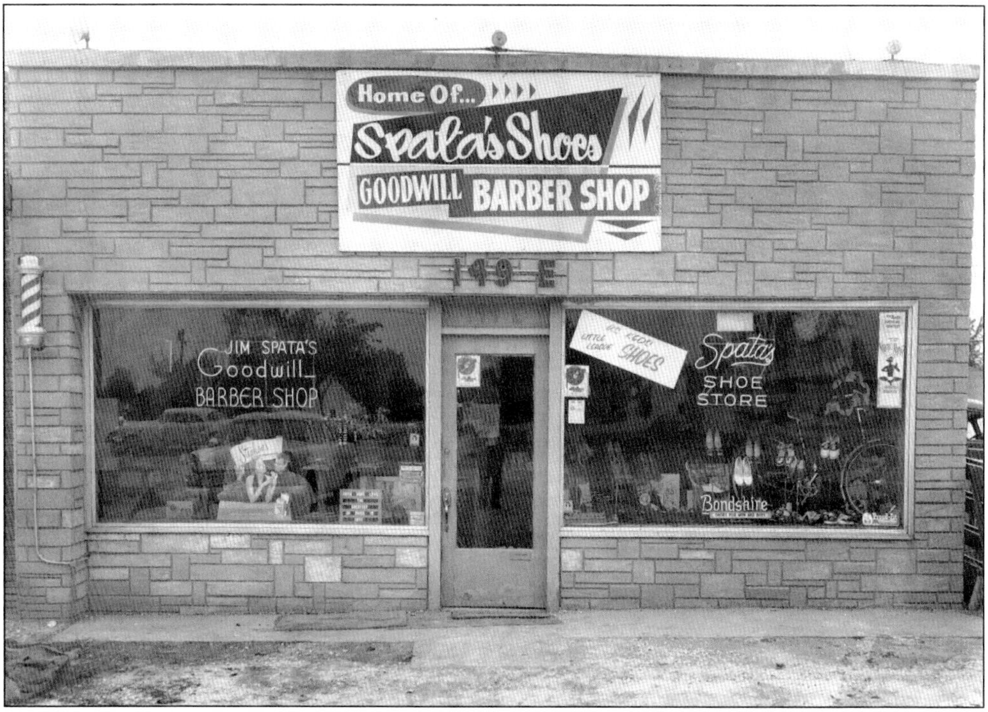

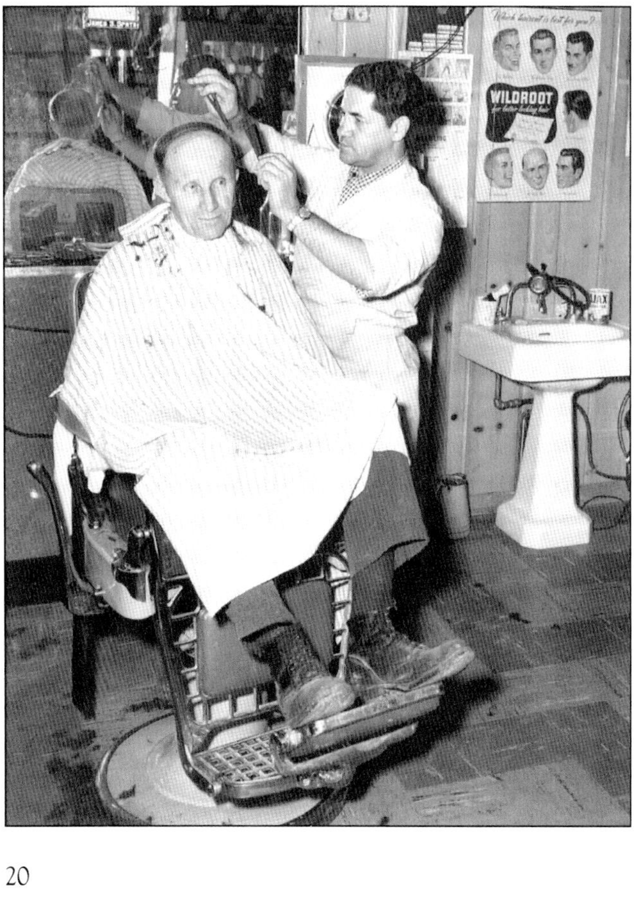

Jim Spata's Goodwill Barber Shop and Spata's Shoe Store. One of the early businesses in town, Spata's featured both stores in one locale. The single-story building had signs on the windows advertising "Bondshire: Shoes for Men and Boys," "Thorogood," and "U.S. Keds." At left, inside the barbershop, James Spata cuts a client's hair. His license is affixed to the mirror and shoeboxes reflect off the mirror from the shoe store. (Both, courtesy of Northlake City Hall.)

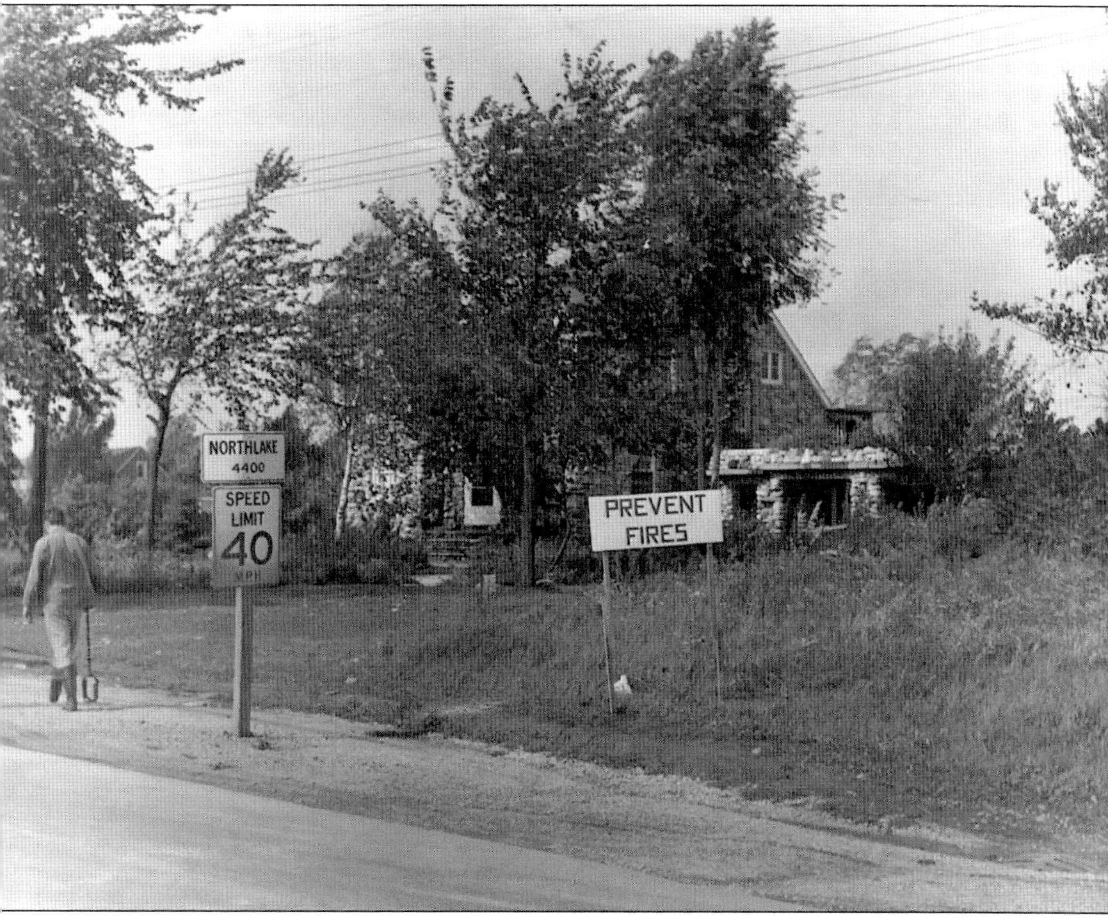

North Avenue. After the town was incorporated in 1949, Northlake's population rose to 4,400, as noted on this sign. This home eventually became Lou's Garden Center, which still stands today. The fire department placed another sign alongside North Avenue warning residents to prevent fires due to the grassy fields. The speed limit is still 40 miles per hour. (Courtesy of Northlake City Hall.)

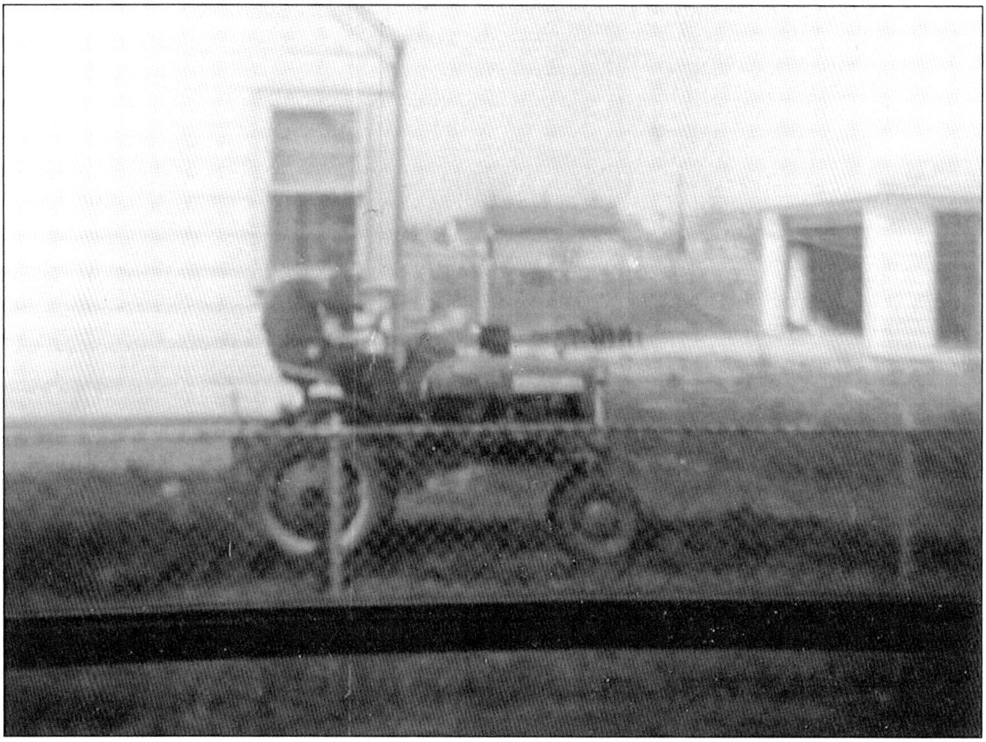

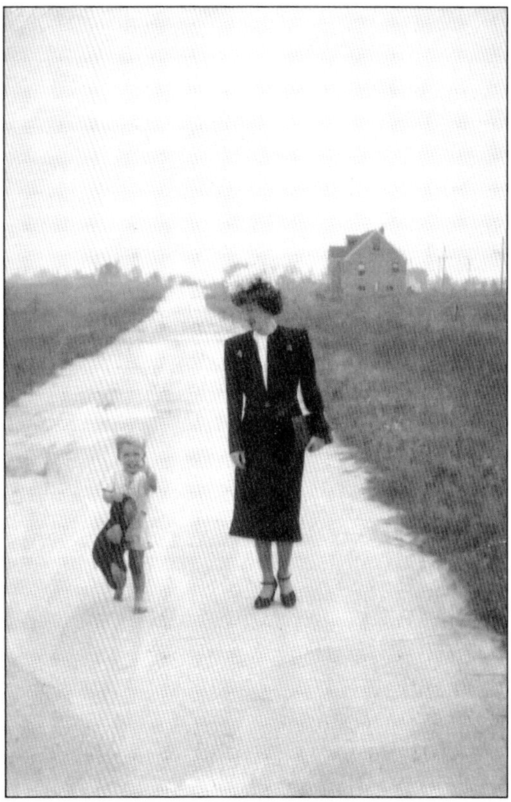

LAWN TRACTOR. Mr. McGuire uses a tractor to landscape his lawn on Wagner Drive. As seen here, garages and lawns were starting to be commonplace as the town continued to grow and establish itself. (Courtesy of Dickson Petzol.)

WESTWARD HO DRIVE, 1947. Monica Kunz walks on the dirt road alongside her son near 147 Westward Ho Drive in 1947. Her husband, Frank Kunz, was the plumbing inspector. (Courtesy of Northlake City Hall.)

Two

From Shell Homes to Incorporation

As more and more residents began to move into the area, several options emerged for residents. One option was to annex to Melrose Park. The second option was to annex to Elmhurst. And the third option was to incorporate, which could lead to many divisions and tense battles. Eventually, the majority of residents voted to incorporate, inviting the challenge of forming a government to rule, creating departments to fight fires and keep civil order, and planning accordingly for the future.

With limited budgets, volunteerism reigned supreme, and the earliest fire stations were built by volunteers. Service organizations assisted one another in any way they could. Slowly, but surely, the town began to form, not only on paper and in principle, but also in practice. Initial mistrust of town leaders began to subside as many residents became involved in ruling their newly formed town.

With many of these challenges came moments that brought smiles and laughter to residents. One such incident was a one-time visitor who rumbled through the streets of town. In a nearby suburb, the Keely and Miller Brothers Circus was performing. According to reports, a low-flying airplane leaving O'Hare Airport startled two elephants, Kay and Barbara. They veered in different directions, with Barbara going northwest. Kay headed straight for Northlake, surprising many residents as she ran through fences, stomped on flowerbeds, and rumbled through town. Northlake police soon caught the 6,500-pound elephant and cuffed him while reinforcements were called in.

The continuing influx of people allowed for more businesses to emerge. During Mayor Ed Neri's term, building was everything. Stores and shopping centers were built and streetlights were placed at busy intersections. Northlake was no longer a small community; it was now a thriving suburb.

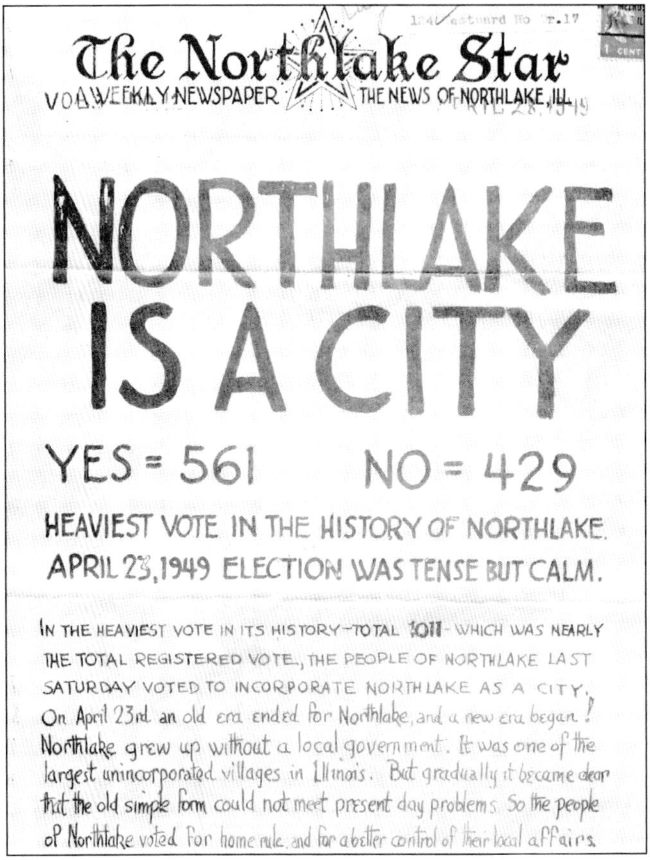

The Northlake Star

A WEEKLY NEWSPAPER — THE NEWS OF NORTHLAKE, ILL.

NORTHLAKE IS A CITY

YES = 561 NO = 429

HEAVIEST VOTE IN THE HISTORY OF NORTHLAKE.

APRIL 23, 1949 ELECTION WAS TENSE BUT CALM.

IN THE HEAVIEST VOTE IN ITS HISTORY—TOTAL 1011—WHICH WAS NEARLY THE TOTAL REGISTERED VOTE, THE PEOPLE OF NORTHLAKE LAST SATURDAY VOTED TO INCORPORATE NORTHLAKE AS A CITY. On April 23rd an old era ended for Northlake, and a new era began! Northlake grew up without a local government. It was one of the largest unincorporated villages in Illinois. But gradually it became clear that the old simple form could not meet present day problems. So the people of Northlake voted for home rule and for a better control of their local affairs.

NORTHLAKE INCORPORATED. The town's newspaper told all its readers that one of the largest unincorporated villages in Illinois was no longer without a local government as residents voted to become incorporated. The vote was taken on April 23, 1949, with 561 Yes votes and 429 No votes. Years later, the town adopted as its logo a circular sign with the two largest streets in town: North Avenue and Lake Street (below). With the motto "City of Friendly People," the four sections show the town's core of local government rule, religious practice, great education, and recreation, as baseball and parks were part of the mission. The town was officially incorporated on July 19, 1949. (Both, courtesy of Northlake City Hall.)

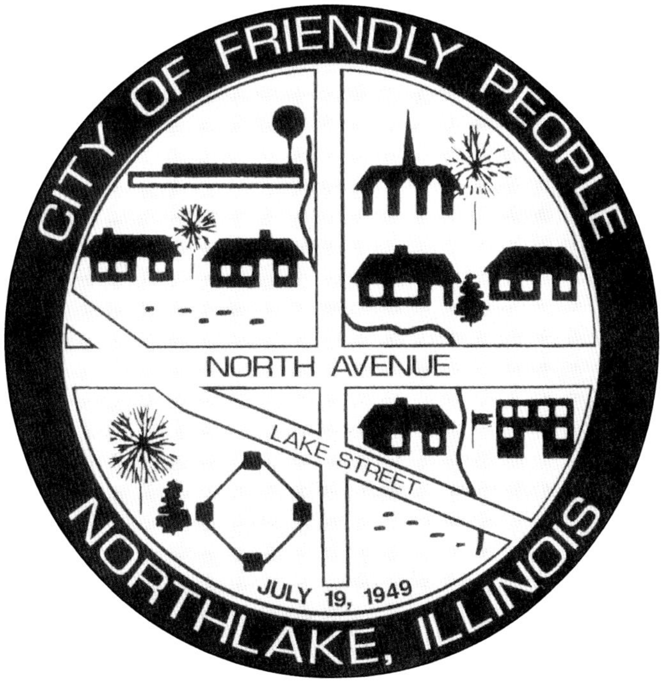

Kay the Elephant. An interesting incident in the town's history occurred when an elephant named Kay rumbled through the streets. In the nearby suburb of Franklin Park, the Keely and Miller Brothers Circus was performing. According to reports, a low-flying airplane leaving O'Hare Airport startled two elephants, Kay and Barbara. Kay came through Northlake, running through fences and stomping on flowerbeds. Northlake police soon caught the elephant. Kay is seen at right chained to a post, cooling herself off. Below, authorities and onlookers stop to get a glimpse of the mammoth animal. (Both, courtesy of *Mont Clare-Leyden Herald*.)

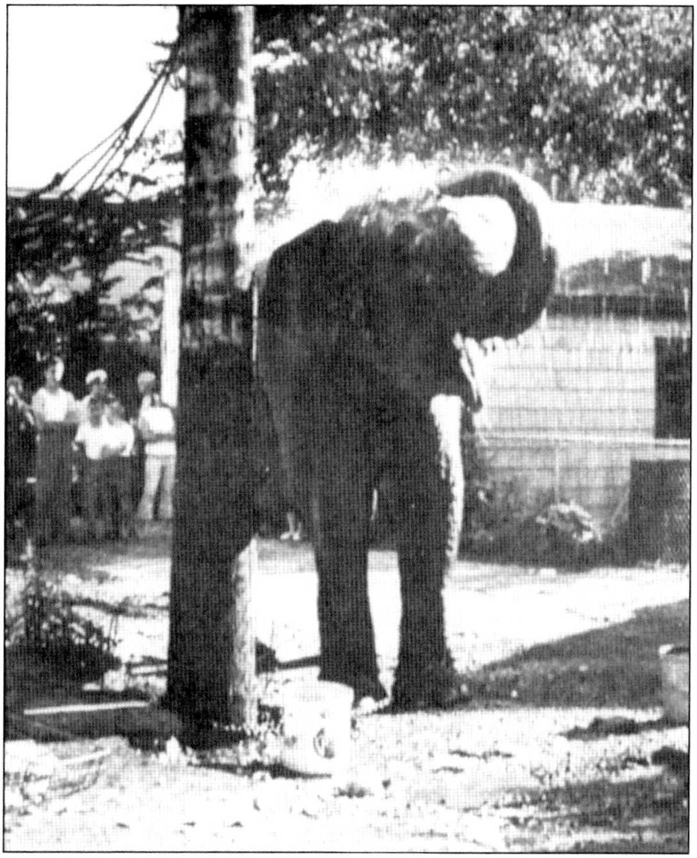

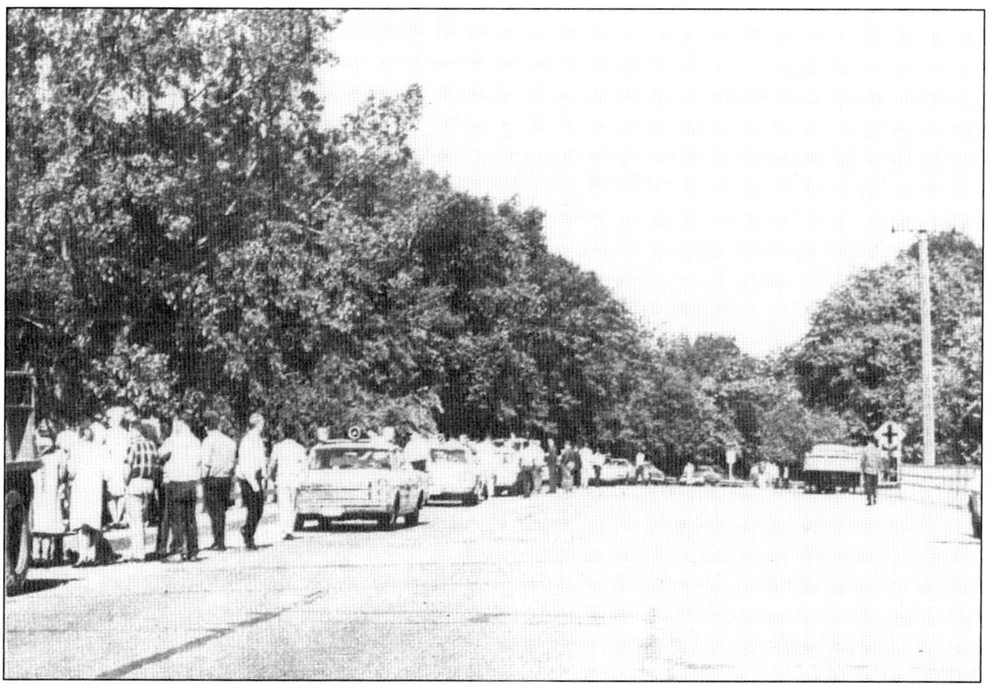

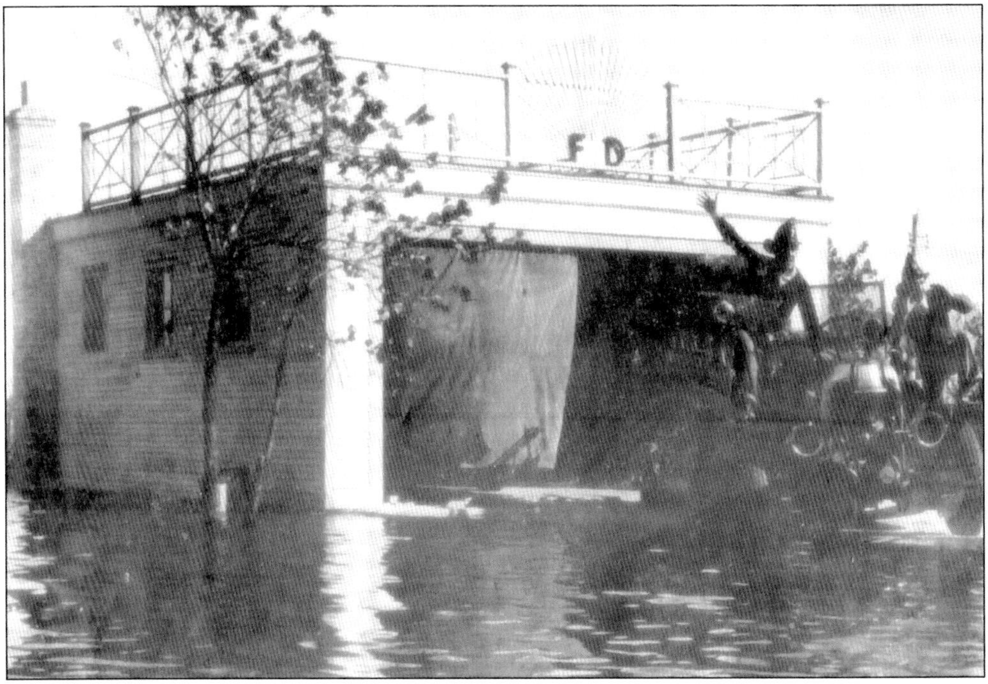

New Fire Station. A few years after incorporation, challenges confronted the newly formed community. But they responded, as volunteers built a new fire station in 1953, replacing the 1941 station, which had also been built by volunteers. (Both, courtesy of Northlake City Hall.)

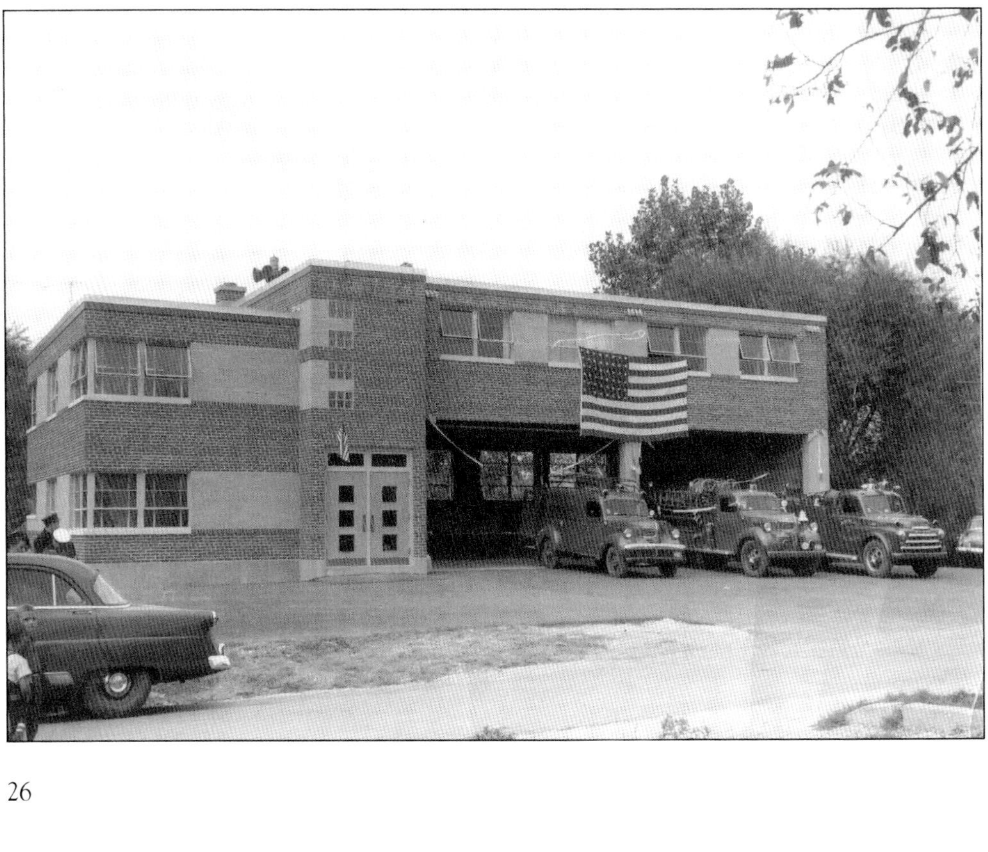

1940

W.F. Fenhaus F.C. Bruns

E. Anderson	F. Gajda	A. Myers
H. Burton	E. Gray	S. Paulson
F. Campea	F. Jacobson	M. Plourde
C. Carlson	C. Jensen	P. Serwich
W. Farmer	D. Kosup	K. Trolle
J. Flickenger	L. Lasky	F. Wenzloff
J. Frost	C. Moore	L. Wollard

VOLUNTEER FIREFIGHTERS. This list provides the names of volunteer firefighters who served the community for many years. Many of those volunteers are in the photograph below, taken in the 1940s. Firefighters went beyond their normal duties by actually building a fire station. (Both, courtesy of Northlake City Hall.)

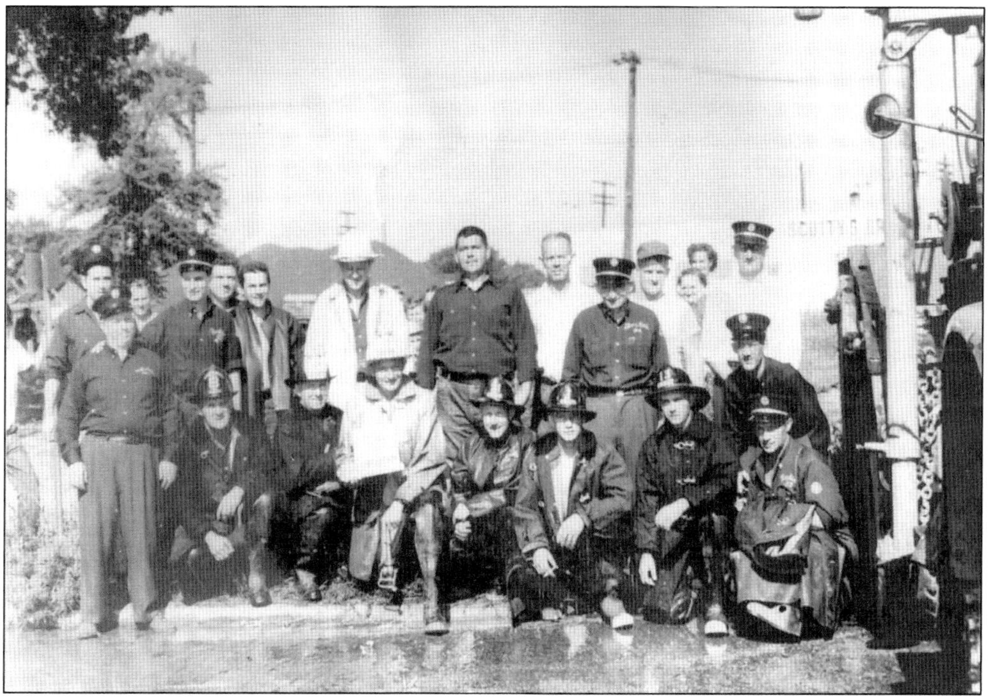

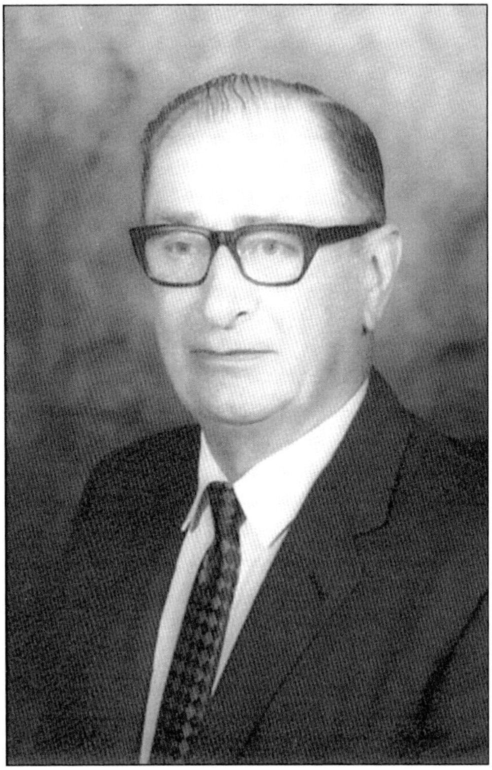

NORTHLAKE FIRE CHIEFS. The first fire chief was Wilbur Fenhaus (left), who served from 1941 to 1951, overseeing many of the early training and fire equipment purchases that laid the foundation for future chiefs and firefighters. The second fire chief, Paul Schroeder (below), served from 1951 to 1959. (Both, courtesy of Northlake Fire Department.)

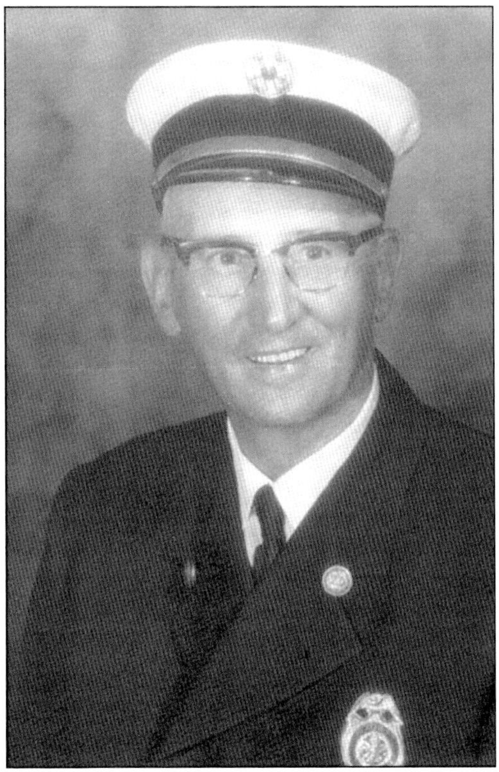

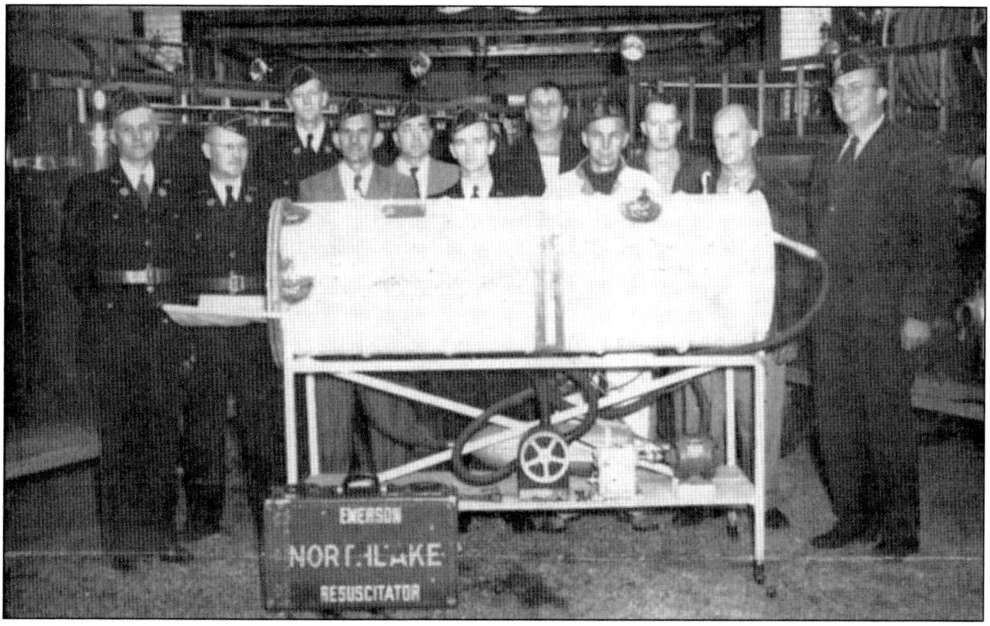

IRON LUNG AND UNDERWATER RECOVERY TEAM. In the 1940s, volunteers from the American Legion Howard H. Rohde Post No. 888 built the iron lung above and donated it to the fire department. The device gives a person who can no longer breathe the ability to breathe by using negative pressure. From left to right are post commander Harry Honeycutt, Clyde Johnson, Evald Skogsberg, Edward Horan, Charles Ellison, Ray Cummings, John Verstad, Walter Padavic, Edgar Hill, Tom Sweet, and Carl Scheel. Below, members of the Northlake Civil Defense Underwater Recovery Team are presented with achievement awards by Mayor Ed Neri for their record 200-foot dive. They are, from left to right, (first row) Lt. William Neal of Northlake, Capt. Richard Longo of Franklin Park, and Mayor Neri; (second row) Sgt. Richard Miller of Elmhurst, Keith Finks of LaGrange, and James Knoll of Elmwood Park. (Both, courtesy of Northlake Fire Department.)

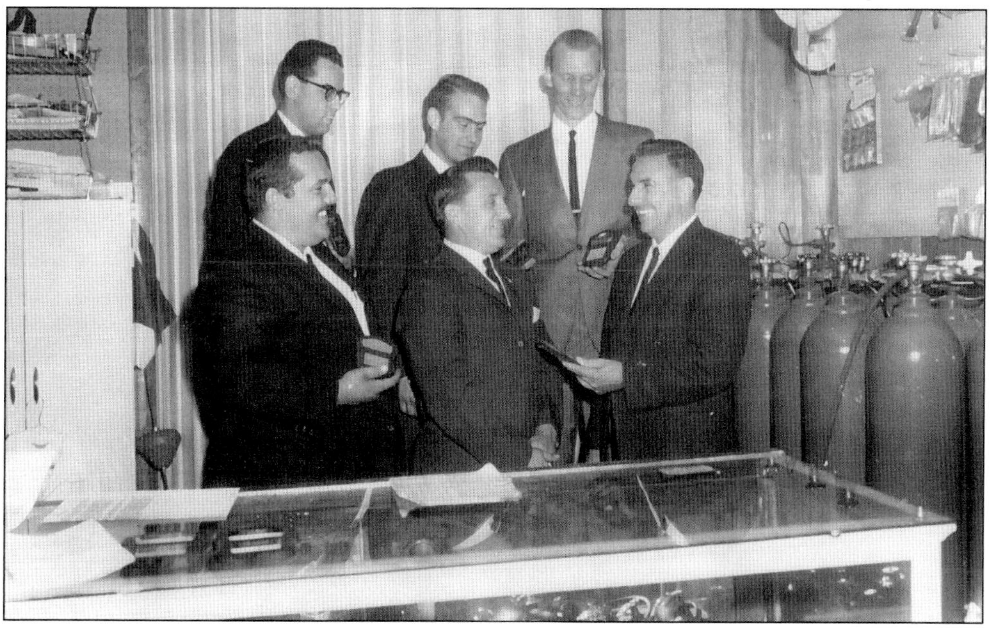

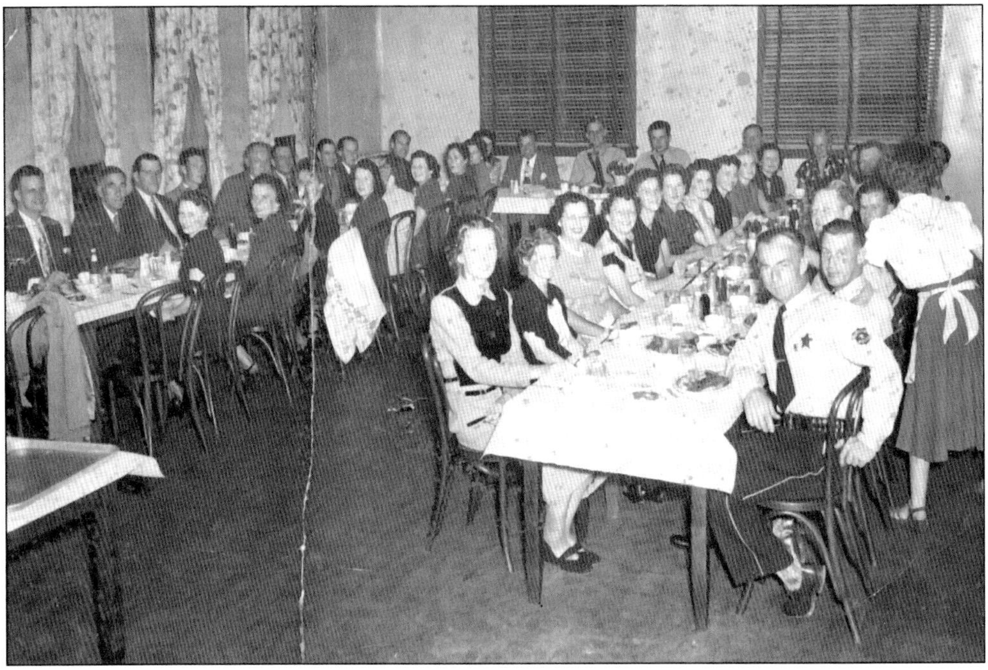

Social Gatherings and Leadership. Above, early residents enjoy a social outing as one of the first police officers (far right) looks straight at the camera with a grin on his face, showing the Northlake police patch on his upper left arm and his badge on the left side of his chest. Behind him are other early Northlake servants, including firemen at the back table and likely political leaders on the opposite side. Below, early leaders gather to lay out plans for Northlake. (Both, courtesy of Northlake City Hall.)

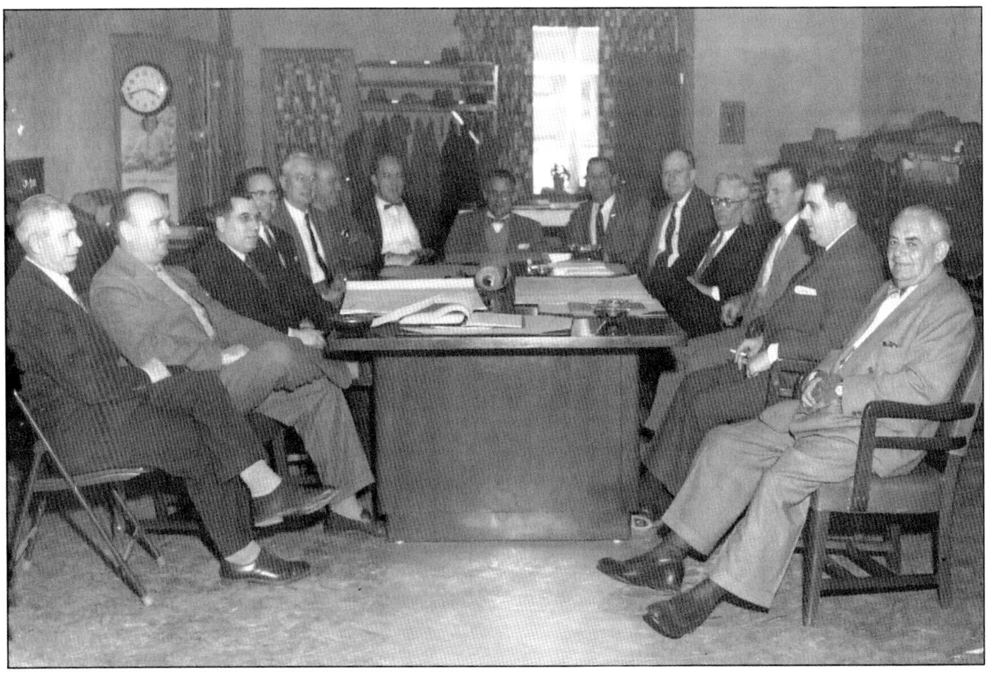

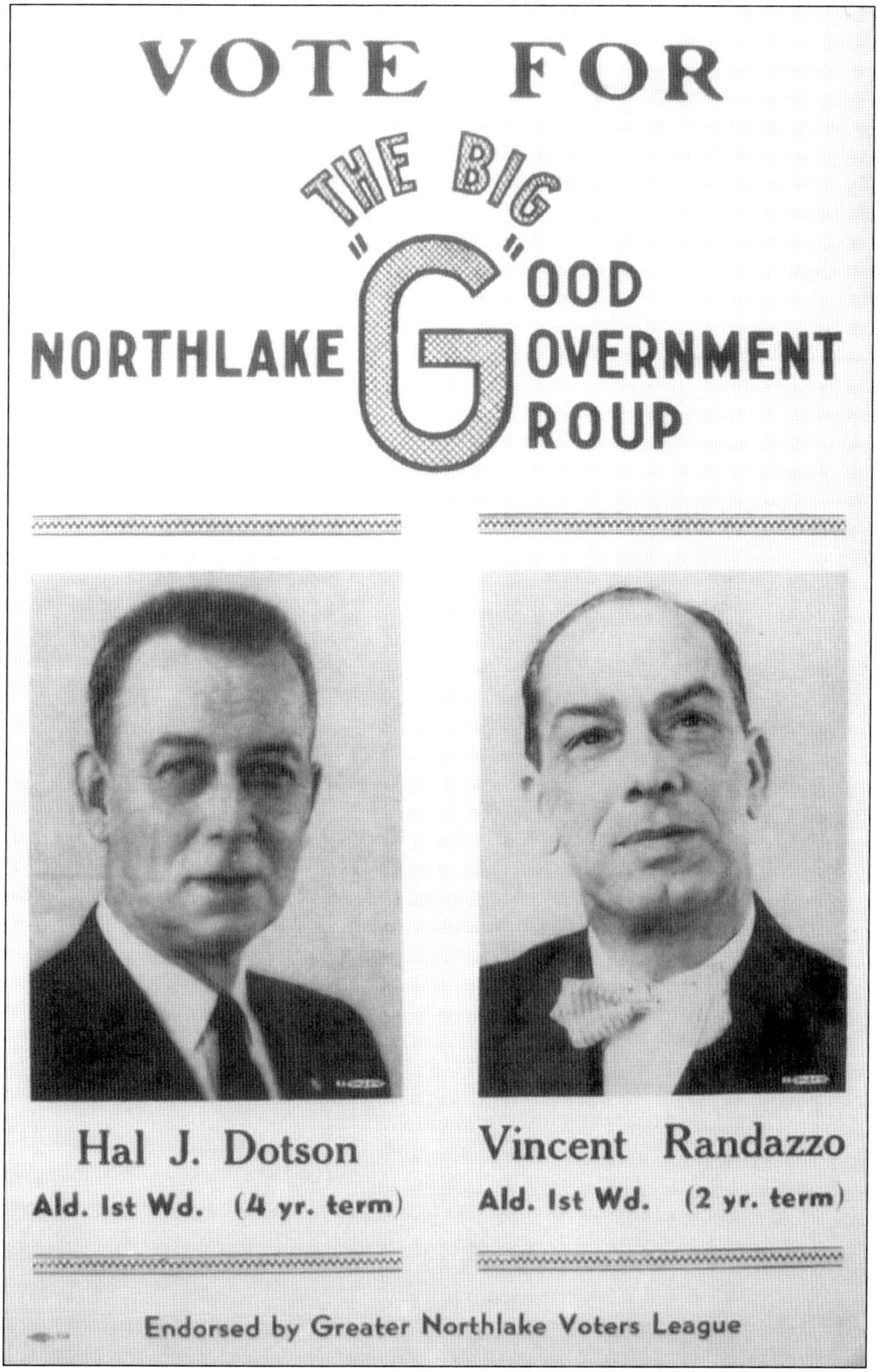

POLITICS. Politics has strong roots in this town. This poster shows two aldermen running for political positions, with Hal Dotson running for a four-year term and Vincent Randazzo running for a two-year term. (Courtesy of Bob Grenier.)

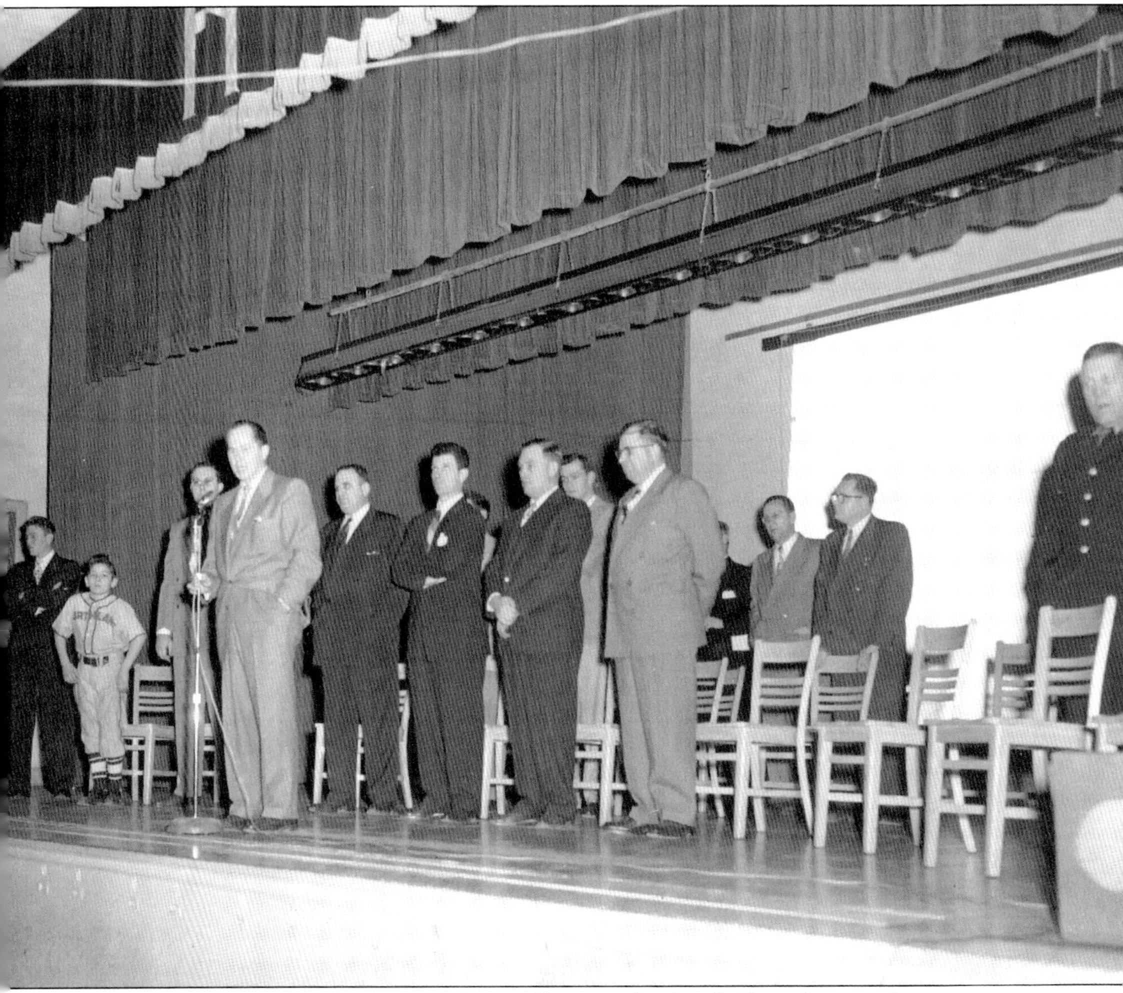

BASEBALL MEETING. The boy at left proudly wears his baseball uniform as the announcement was made that Northlake baseball would be officially organized, providing a sport for the town's youth to compete with neighboring towns. The meeting was held in the Riley School gymnasium. (Courtesy of Northlake City Hall.)

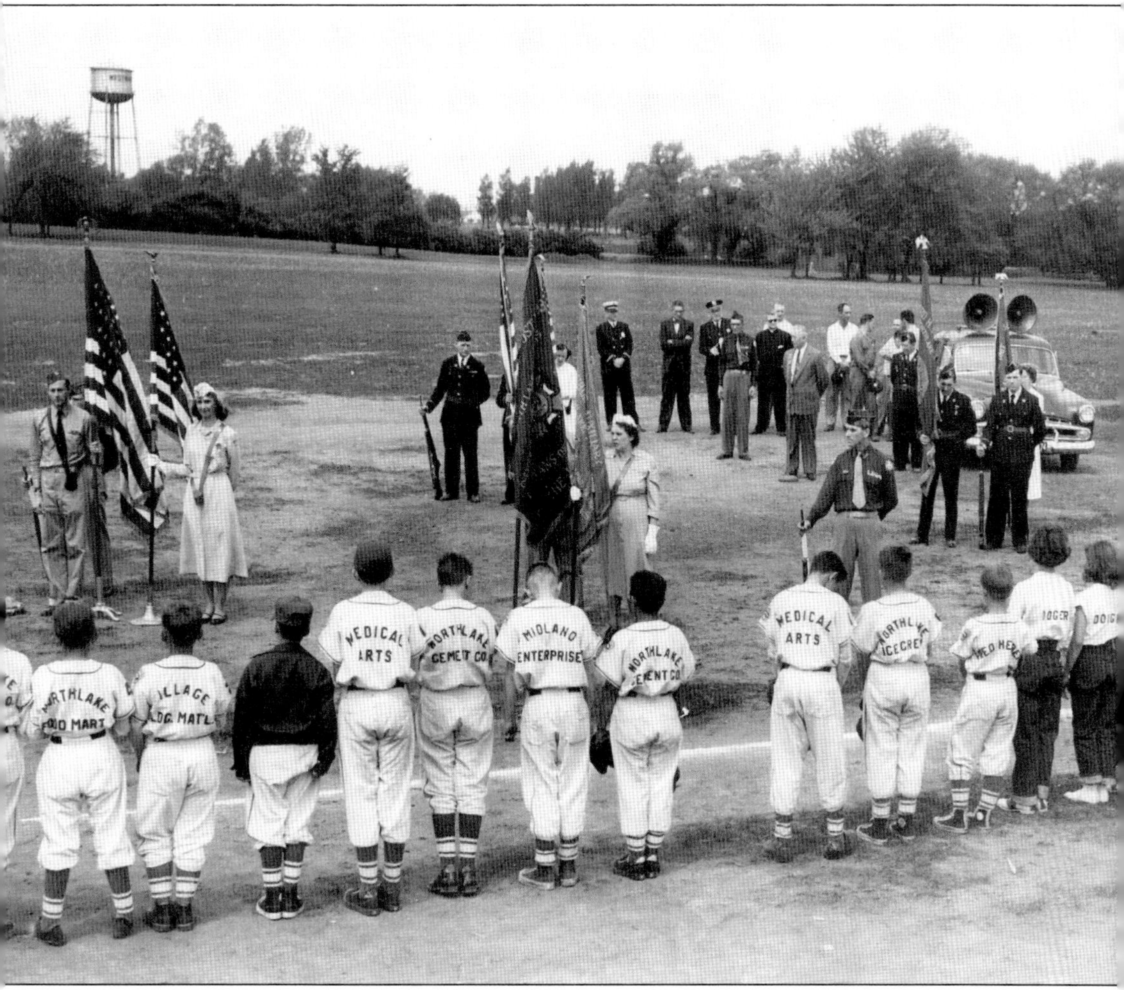

Opening Day 1952. On opening day, a special ceremony was held in the park to commemorate its inaugural season. The field was marked with chalk and players wore uniforms with sponsor's names on the back of their jerseys. Some of the original sponsors were Medical Arts, Northlake Ice Cream, Midland Enterprise, Northlake Food Mart, and Northlake Cement Company. Northlake Baseball celebrated its 60th anniversary in 2012. (Courtesy of Northlake City Hall.)

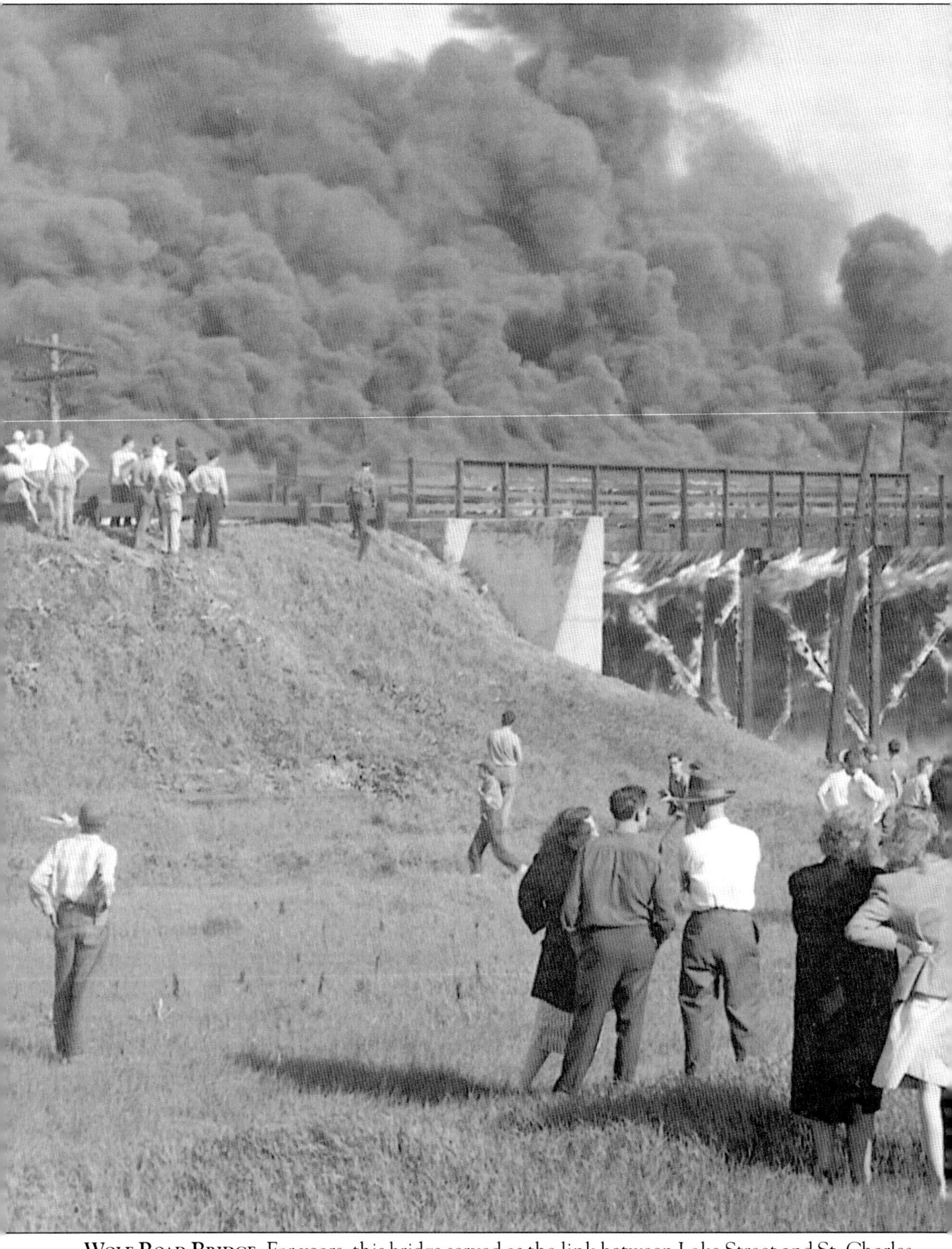

WOLF ROAD BRIDGE. For years, this bridge served as the link between Lake Street and St. Charles Road on Wolf Road. But the wooden bridge burned to the ground on May 22, 1948, and was never replaced. The likely cause of the fire was sparks from a passing train underneath the bridge.

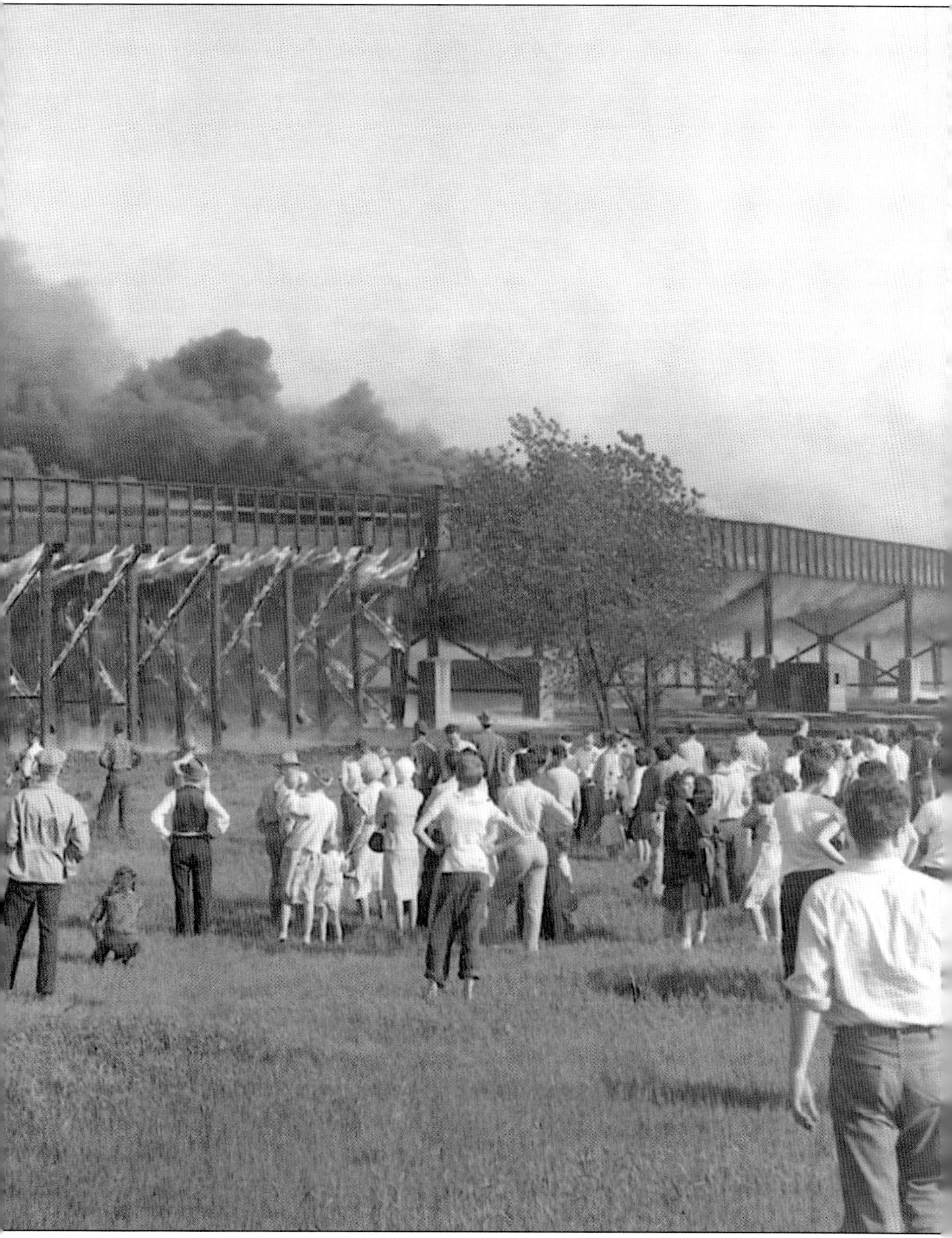

Schoolchildren who had to travel to Sunnyside Junior High School had to take the two-lane wooden bridge on Mannheim Road, which provided many adventures for them. (Courtesy of Northlake City Hall.)

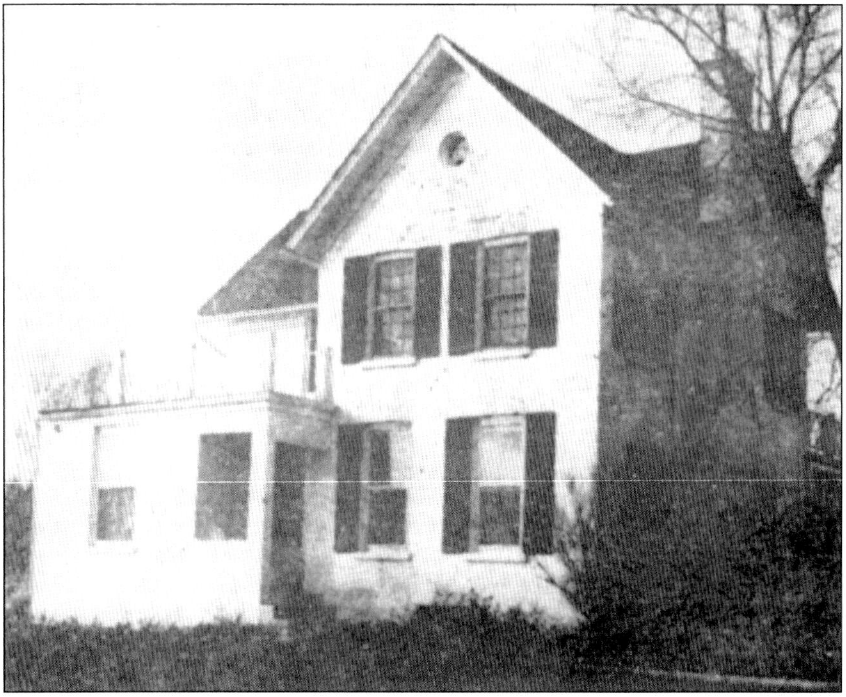

Northlake Library and Brochure. The house above, at 149 East North Avenue, served as the main site for the library. In 1958, it moved to 402 North Wolf Road, and eventually to its permanent location at 231 North Wolf Road. Below is the brochure of the new library. By 1963, the library's book capacity was 23,000 and the main reading room was 3,400 square feet. (Both, courtesy of Northlake City Hall.)

PROGRAM

POSTING OF COLORS — NORTHLAKE AMERICAN LEGION AND VFW POSTS

PLEDGE OF ALLEGIANCE

WELCOME AND INTRODUCTIONS — EDWARD LUNDGREN, PRESIDENT OF LIBRARY BOARD

GUEST SPEAKERS

MAYOR HENRY NERI — REVEREND MICHEALSON

DAN WARD, STATES ATTORNEY

GEORGE COX, PRINCIPAL WEST LEYDEN HIGH SCHOOL

REVEREND MILAN SWASKO

PRESENTATIONS

JOHN H. GEIGER, ARCHITECT

NORTHLAKE LIONS CLUB

NORTHLAKE VOLUNTEER FIRE DEPT., GEORGE HAMBY

THOUGHTS FOR A SPECIAL DAY — REVEREND FR. EDWARD BOYLE

REFRESHMENTS — TOUR OF THE LIBRARY

FLOWER AND TABLE ARRANGEMENTS — NORTHLAKE GARDEN CLUB

MRS. HAROLD OSBORN — MRS. ZOEL CARON

PROGRESS CHART 1957 THRU 1963

LOCATION	CIRCULATION	BORROWERS
149 E. NORTH AVE.	NOT RECORDED	848
149 E. NORTH AVE.	13,196	1,384
149 E. NORTH AVE.	14,504	2,448
402 N. WOLF ROAD	23,240	3,639
402 N. WOLF ROAD	22,729	3,209
18 N. WOLF ROAD	26,294	4,385
231 N. WOLF ROAD	PERMANENT LOCATION	

FACTS YOU SHOULD KNOW ABOUT THE LIBRARY

ARCHITECTS AND ENGINEERS — JOHN H. GEIGER & ASSOCIATES

CONTRACTOR — EGYPTIAN CONSTRUCTION CO.

COST OF BUILDING — $83,000.00

BOOK CAPACITY — 23,000

MAIN READING ROOM AREA — 3,400 SQUARE FEET

TOTAL GROSS FLOOR AREA — 5,800 SQUARE FEET

MATERIALS

FACE BRICK EXTERIOR, ALL FLOORS FINISHED WITH VINYL ASBESTOS TILE, ACCOUSTICAL CEILINGS, SOME ROOMS AIR-CONDITIONED.

FEATURES

ACTIVITY ROOM WITH BUILT-IN KITCHENETTE

LIBRARIANS OFFICE

MEETING ROOM IN BASEMENT ACCOMODATES 85 PEOPLE

TOILETS UPSTAIRS AND DOWN

HEAT

HOT WATER BOILER PLANT — WALL-FIN RADIATORS

CLASS-ROOM UNIT VENTILATORS

PARKING

30-CAR, BLACK-TOPPED PARKING LOT

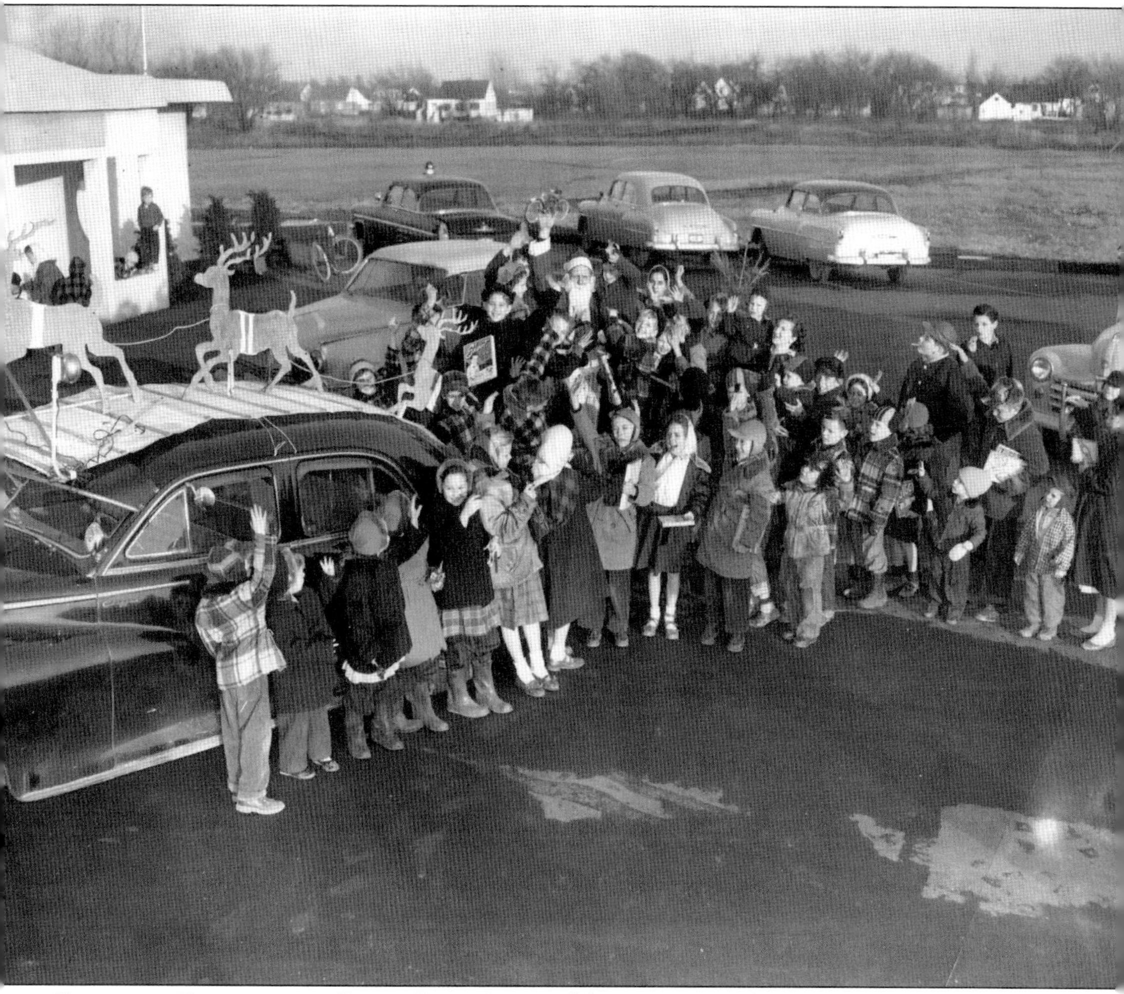

Christmas Festivities at Grant Park. Many of the younger residents enjoy the festivities of Christmas. Santa Claus makes an appearance with his reindeer as children cheer him on at the outskirts of Grant Park. The field house to the left was eventually replaced with a brick structure. Christmas festivities continue to this day, with carriage rides and games for children. (Courtesy of Northlake City Hall.)

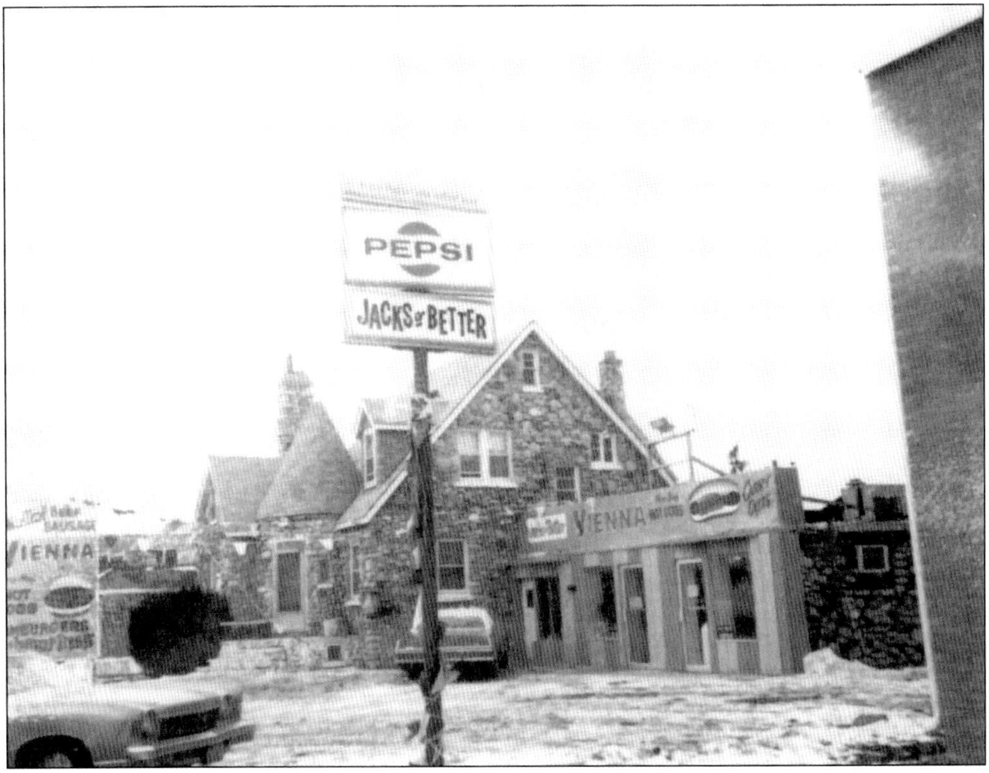

JACK'S OR BETTER AND NORTHLAKE SHOPPING CENTER. No town is complete without a hot dog stand. Next to the house that is now Lou's Garden Center stands Jack's Or Better hot dog stand (above), selling Vienna hot dogs and burgers. One of the first shopping centers was the Northlake Shopping Center (below, in 1968) on the northeast corner of North Avenue and Wolf Road. National Food Stores competed with Northlake Foods down the street on Wolf Road. National Foods anchored the shopping center, which included a Brown's Chicken and a medical center. (Both, courtesy of Northlake City Hall.)

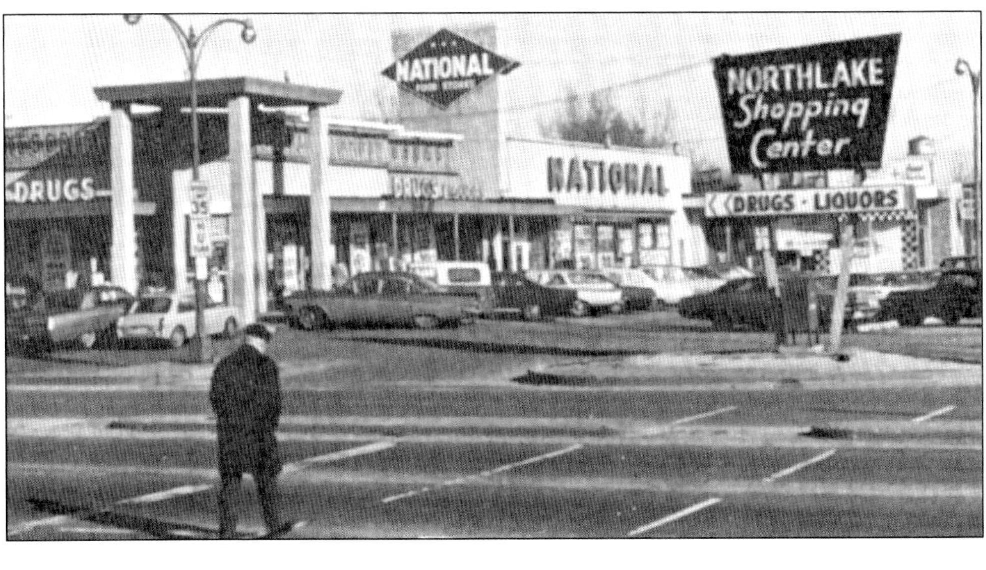

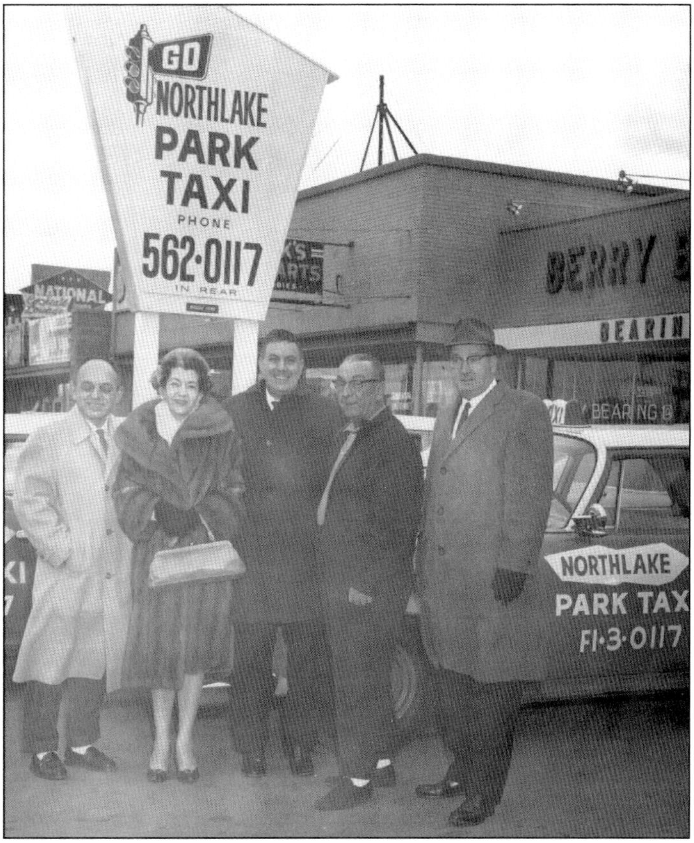

Go Northlake Park Taxi and Brown's Chicken. In front of the North Avenue shopping center stood the Go Northlake Park Taxi. At right, Mayor Neri (center) joyfully puts his arms around two residents as Alderman Wayne Seidler (right) looks on. This shopping center was the largest revenue-producing strip of businesses since the town's inception. One of those revenue producers was Brown's Chicken (below). (Both, courtesy of Northlake City Hall.)

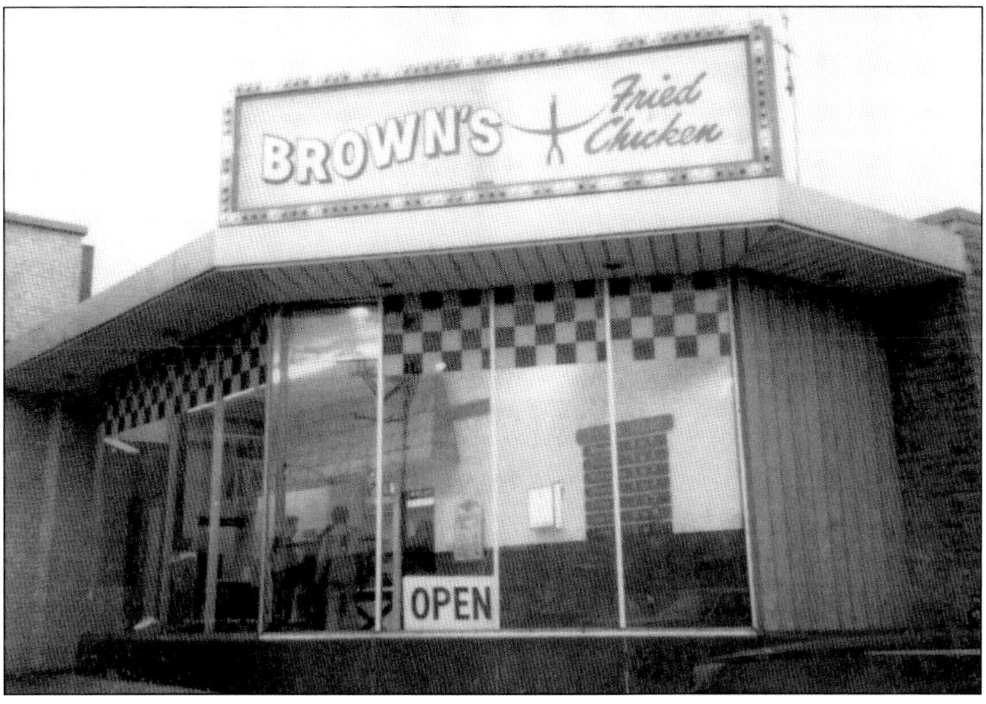

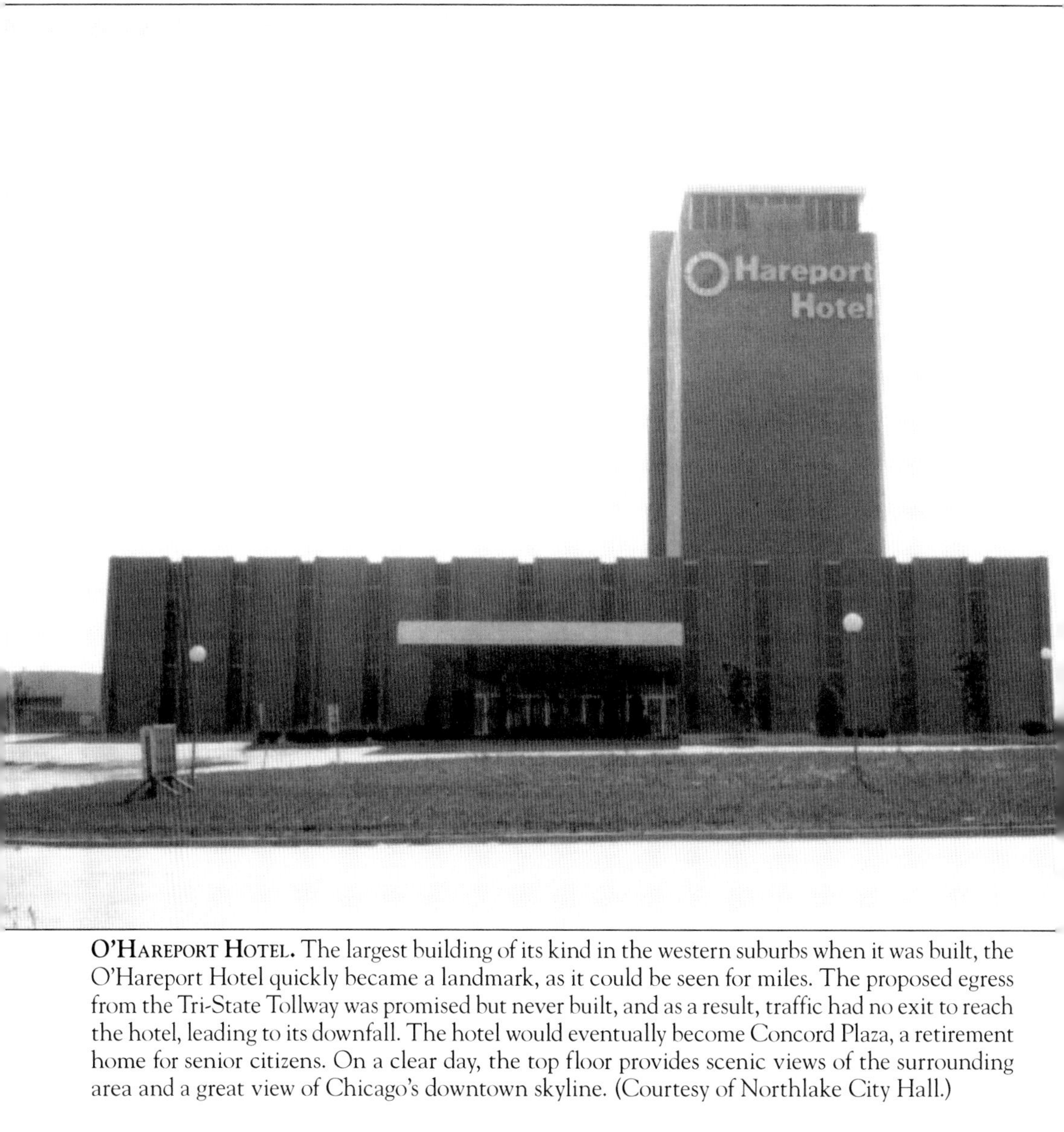

O'HAREPORT HOTEL. The largest building of its kind in the western suburbs when it was built, the O'Hareport Hotel quickly became a landmark, as it could be seen for miles. The proposed egress from the Tri-State Tollway was promised but never built, and as a result, traffic had no exit to reach the hotel, leading to its downfall. The hotel would eventually become Concord Plaza, a retirement home for senior citizens. On a clear day, the top floor provides scenic views of the surrounding area and a great view of Chicago's downtown skyline. (Courtesy of Northlake City Hall.)

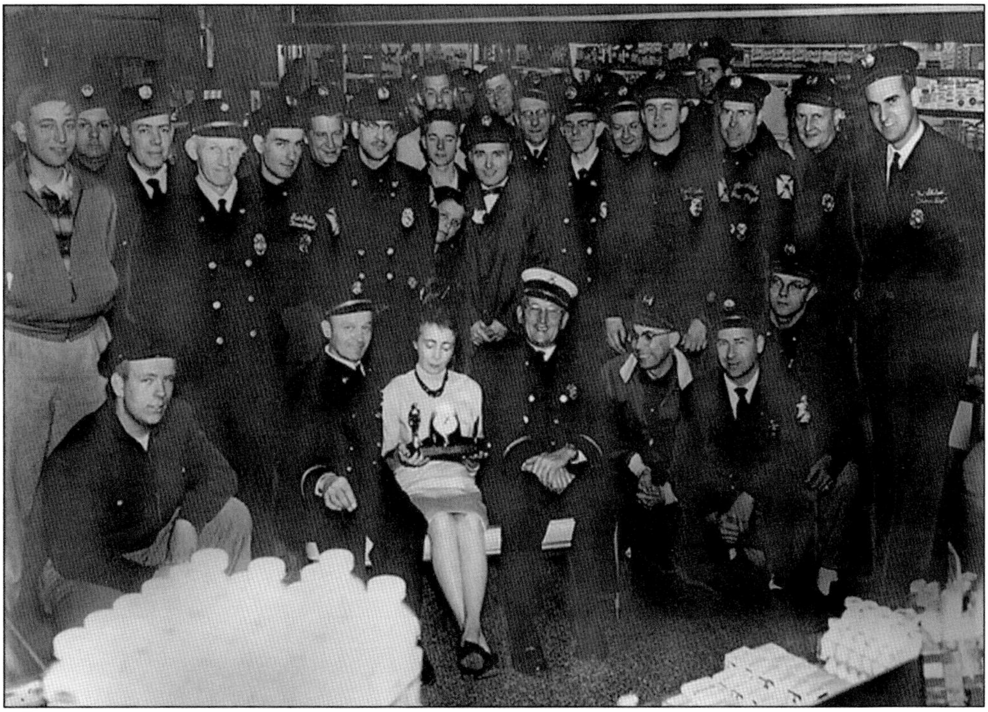

GRAY'S DRUG STORE AND FULL FORCE FIRE DEPARTMENT. One of the earliest businesses on the eastern edge of town was Gray's Drug Store on the corner of North Avenue and Roy Street. Above, Mrs. Gray receives an award from firefighters for her efforts in helping the newly formed fire department. By 1970, the fire department had hired its first five firefighters—all standing below in blue shirts—and had become a full-time force. (Both, courtesy of Northlake City Hall.)

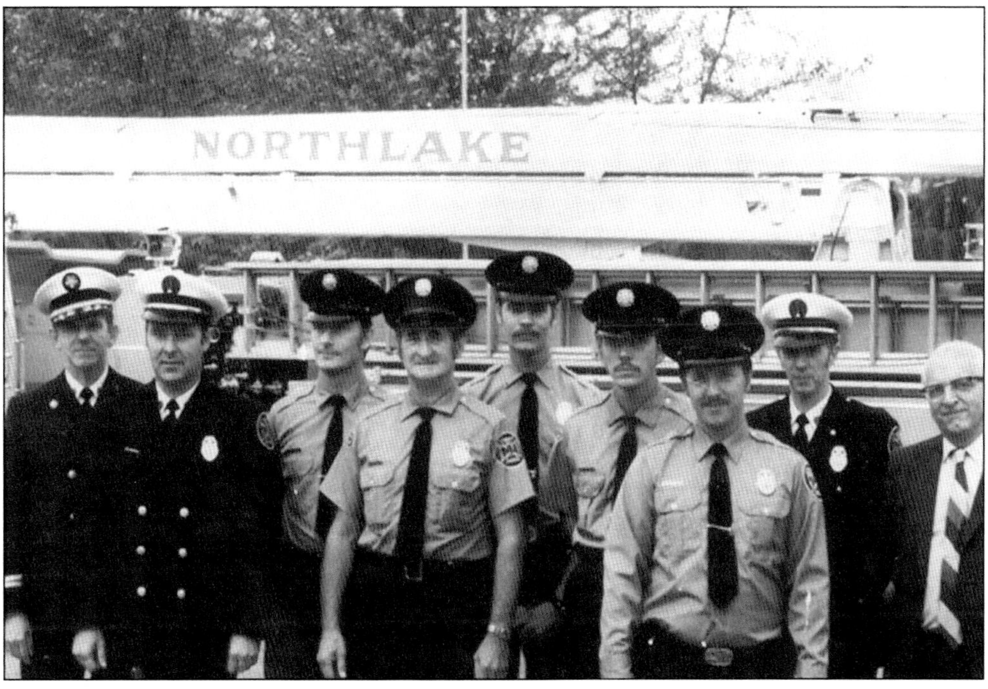

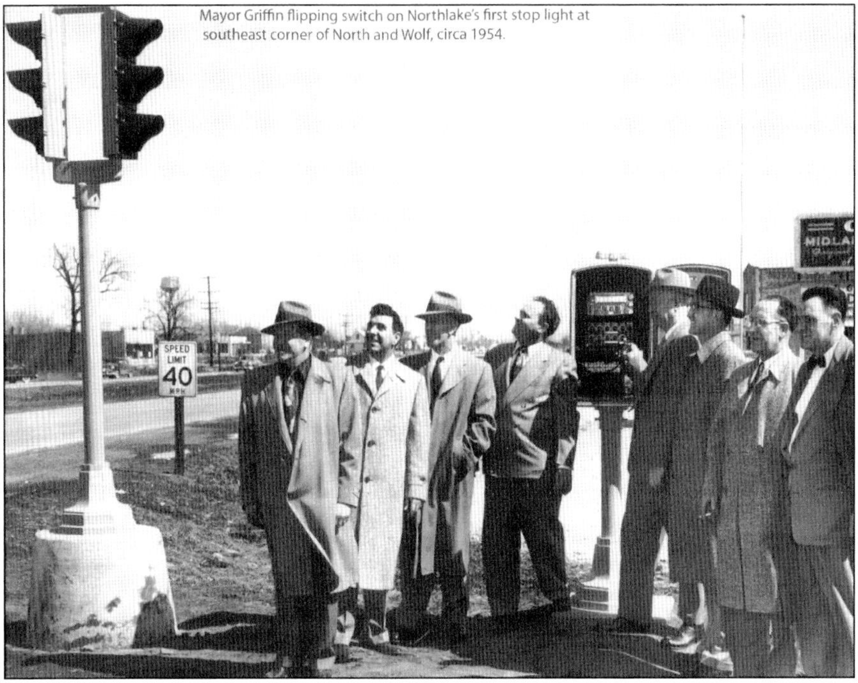

First Stoplight and Police Force. The town's first stoplight (above) was on the southeast corner of North Avenue and Wolf Road, near McDonald's. Mayor Joseph Griffin flips the switch as future mayor Ed Neri (second from left) looks up. This continues to be the town's busiest intersection and the heart of Northlake; today, the town is in the process of modernizing its stoplights. Northlake also developed a police force (below) to provide for the safety of its residents. Today, the police force has 40 officers. (Both, courtesy of Northlake City Hall.)

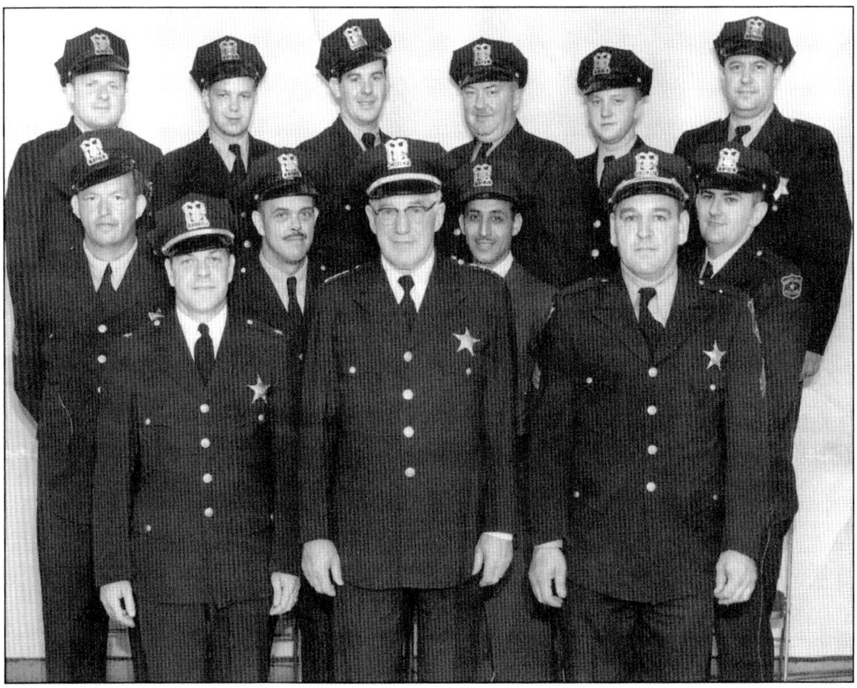

Automatic Electric Moves In. The large size of Automatic Electric meant that equipment had to be relocated to Northlake. Here, Mayor Ed Neri (center) assists Joyce Brothers Movers as a company executive stands to the right. The number of workers at Automatic Electric doubled the town's population. For more than 20 years, the company played a big part in the lives of Northlake residents. (Courtesy of Northlake Public Library.)

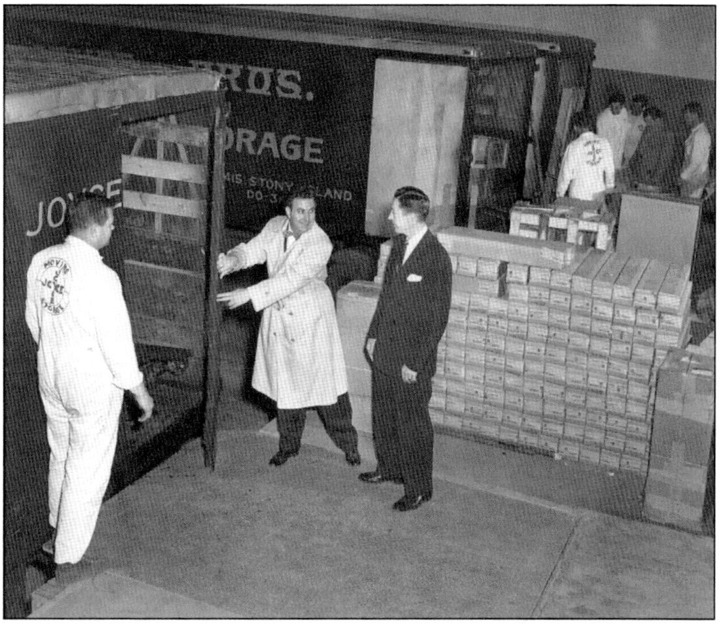

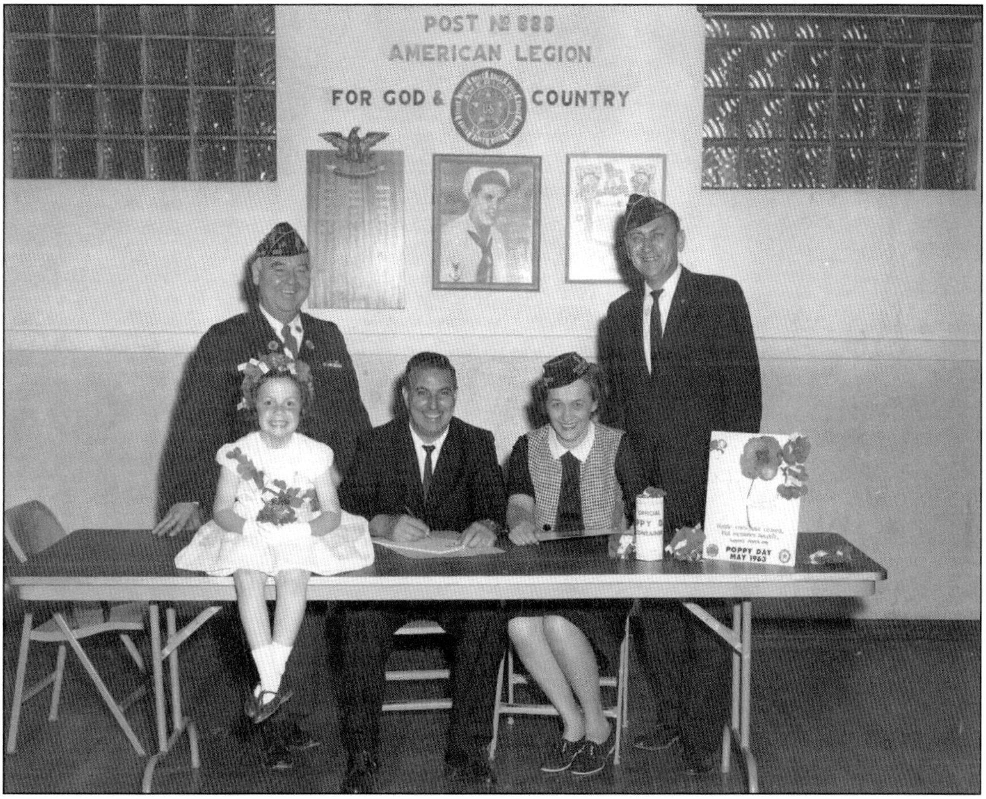

Poppy Day, May 1963. Mayor Neri (center) signs a document recognizing Poppy Day in May 1963 as a girl sits on the table and smiles widely. By this time, the American Legion hall had been named for Howard H. Rohde, whose picture hangs proudly on the wall. This date of remembrance has been observed since the end of World War I. (Courtesy of Northlake Public Library.)

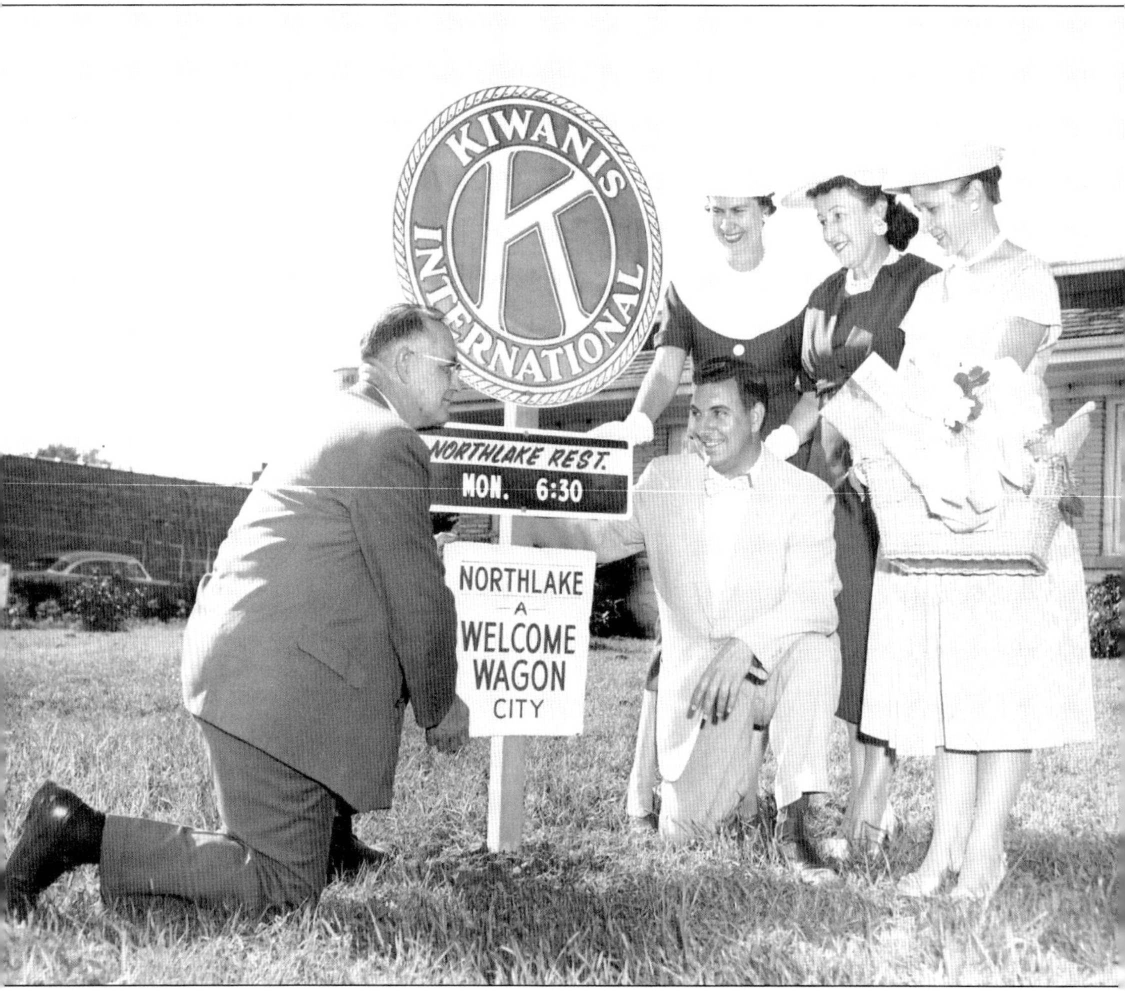

NORTHLAKE KIWANIS CLUB. The Kiwanis Club has had a strong presence in the community since its charter in December 1955. Here, Mayor Neri kneels next to a sign indicating the time of their meetings. Northlake Kiwanis remains important today, serving many children and residents through scholarships and other educational efforts. The community feels the club's presence when it enjoys the Grant Park gazebo and playground, which the Kiwanis helped create. (Courtesy of Northlake City Hall.)

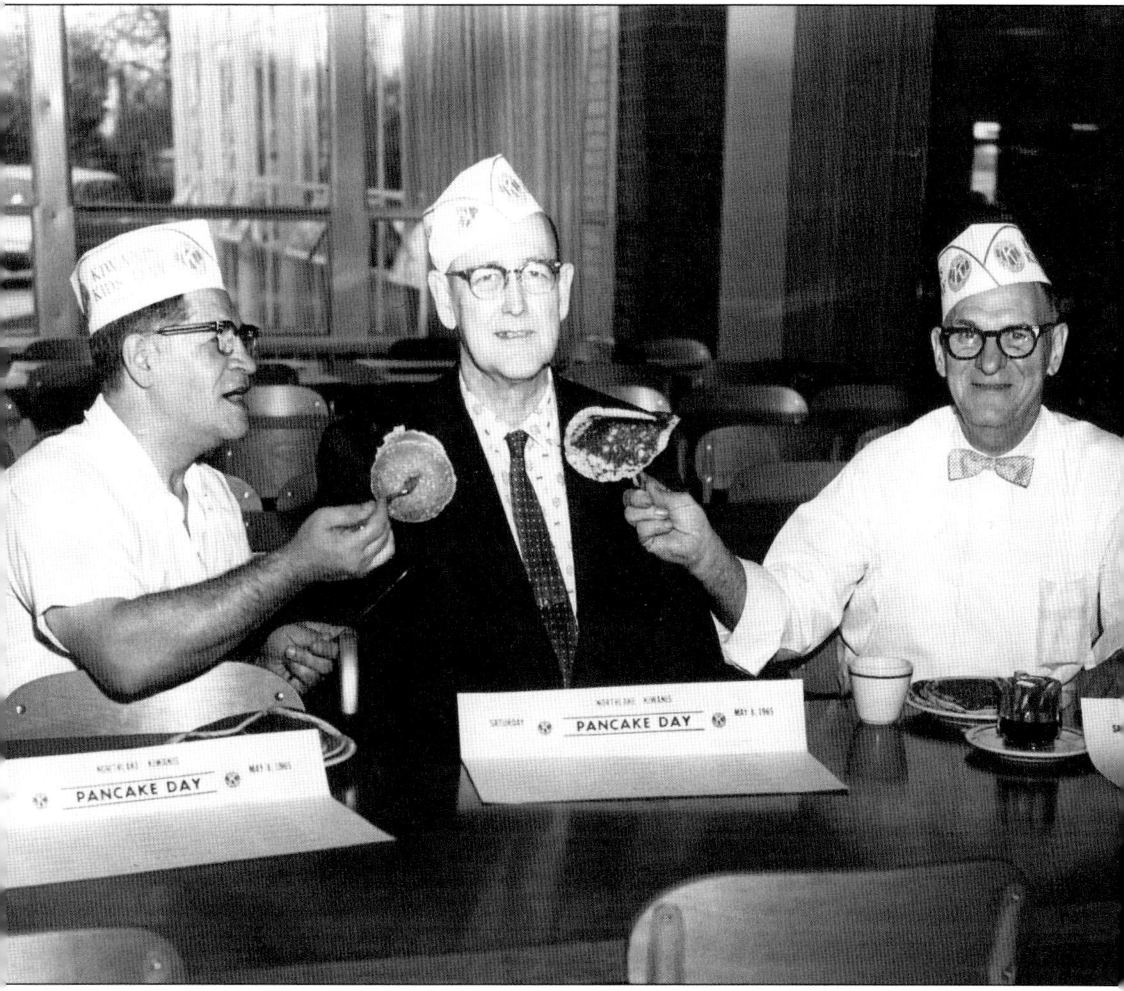

NORTHLAKE PANCAKE DAY. One of the longest-lasting fundraising events in Northlake has been the Kiwanis Pancake Day, seen here in May 1965. Area residents who have labored tirelessly for the fundraiser over the years include Vice President Nancy Tobin and William Piper, both graduates of West Leyden High School and longtime Kiwanis Club leaders. (Courtesy of Northlake Public Library.)

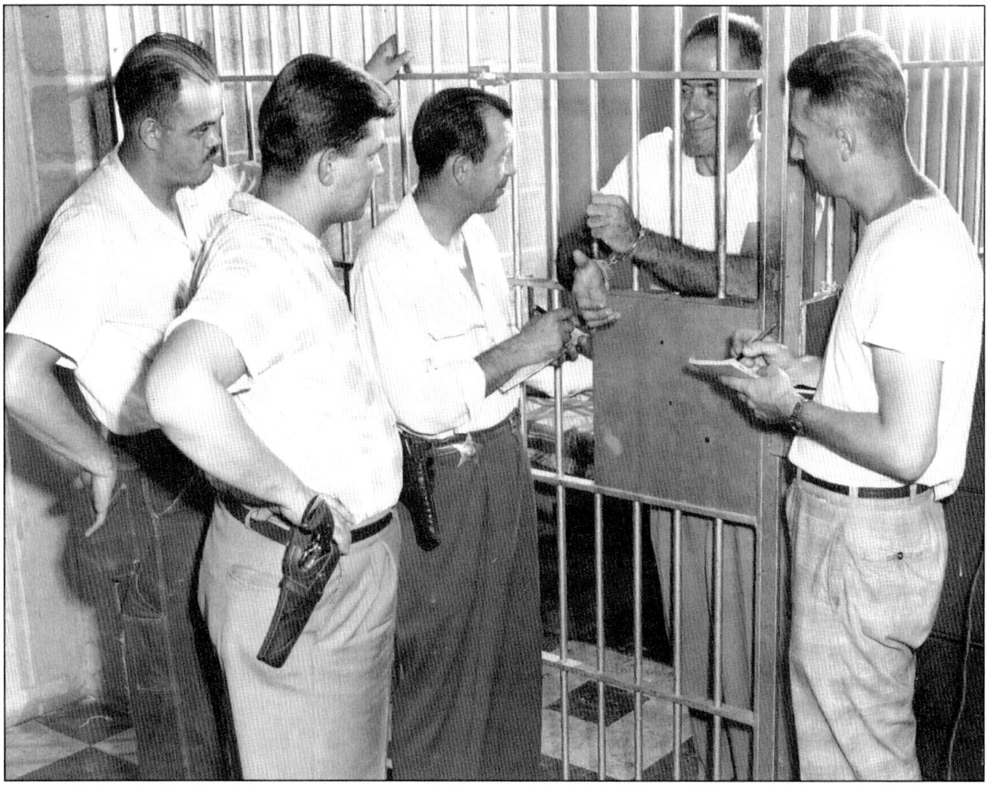

NORTHLAKE JAIL. Once the Northlake Police Department had enough space, a holding cell was added. This man is temporarily handcuffed as he is interviewed by policemen. The cell had nothing more than a small window and a cot. (Courtesy of Northlake City Hall.)

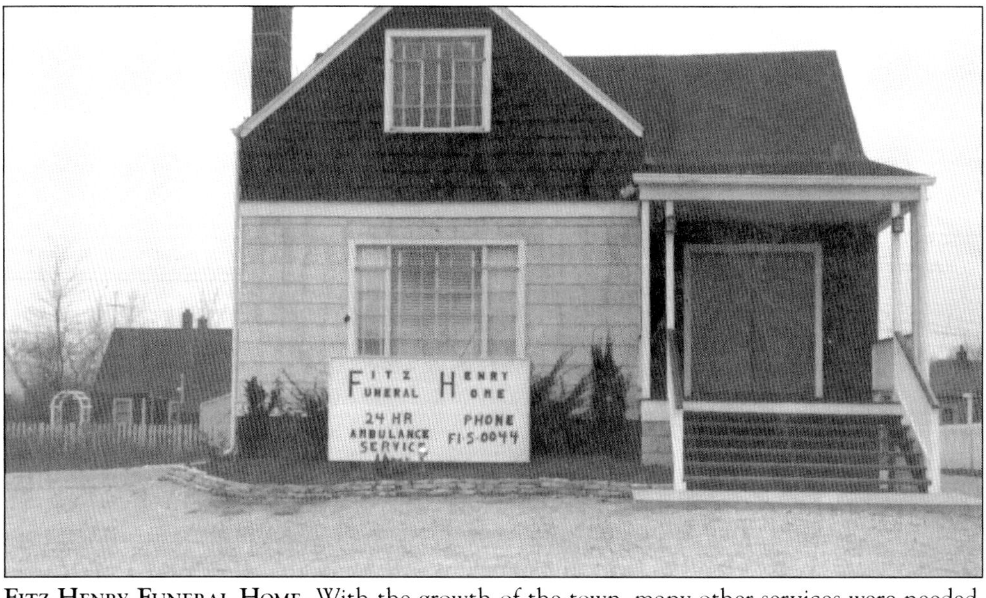

FITZ HENRY FUNERAL HOME. With the growth of the town, many other services were needed. The Fitz Henry Funeral Home displays a sign advertising its 24-hour ambulance service. (Courtesy of Connell family.)

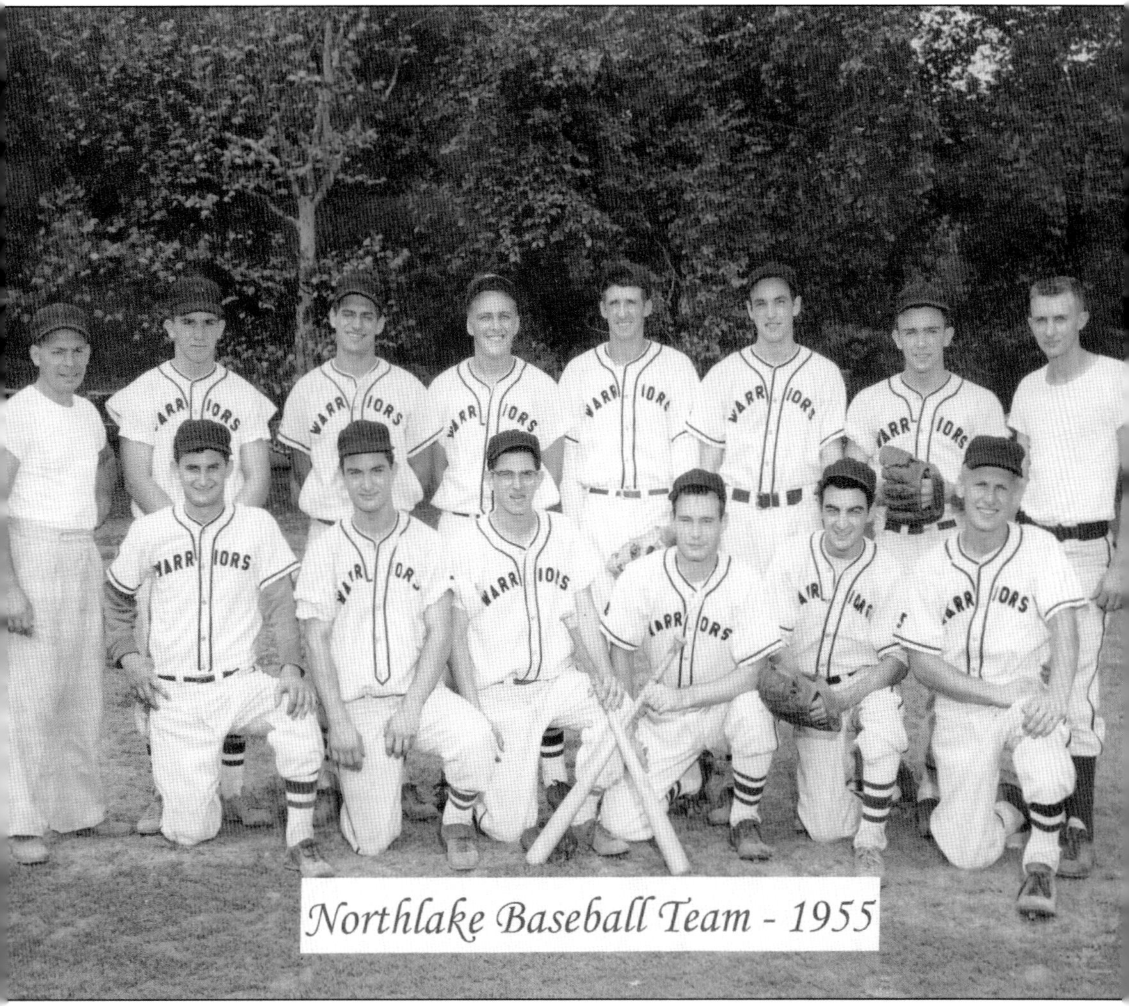

1955 Northlake Baseball Team. Sports continued to be a passion for many in Northlake. After Northlake Baseball was founded in 1952, it attracted a growing following. The 1955 Northlake Warriors are seen here. (Courtesy of Northlake City Hall.)

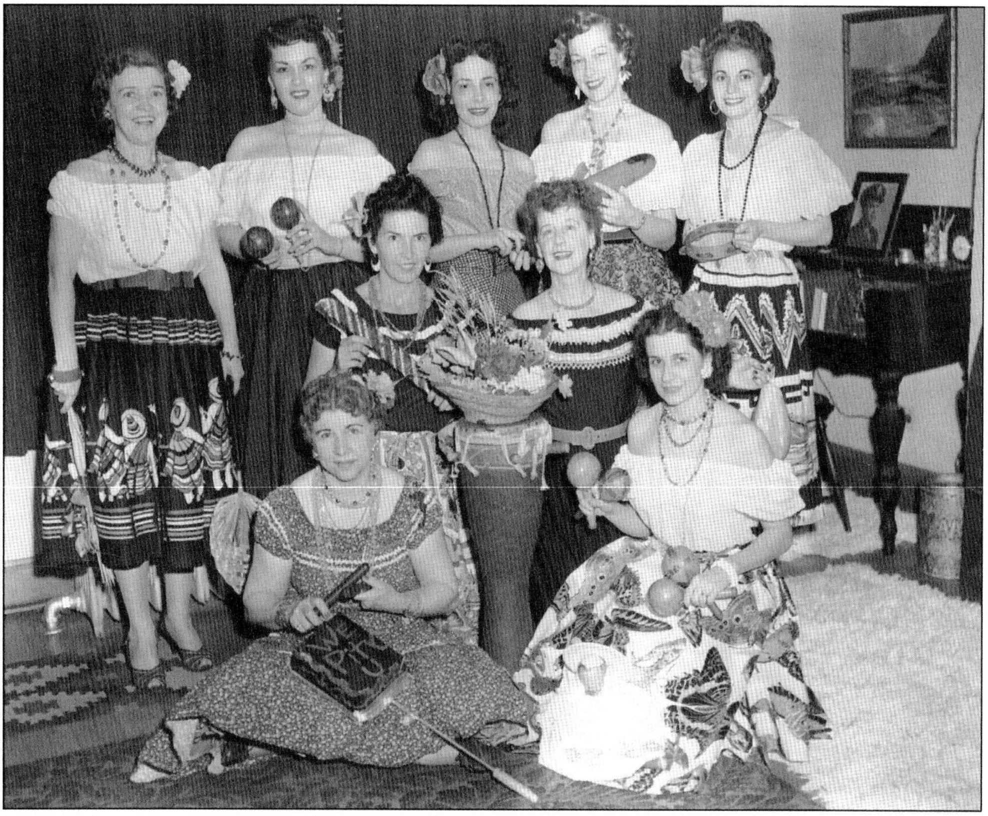

LADIES' CULTURE GROUP. Involvement in the community was always important. This ladies' group gathers wearing international attire, representing their interest in other cultures with maracas and skirts from foreign countries. (Courtesy of Northlake City Hall.)

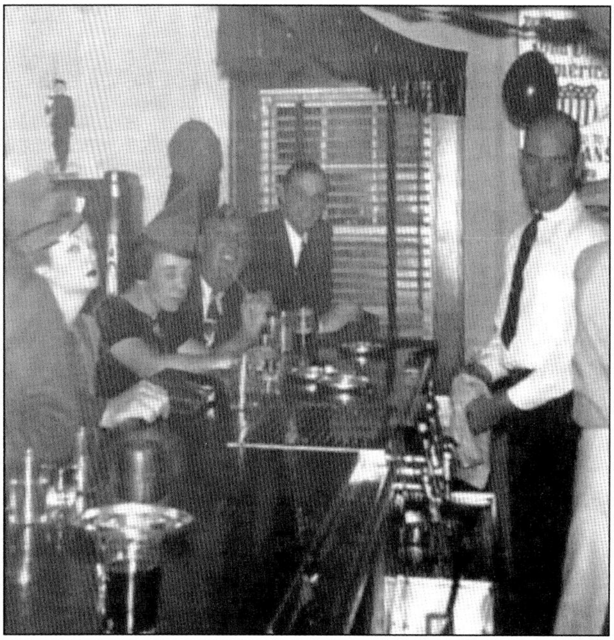

NORTHLAKE BAR PARTY. Socializing has always been important in Northlake. Here, residents gather at a local tavern, celebrating in their finest attire. Notice the "God Bless America" poster on the back wall. (Courtesy of Northlake City Hall.)

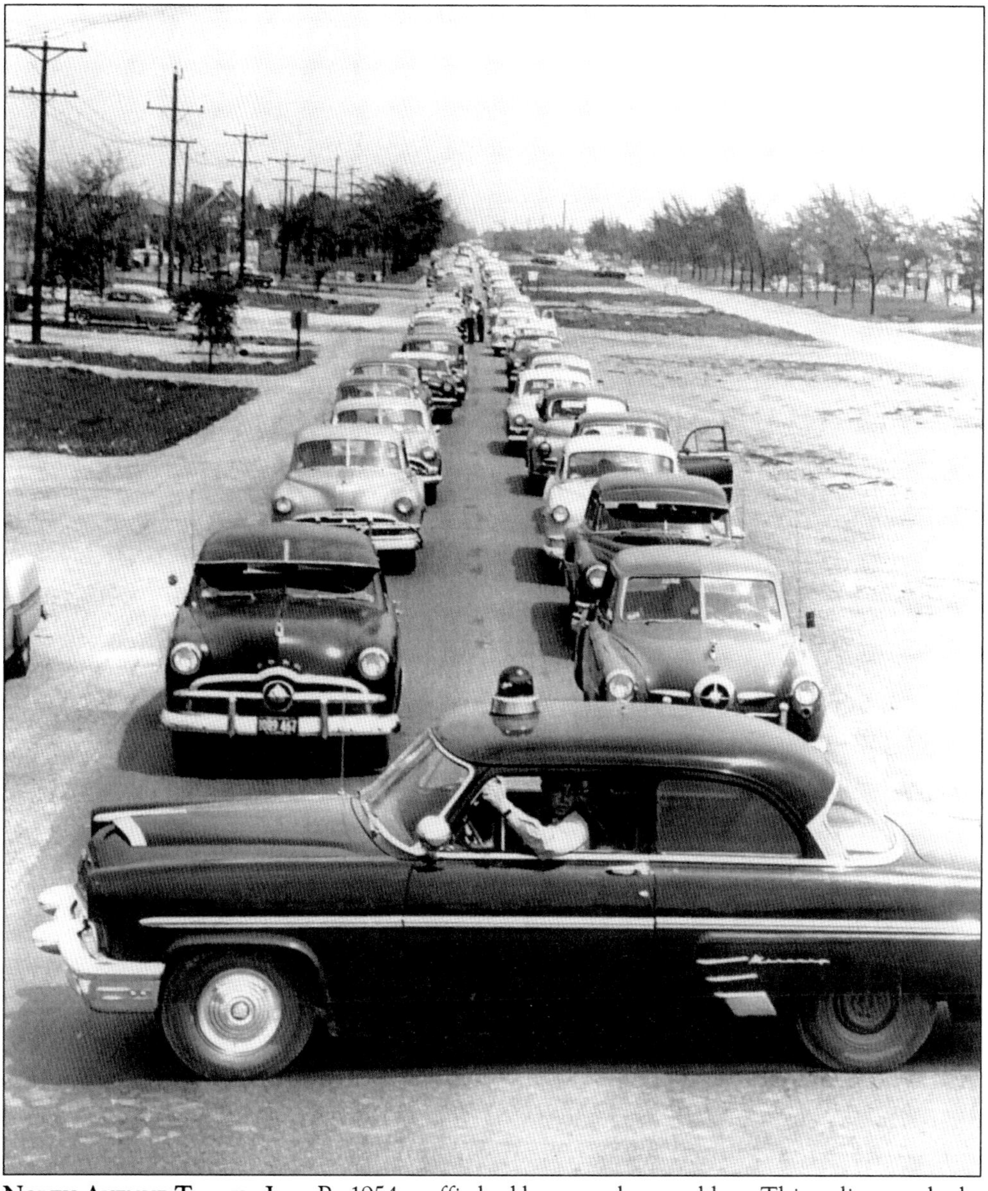

NORTH AVENUE TRAFFIC JAM. By 1954, traffic had begun to be a problem. This policeman looks eastward on North Avenue as he blocks traffic during a jam. Notice the abundance of grass in the background, as there were still more residences on the main street than there were commercial buildings at the time. (Courtesy of Northlake City Hall.)

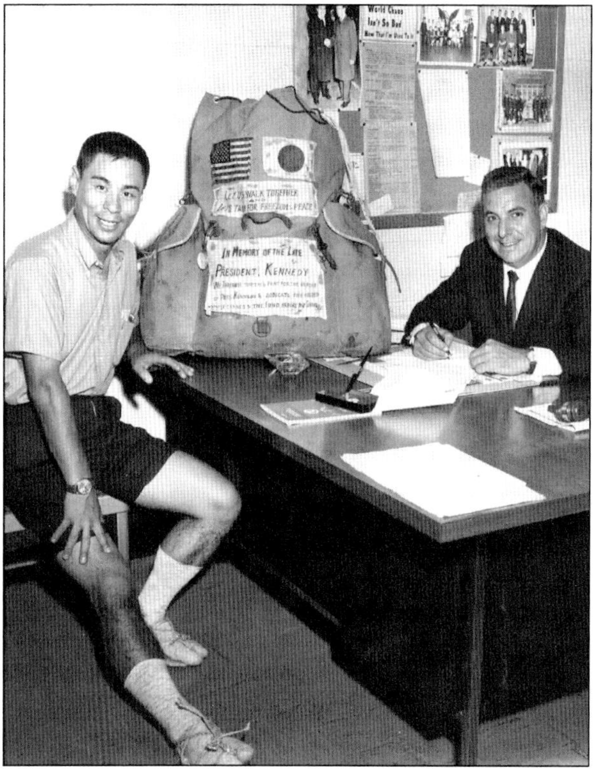

Mayor Neri, 1960s. Mayor Ed Neri sits at his desk with a man and a bag that reads, "In Memory of the Late President Kennedy." Notice the paper pinned to the bulletin board that reads "World Chaos Isn't So Bad Now That I Am Used To It," reflecting the diverse movements and world events of the 1960s. (Courtesy of Northlake City Hall.)

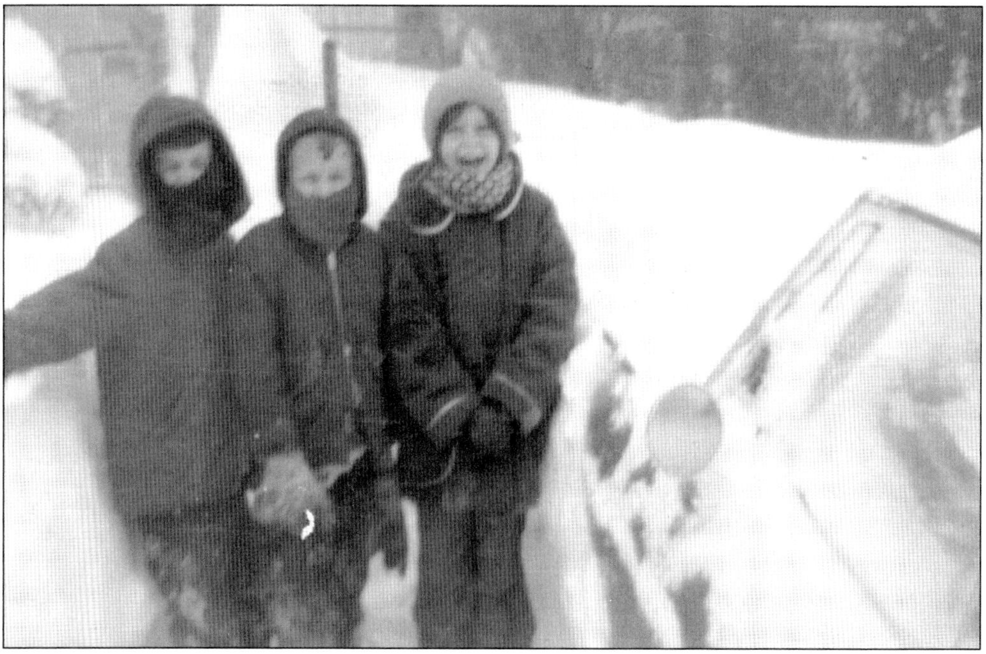

Blizzard of 1967. Weather has provided many challenges for residents of Northlake. However, snowstorms such as the Blizzard of 1967, seen here, also made for great playtime outside. From left to right, Bob, Rusty, and Jeanmarie Grenier stand in the driveway ready for sledding, snowball fights, and snowmen. (Courtesy of Bob Grenier.)

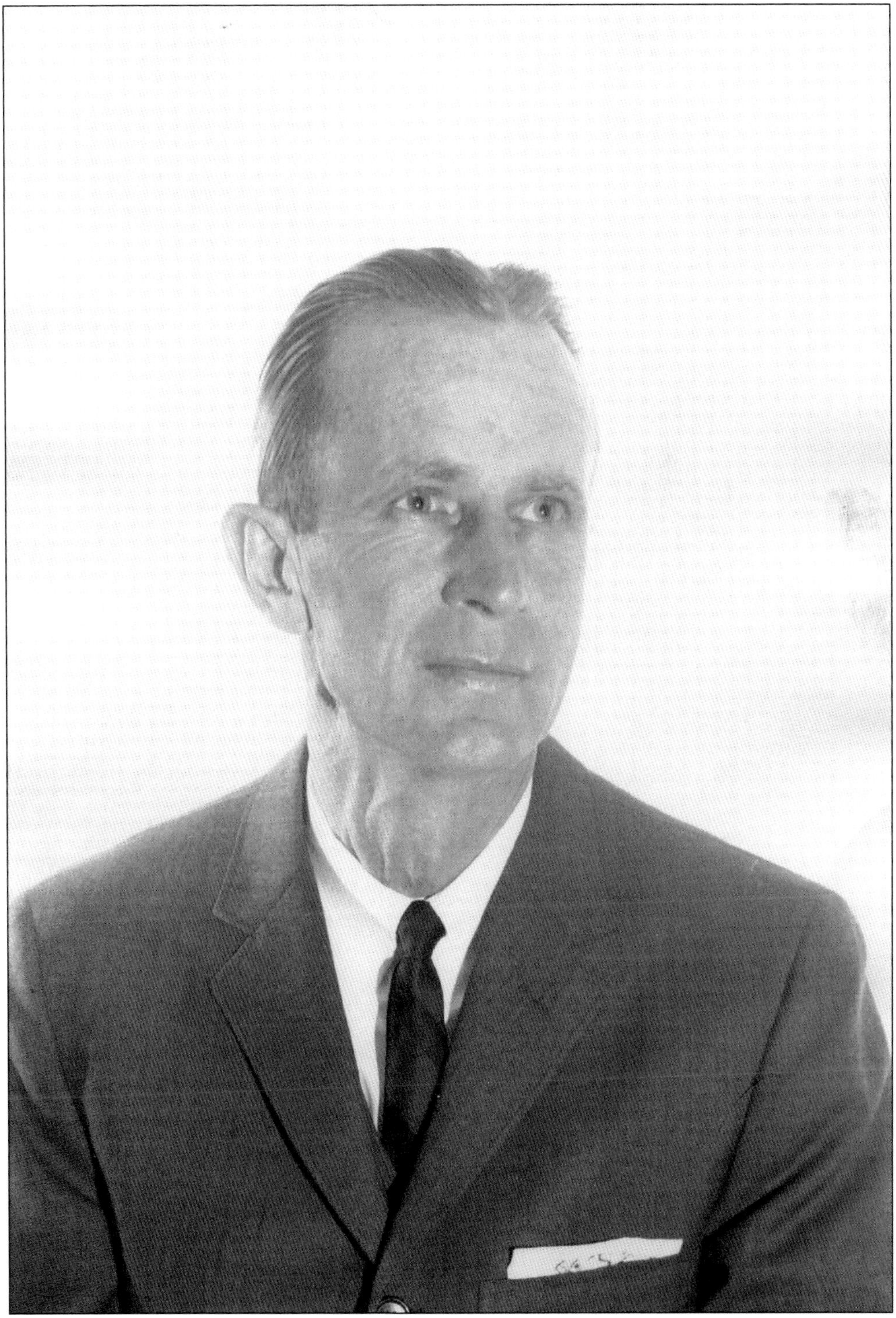

Joe Smith. A respected businessman and the owner of Pure Oil on the corner of North and Wolf Streets, Joe Smith is seen here in 1957. He served as a third ward alderman and as president of the Northlake Chamber of Commerce. (Courtesy of Northlake City Hall.)

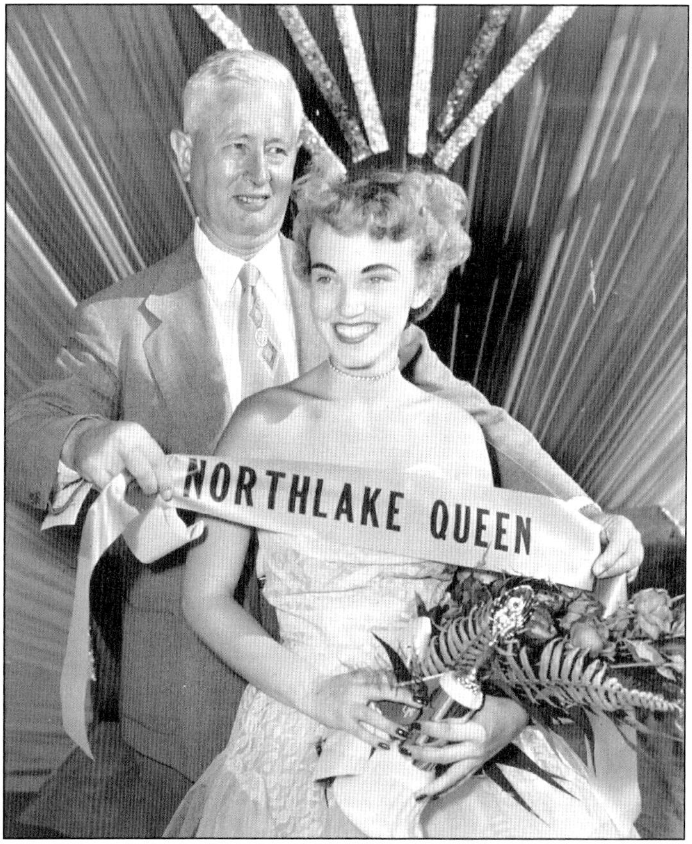

Miss Northlake with Mayor Griffin. One of the many queens in the early Northlake era gets a sash placed around her by Mayor Joseph Griffin in the 1950s. Miss Northlake's responsibilities included attending official Northlake events and ribbon cuttings. Given the explosive growth of Northlake in the 1960s, Miss Northlake played an important role as a city representative. (Courtesy of Northlake City Hall.)

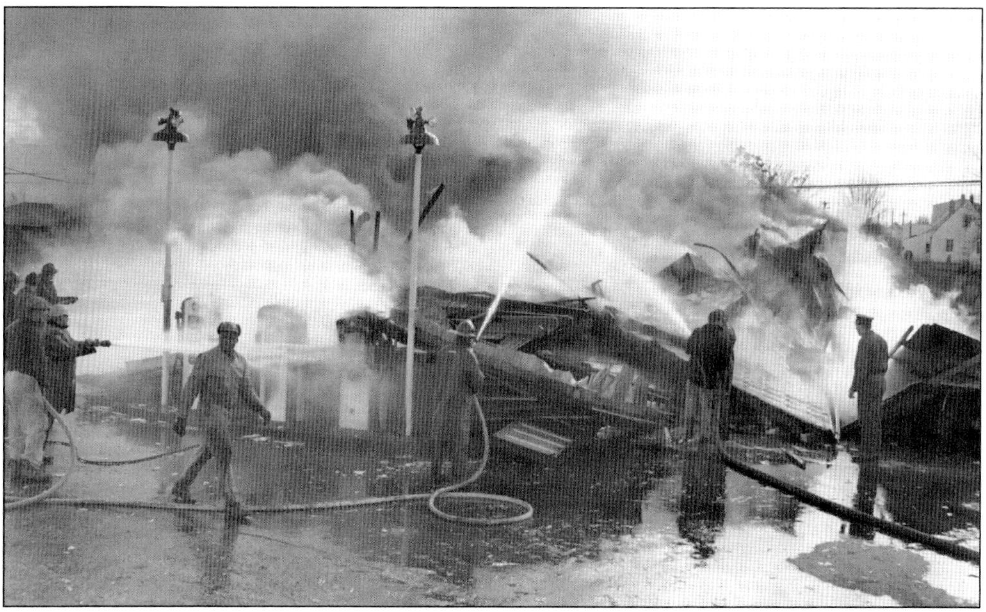

Fire at Jack's Service Station. Around 1950, Jack's Service Station, on the corner of North Avenue and Prater Avenue, burned down. The smoke billowing from the site could be seen for miles around. (Courtesy of Northlake City Hall.)

Three
The Changing Face of Northlake

At the end of Mayor Neri's term, many newsworthy developments were emerging. A local bank robbery grabbed the attention of the nation as two police officers were killed in the line of duty. A national manhunt ensued and the community came together.

Many restaurants gained spots in the hearts of locals, as beer gardens became popular for customers to enjoy the nice weather and socialize. Large-screen televisions brought people into restaurants to watch sports, especially the Chicago teams of the late 1980s and 1990s, when the Bulls won six championships. Talking sports over a few drinks became the norm.

Northlake baseball teams had changing names and faces as more Latinos moved into the area, many of whom followed in the footsteps of the early Italian American residents. Soccer became a popular sport in the area. Spanish services were soon provided for Spanish-speaking residents at nearby churches. Supermarkets began to stock items from foreign countries, especially Mexico, to meet the needs of their changing customer base.

Restaurants also began to diversify, with a few Mexican restaurants opening. Northlake was no longer a homogenous community, but in so many ways, the "City of Friendly People" continued to be just that.

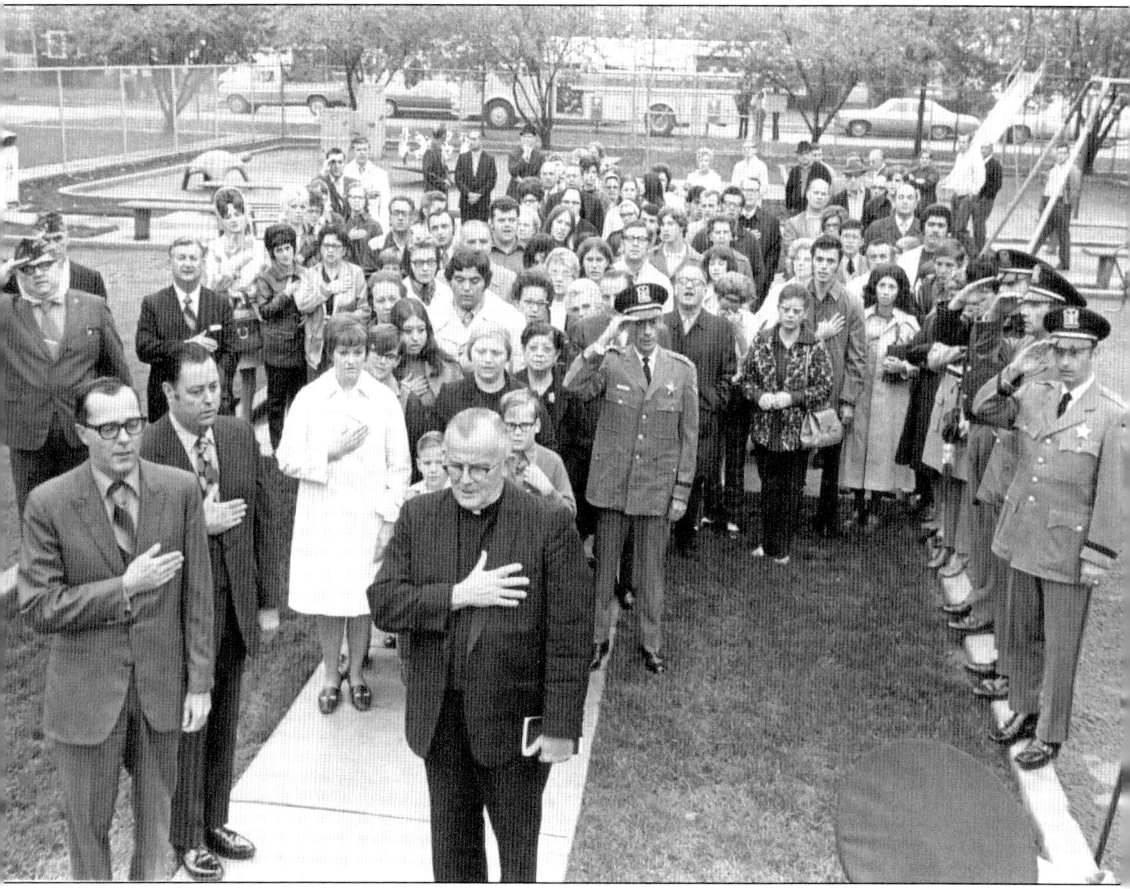

Deaths of Officers Nagle and Perri. Tragedy occurred in October 1967 when three bank robbers entered Northlake Bank with semiautomatic weapons and walked out with bags full of money. Two officers, John Nagle and Anthony Perri, responded to the bank alarm and received a hail of bullets, both ultimately dying from multiple gunshot wounds. (Courtesy of Northlake City Hall.)

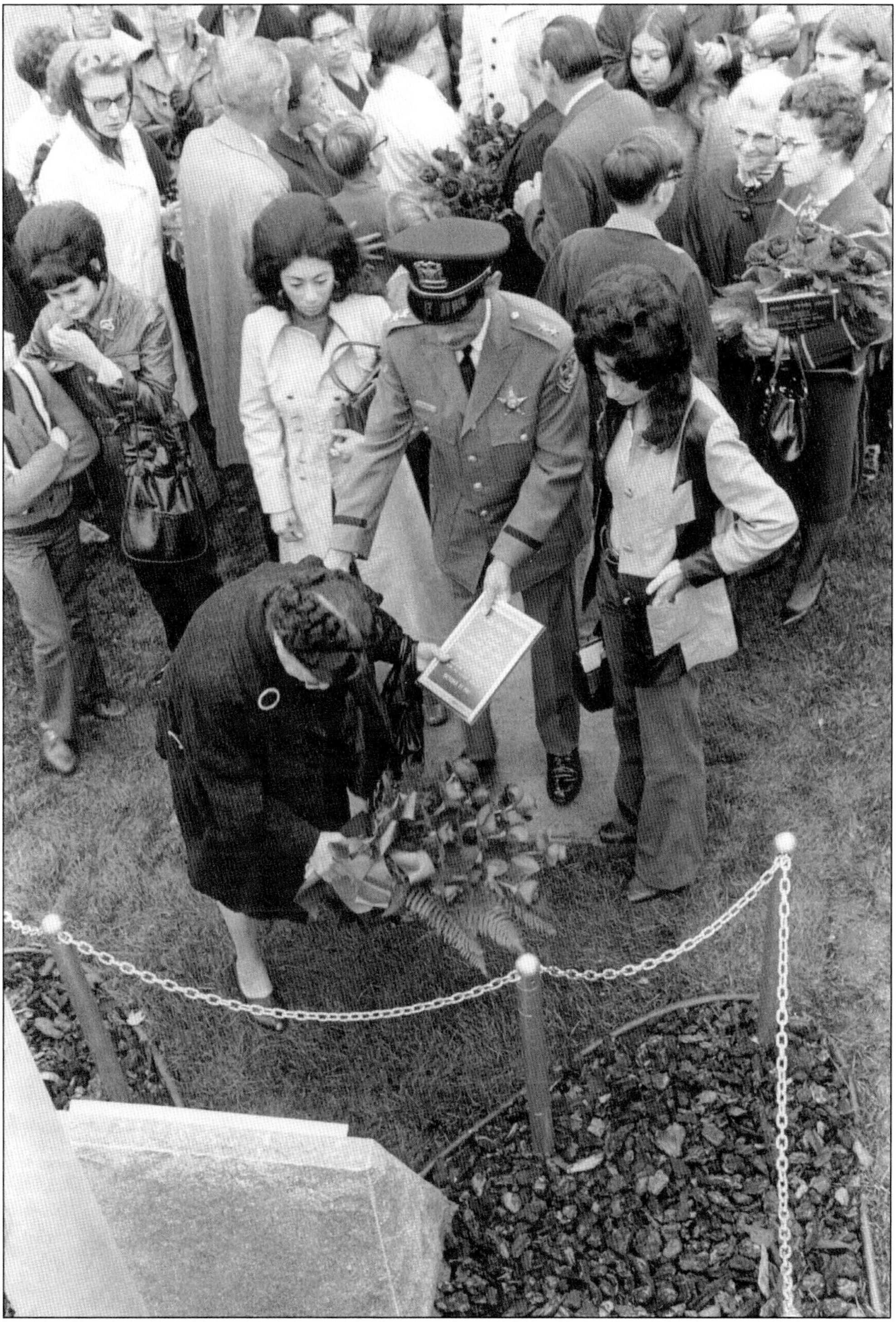

NAGLE-PERRI PARK. Four years after the deaths of Officers Nagle and Perri, a park was named in their honor and a special ceremony commemorated their lives. Here, Antoinette Perri places flowers near the plaque honoring the two fallen officers. (Courtesy of Northlake City Hall.)

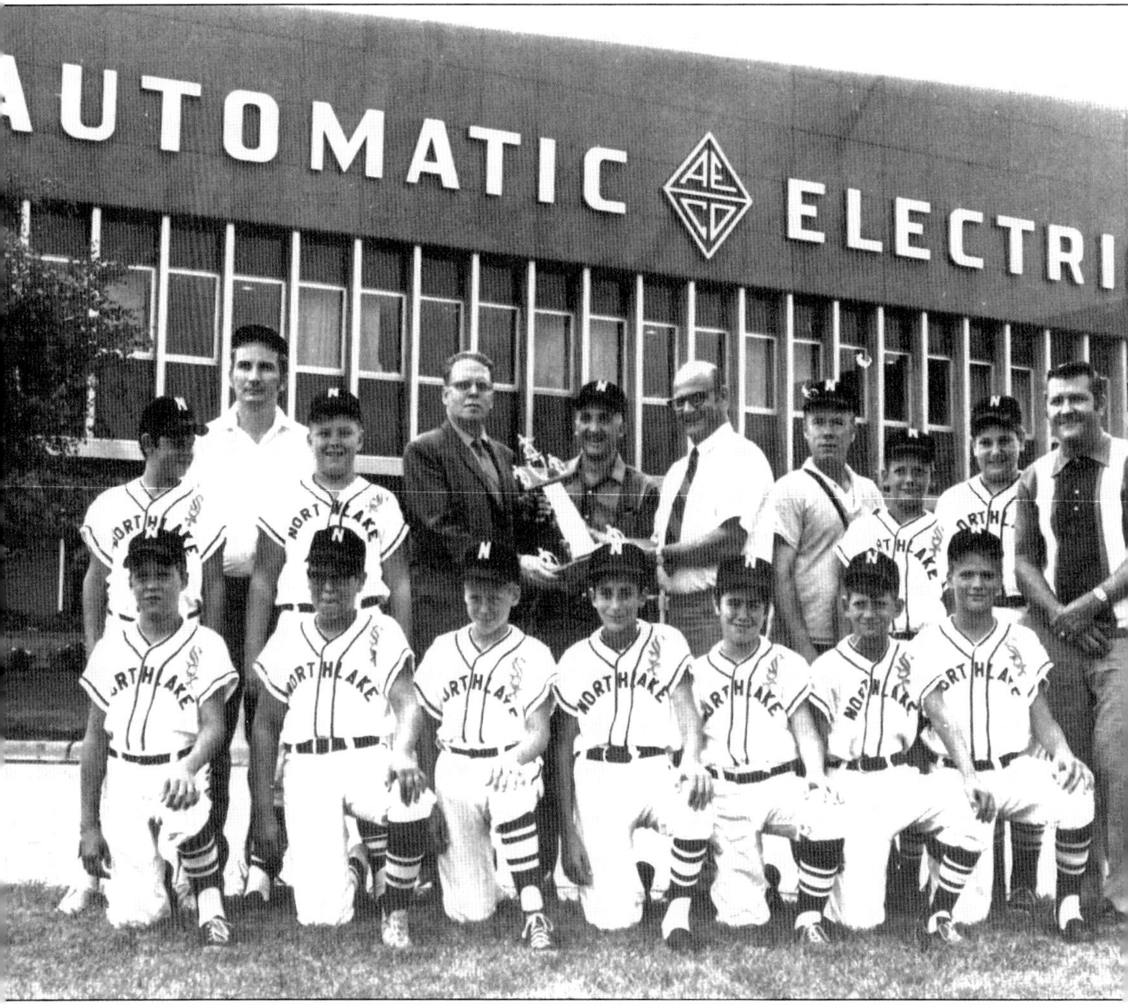

Automatic Electric Baseball Team. Baseball remains a strong local tradition to this day with teams like the Automatic Electric plant team, seen here with their coach and a company representative holding the trophy. (Courtesy of Northlake City Hall.)

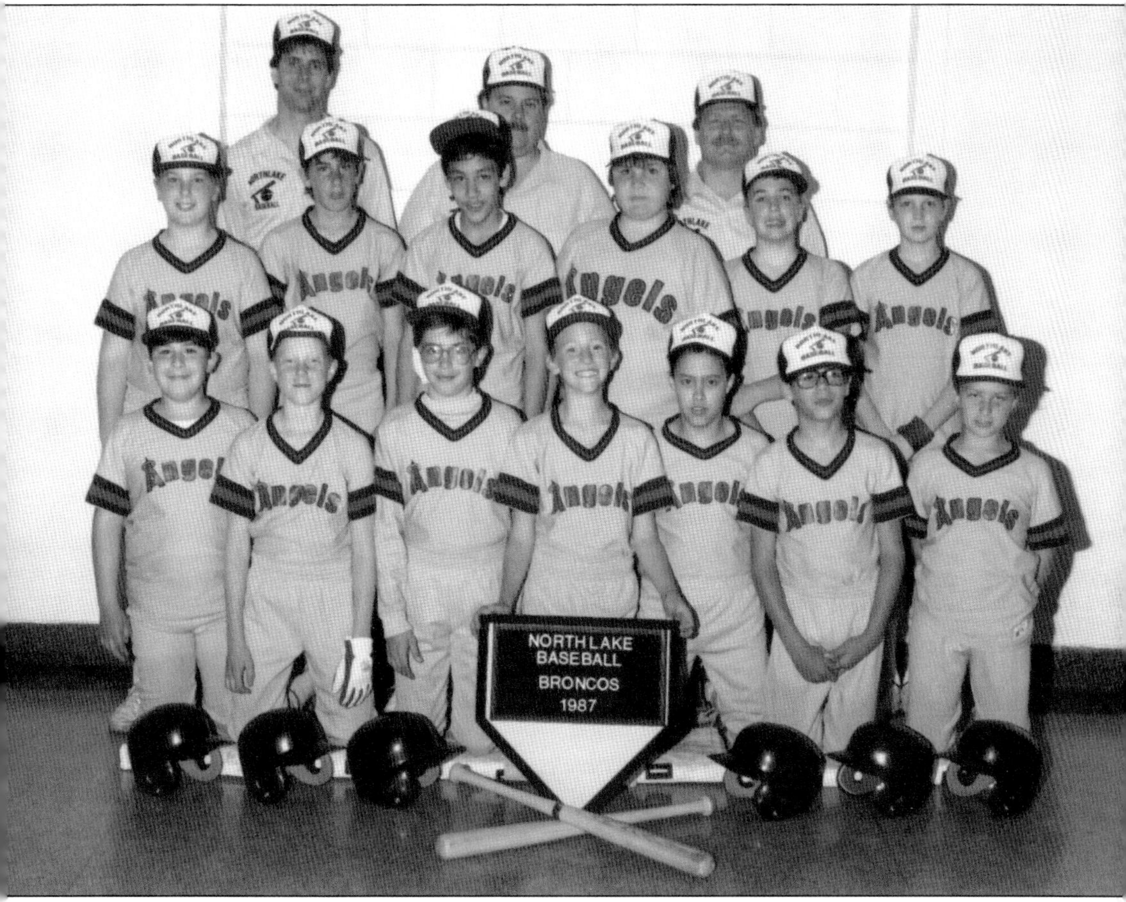

1987 Northlake Team. This photograph of a local youth baseball team shows the addition of Latinos and other minority groups that had started moving into the area. Competition came from surrounding suburbs such as Bellwood and Broadview. (Author's collection.)

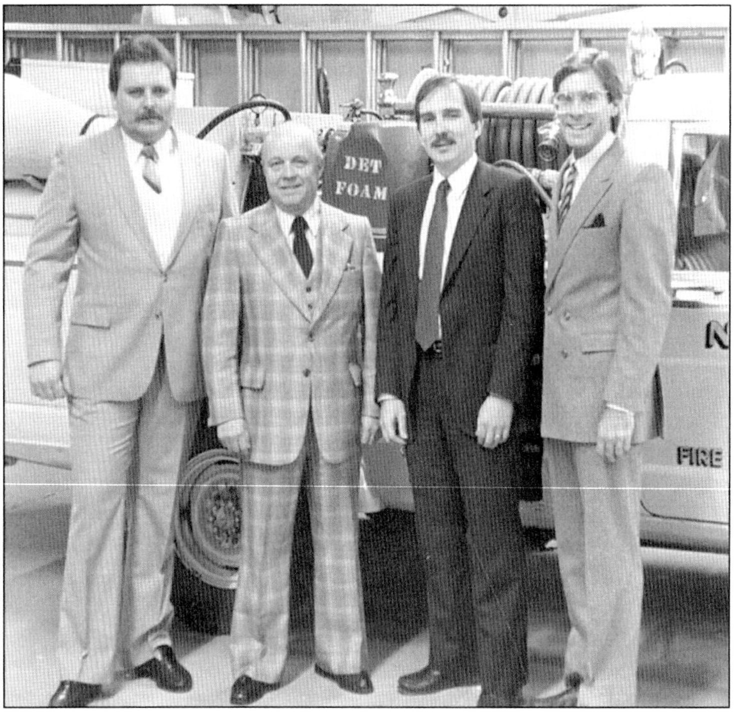

NORTHLAKE'S FIRST ELECTED TRUSTEES. In 1985, Northlake elected its first trustees (from left to right): Jeffrey Ferguson, Frank Sullivan, Jeffrey Sherwin, and Greg Zito. More than 10 years later, Sherwin became mayor of Northlake. (Courtesy of Northlake City Hall.)

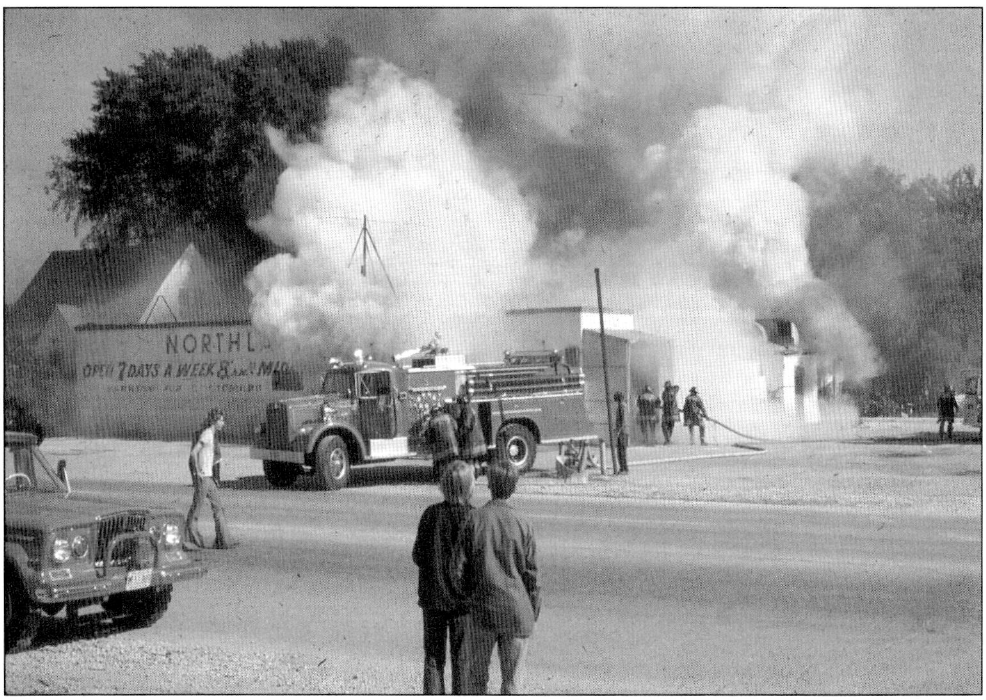

NORTHLAKE FOODS FIRE. One of the earliest grocery stores, Northlake Foods on Wolf Road, burned to the ground in 1970. Smoke could be seen for miles around as onlookers watched the end of the popular grocery store. After the fire, National Foods, a block north, no longer had a competitor. (Courtesy of Northlake Fire Department.)

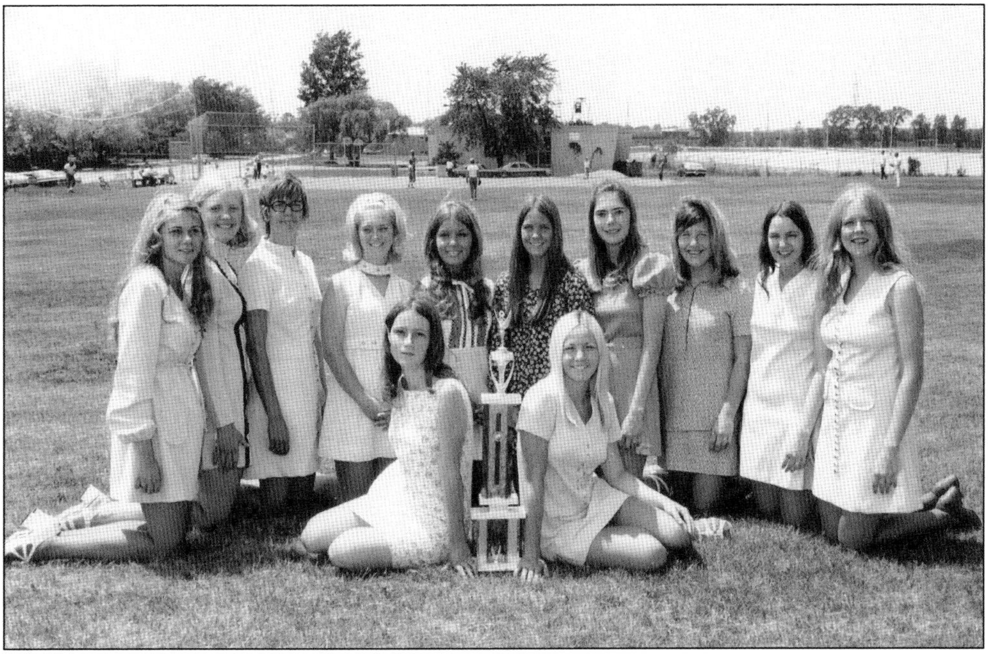

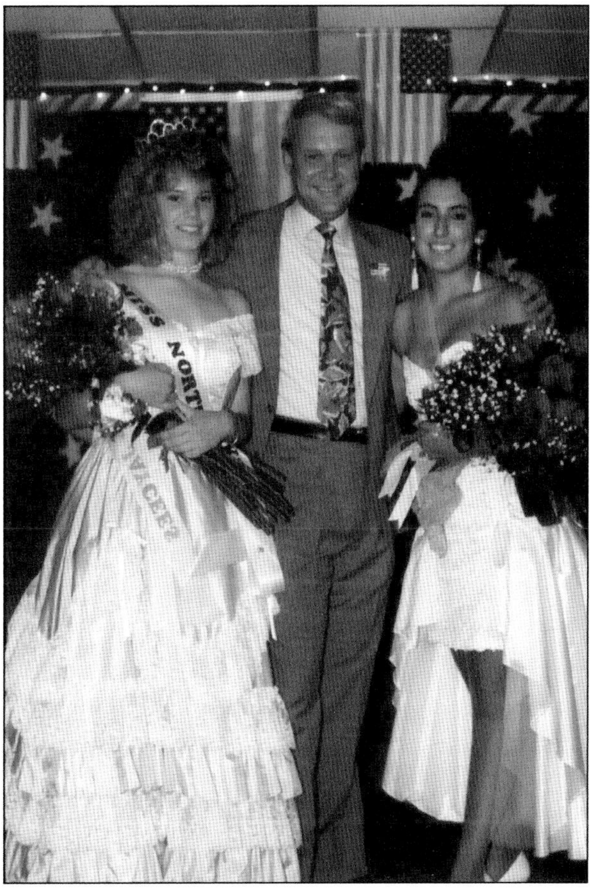

NORTHLAKE BEAUTY CONTEST AND MISS NORTHLAKE. Beyond the normal athletic competitions, Northlake loved its Miss Northlake contests. Above, 15 contestants pose for a photograph in Grant Park with the winning trophy placed in their midst. At right, Mayor Reid Paxson poses with Miss Northlake in the early 1990s. (Both, courtesy of Northlake City Hall.)

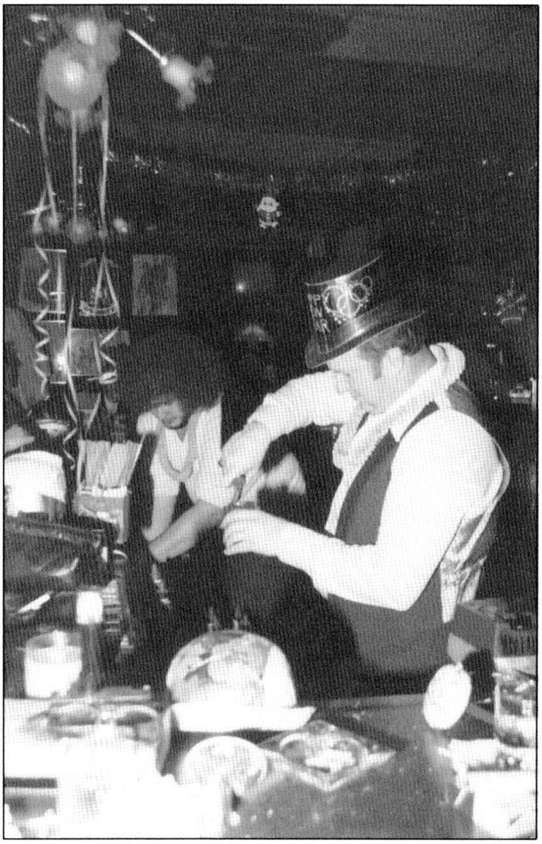

Perry's Pizza Joynt and New Year's Eve Party. The ever-popular Perry's Pizza Joynt near the center of town continues to be a permanent fixture in the community. Owner Jack Perry prepares a drink for New Year's Eve party guests as streamers and ribbons hang from the wall. Aside from the bar and restaurant seating area, there is a room for special events like birthday parties. Perry's continues to be a popular place for baseball teams to grab a bite to eat after games. As for local residents, watching games on the big screen still remains a popular choice. (Both, courtesy of Jack Perry.)

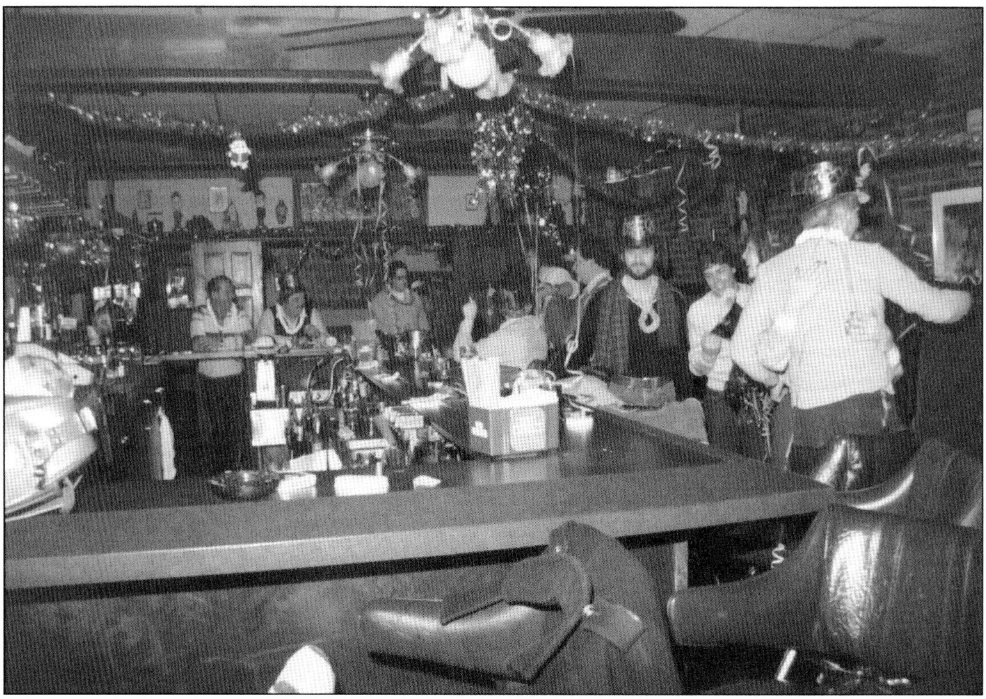

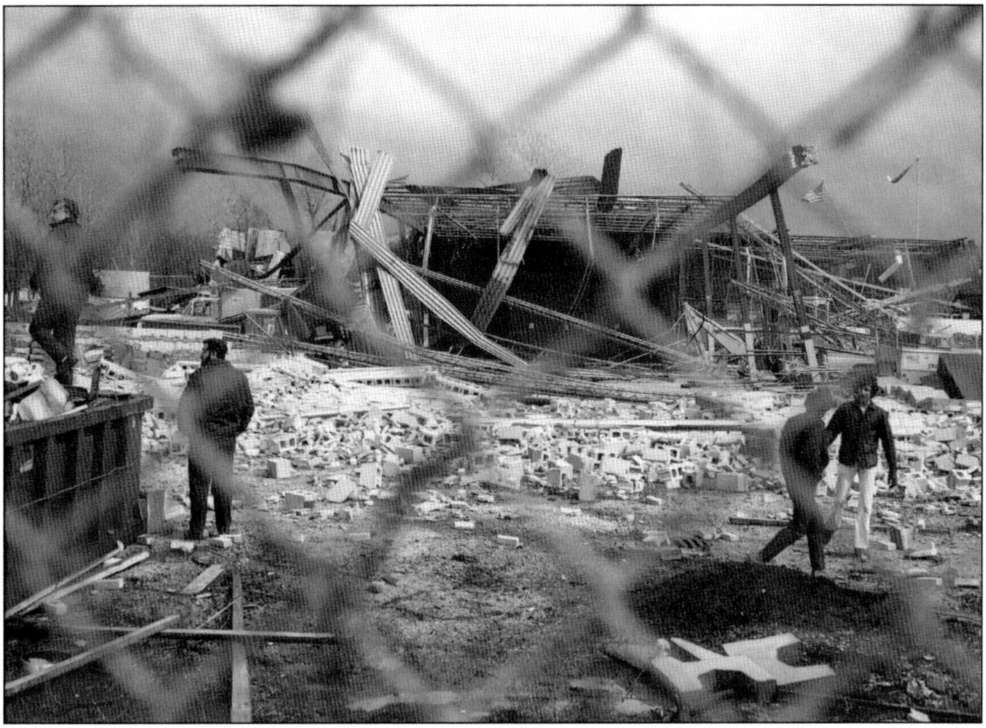

PUBLIC WORKS BUILDING DESTROYED. Natural events have left their mark on Northlake. In addition to frequent floods, tornadoes have ripped through the area, leaving destruction in their path. Such was the case on March 12, 1976, when a tornado left the public works building shattered. The only standing markers were the flags flapping in the air. The new Northlake Public Works Building (below) was built with brick walls to prevent a future disaster. (Both courtesy of Northlake City Hall.)

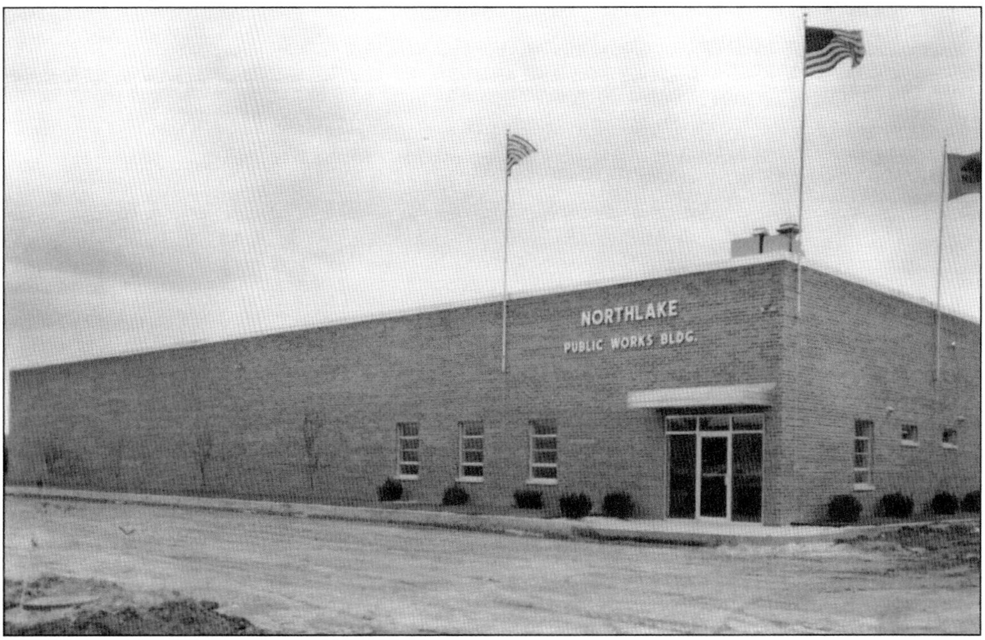

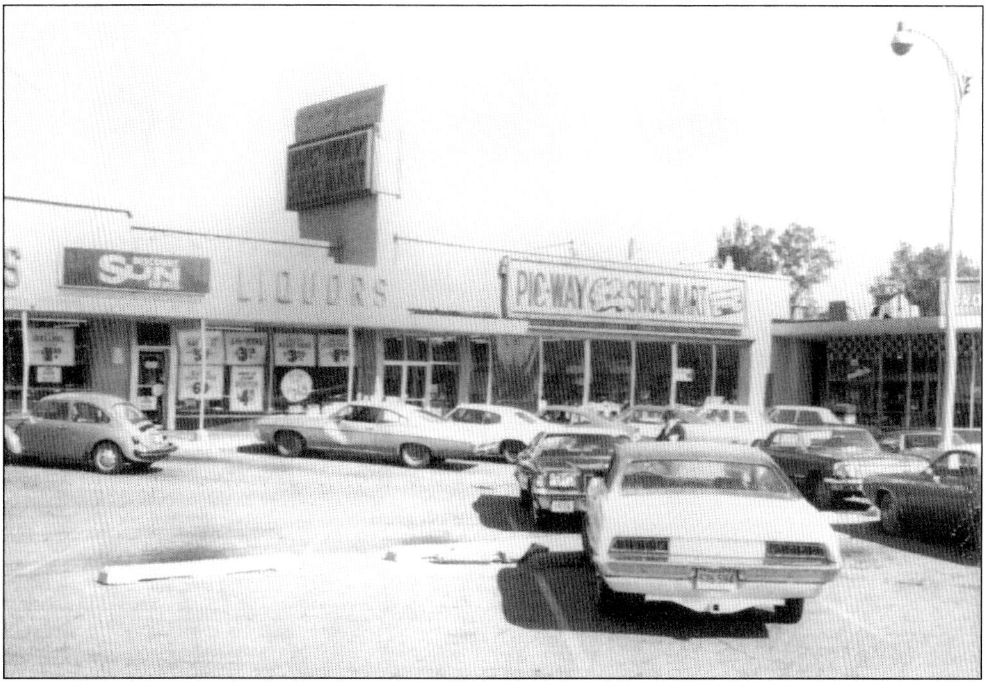

The Shopping Center Evolves and Stores Open. The shopping center continued to evolve and change to meet customer demand. Pic-way Shoe Mart (above) and a drugstore soon emerged. The video store below was in step with the times, advertising Atari video game competitions as well as VHS movie rentals. At the store's grand opening, Mayor Doyle stood in front selecting raffle winners as a band beckoned passersby to visit the latest business in town. (Both, courtesy of Northlake City Hall.)

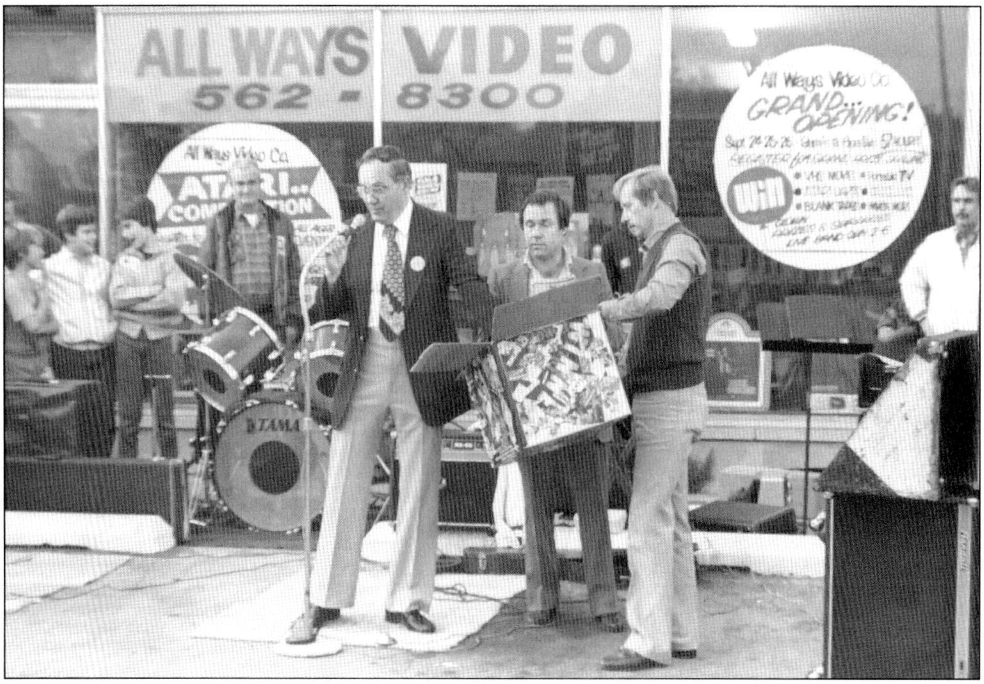

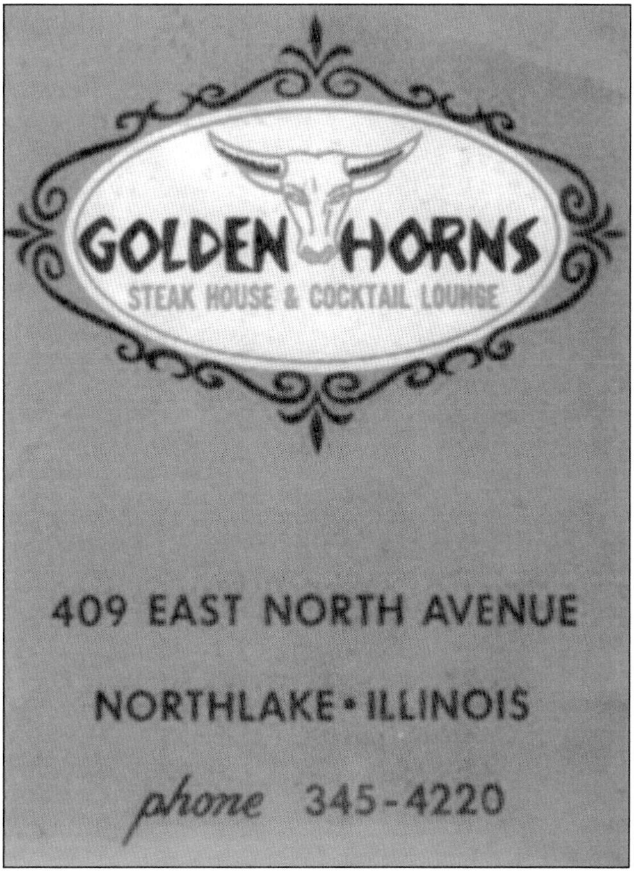

GOLDEN HORNS STEAKHOUSE AND CHRIS' PLACE. Many restaurants were local fixtures in the 1980s. Two iconic places were Golden Horns Steakhouse, near the eastern part of town, and Chris' Place, near the center of town. Chris' Place had billiards, game rooms, and a beer garden. Unfortunately, Chris' Place burned down, leaving only great memories. (Right, courtesy of Rudy Galfi; below, courtesy of Northlake City Hall.)

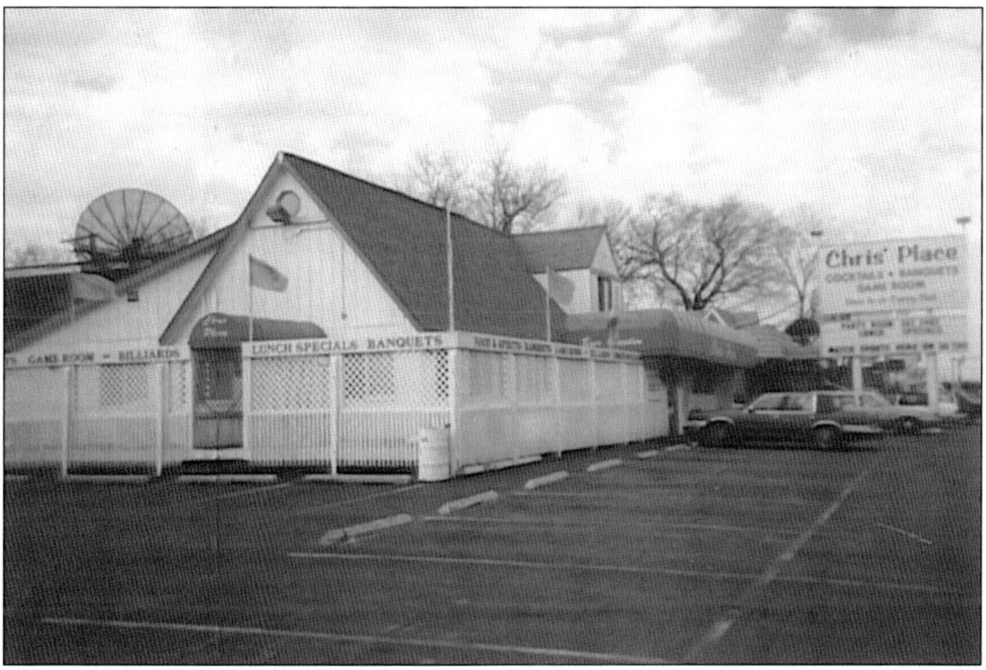

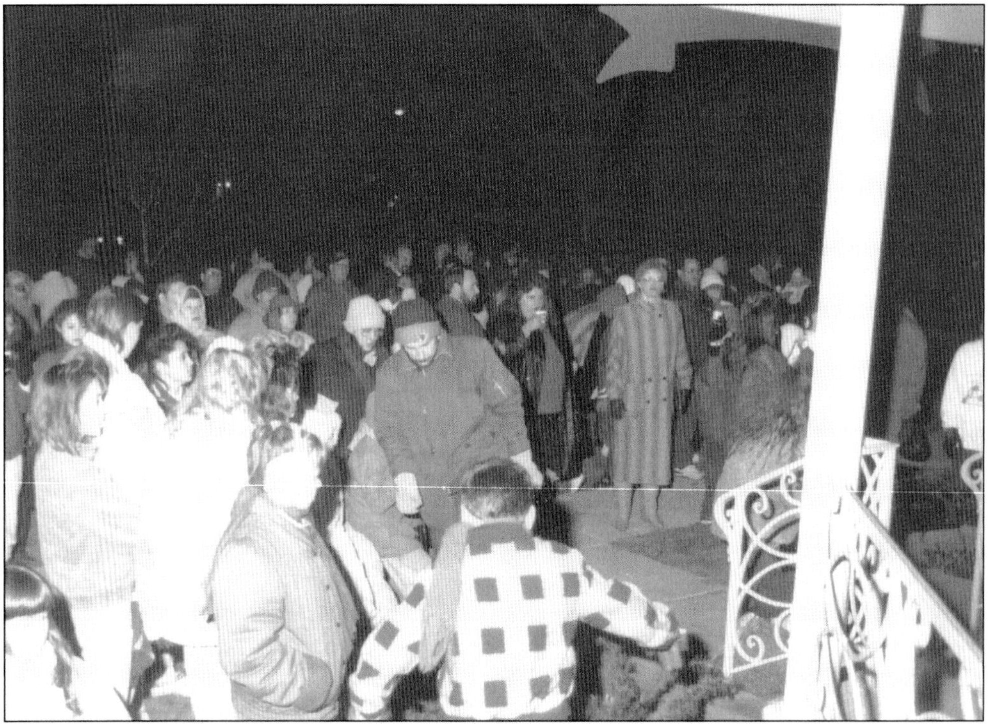

Tree Trimming and Carriage Rides. Two local traditions remained strong: the annual tree trimming and the annual carriage ride, seen here. The carriage ride is part of Northlake's holiday celebrations in December, entertaining children and adults alike. (Both, courtesy of Northlake City Hall.)

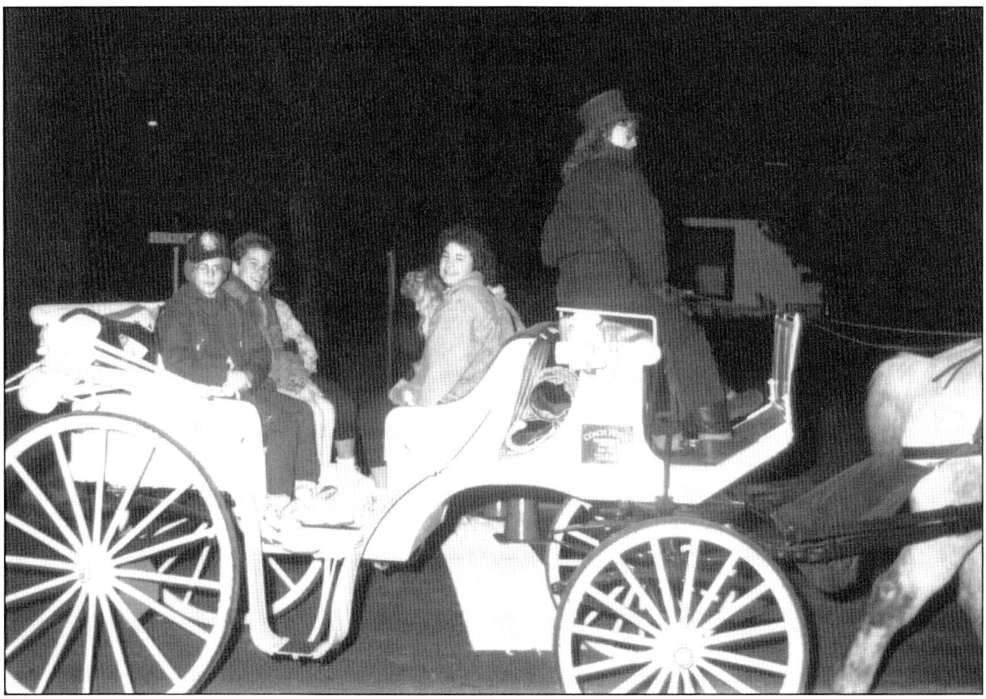

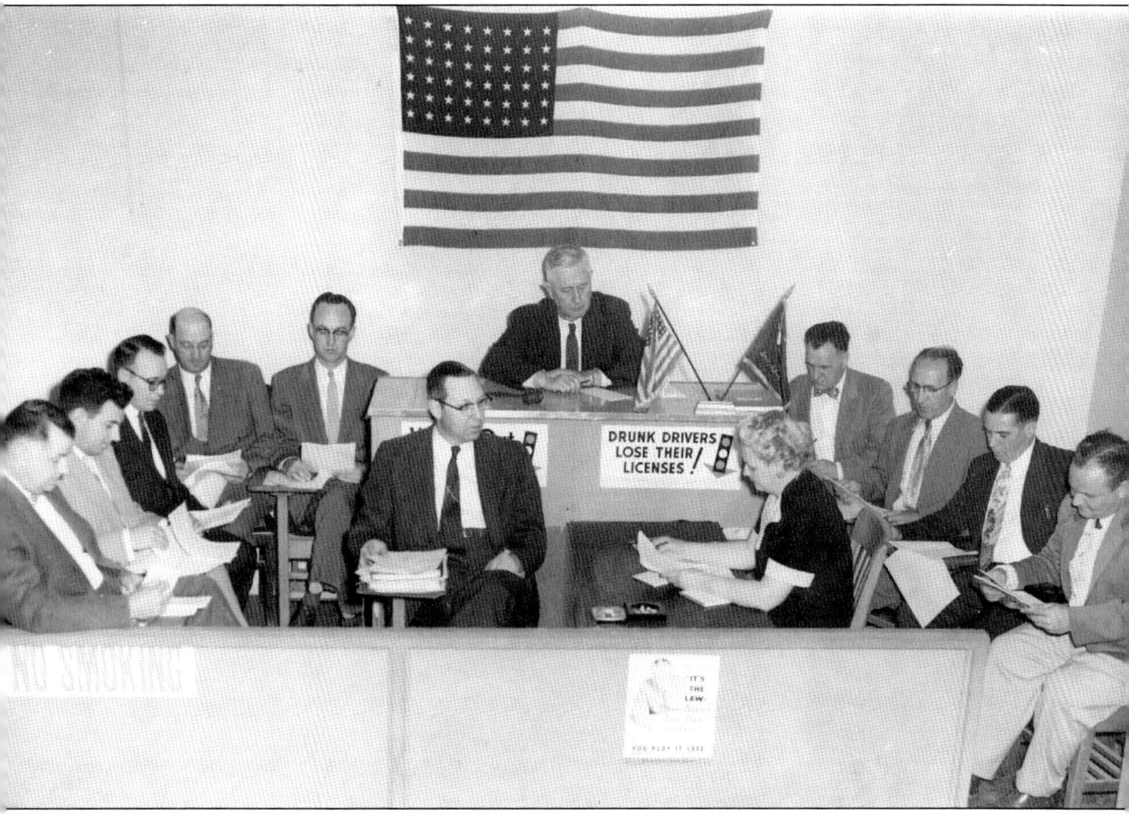

Mayor Joseph Griffin. Here, Mayor Griffin leads the first city council meeting on May 19, 1955, in the tight quarters of Northlake's city hall. This sign declares that, "Drunk Drivers Lose Their Licenses!" Future mayor Ed Neri (seated second from left), an alderman at the time, was poised to lead Northlake in many of its future programs. (Courtesy of Northlake Public Library.)

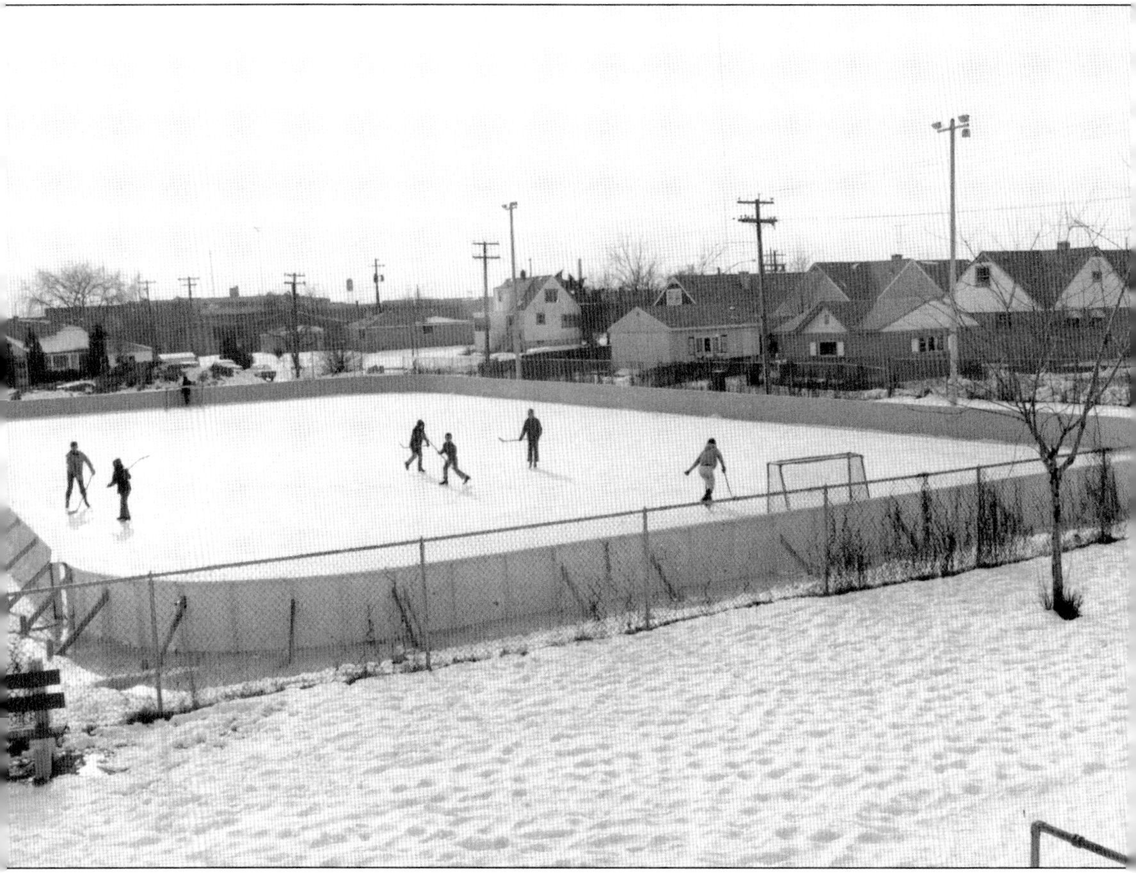

NORTHLAKE ICE RINK. Under the leadership of Mayor Eugene Doyle, Northlake built an ice rink for its youth. The rink provided a place for kids to enjoy themselves, skating around, playing hockey, and taking advantage of the cold winters in the area. (Courtesy of Northlake City Hall.)

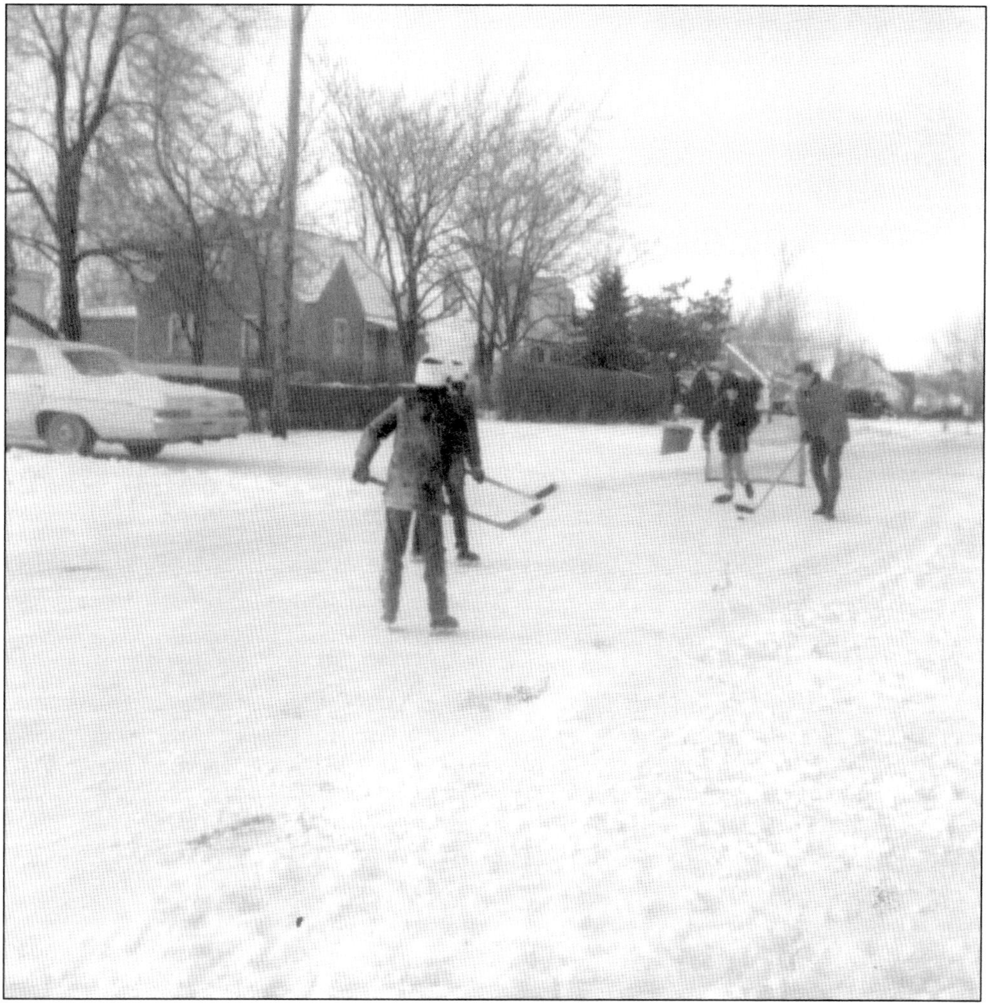

Hockey in the Streets. Before the ice rink was built, kids took great joy in playing hockey in the streets. Here, the Grenier and Coconate families play ice hockey on LaVergne Street in the early 1970s. (Courtesy of Bob Grenier.)

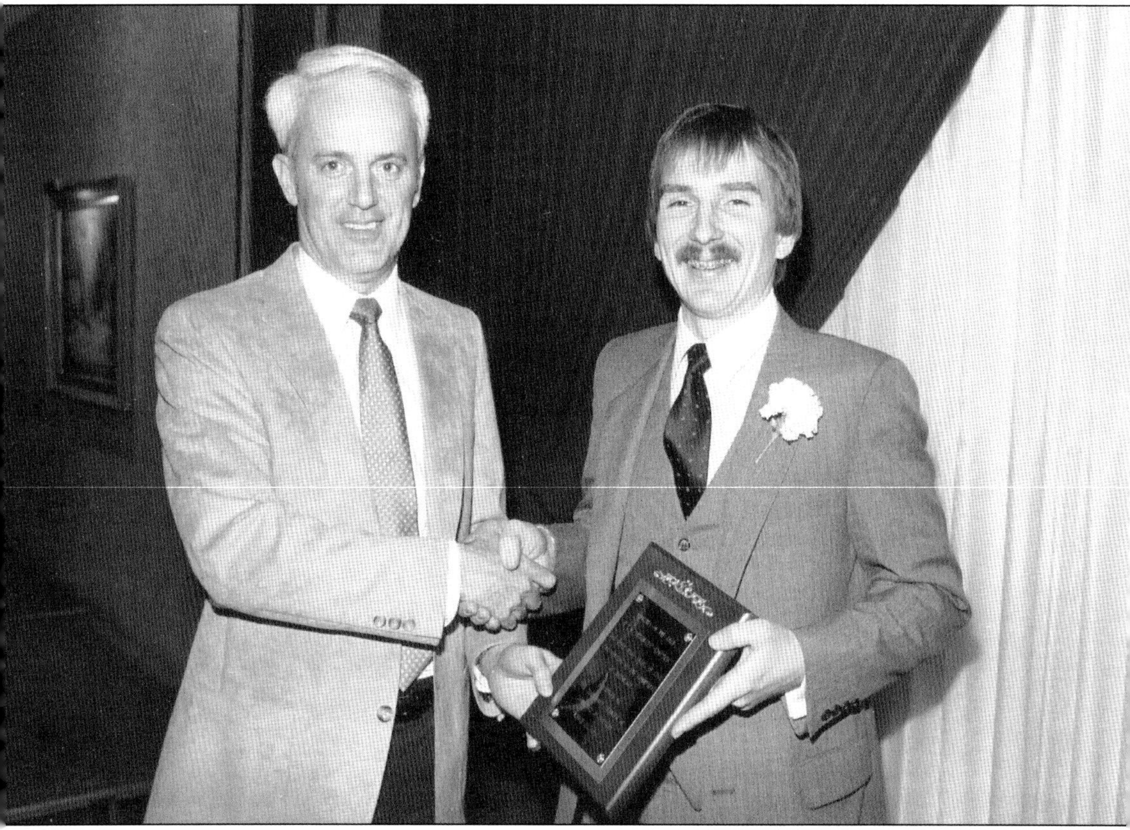

Jeff Sherwin and Jack Kirker. Northlake Chamber of Commerce president Jeffrey Sherwin (right) shakes the hand of Automated Electric president Jack Kirker as they hold a plaque. Automated Electric eventually left town in the 1980s after consolidating operations. (Courtesy of Northlake City Hall.)

Four

Northlake Days, Parades, and Floats

The town's best-known event is its summer festival, known as Northlake Days. It has continued for decades, serving its primary purpose of bringing local Northlake residents and residents of nearby communities to celebrate our nation's independence.

The week provides vast amounts of entertainment, as the carnival atmosphere allows children to ride roller coasters, play games for prizes, and get their fill of cotton candy. Artists set up tents and paint kids' faces with images of tigers, lions, and other animals. Clowns perform magic tricks and give away balloons shaped like dogs, birds, and giraffes, making them one of the more popular acts. There is also a fireworks display on the Sunday night leading up to the Fourth of July.

The adults have plenty of entertainment as well, with live music, a beer garden, and food vendors of all types. Chairs, blankets, and picnic tables cover the grassy field as adults gather around to catch up on the summer's events. Many come back from the surrounding area to reminisce about their childhood and let their children enjoy the same carnival games they played.

Performers in the past have included Chubby Checkers and the rock band Three Dog Night. Politicians frequent this event, getting to know their constituents and interacting with them in order to learn more about their expectations. Without a doubt, Northlake Days is the highlight of many wonderful local activities.

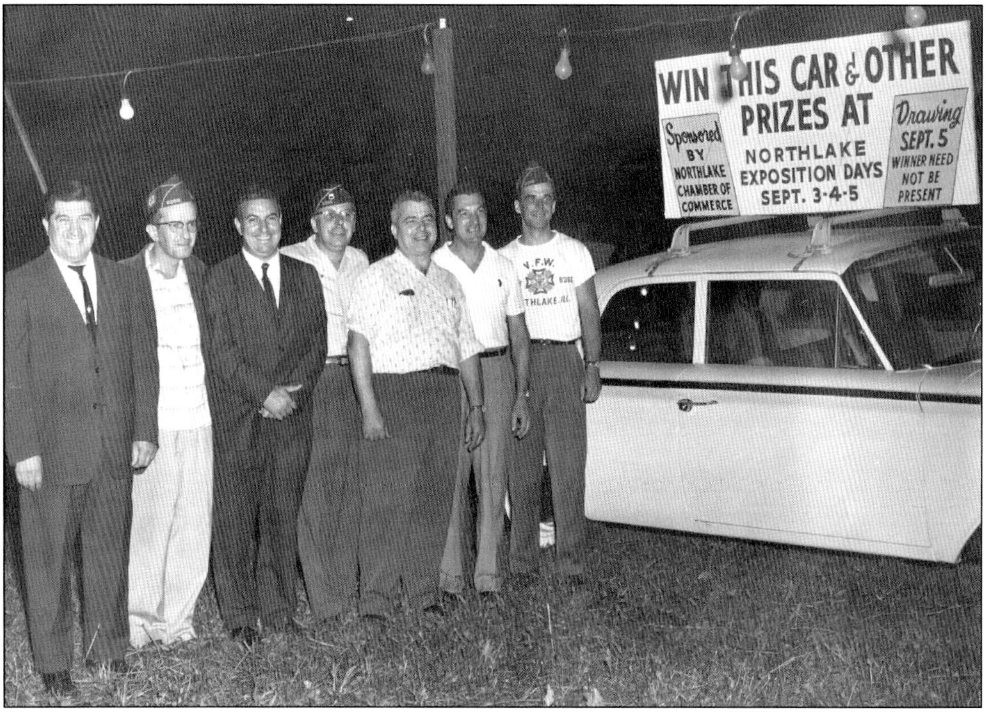

NORTHLAKE DAYS WITH NERI. Mayor Neri (center) stands with other individuals promoting the raffle of this car during the exposition. There are still frequent raffles for former police cars. (Courtesy of Northlake City Hall.)

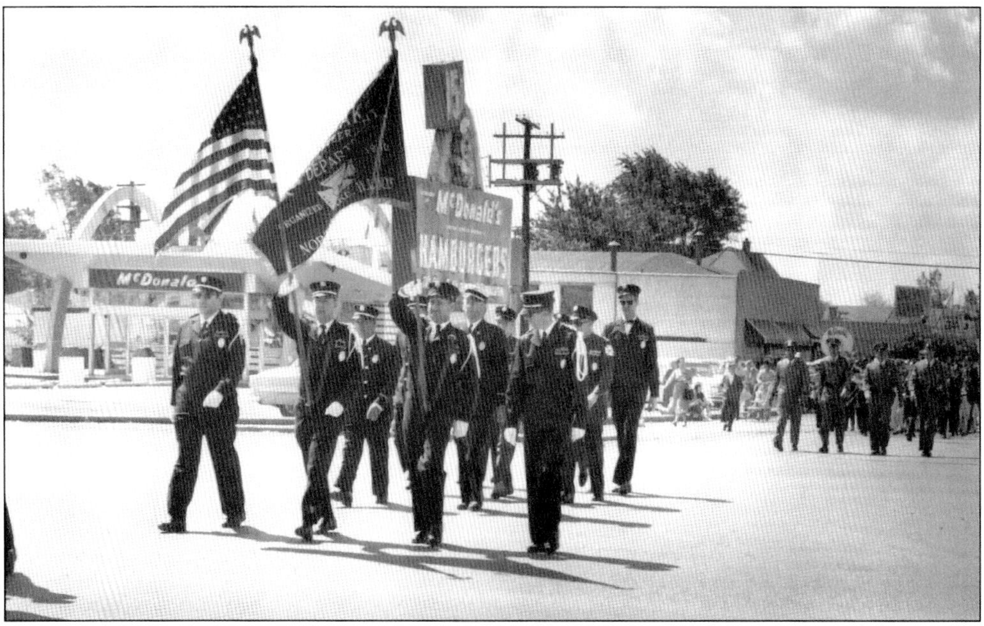

NORTHLAKE FIRE PARADE. The Fire Prevention Parade marches northbound on Wolf Road past one of the earliest McDonald's built, on the corner of Wolf Road and North Avenue, in 1960. Notice the 15¢ hamburgers and Speedee, the McDonald's mascot prior to Ronald McDonald, on the sign. (Courtesy of Northlake City Hall.)

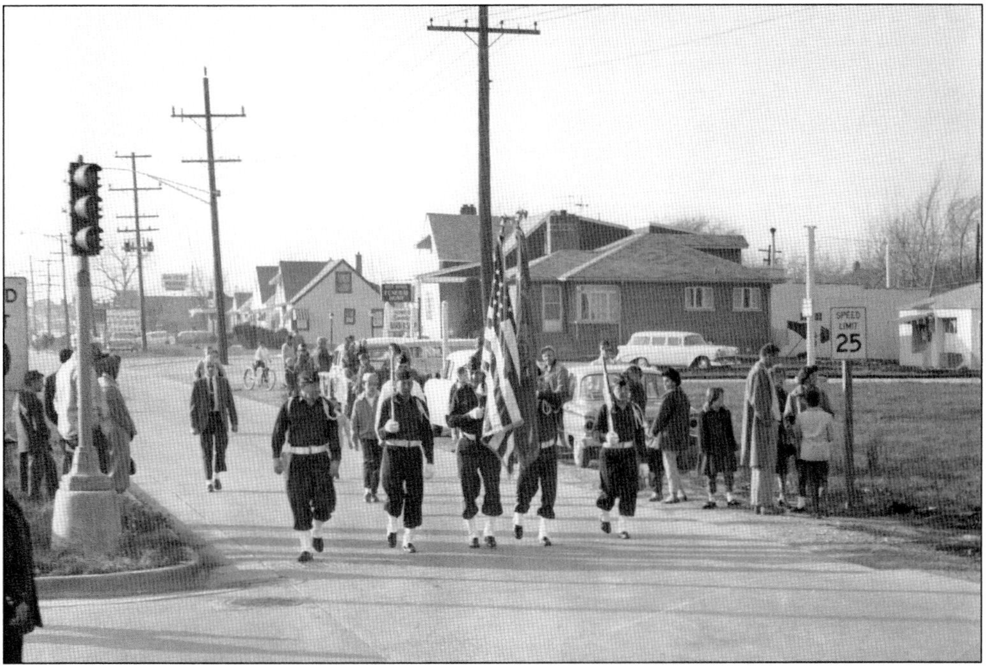

1940s Parade. This parade marches along the shoulder of North Avenue as it goes past some early businesses in the 1940s. Servicemen march eastbound past Fitz Henry Funeral Home and Spata's Barber Shop. In the background is the Shell gas station, which is still there today. (Courtesy of Northlake City Hall.)

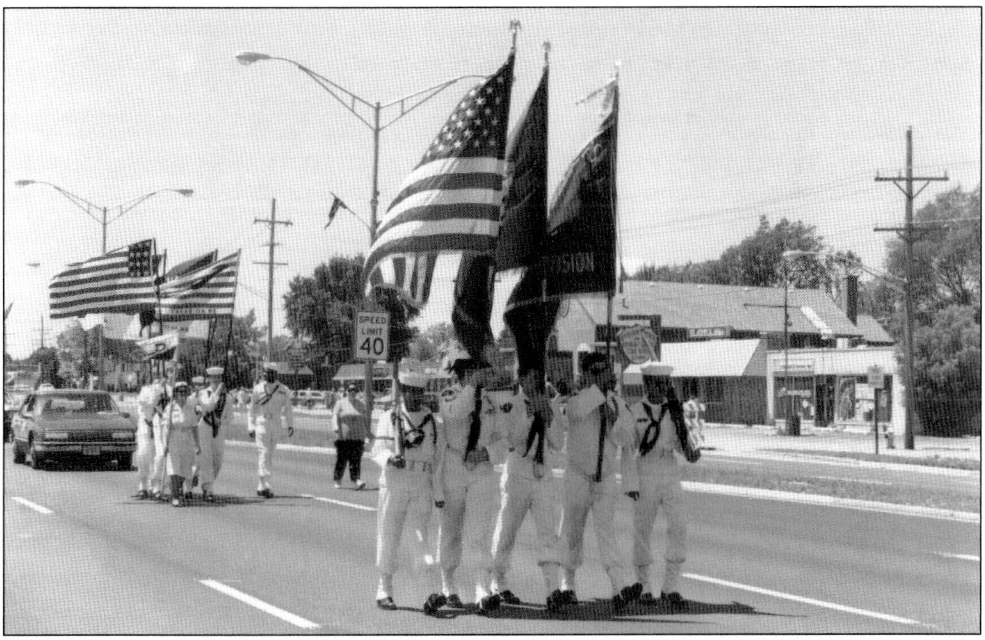

1980s Parade. These serviceman march down North Avenue in the 1980s. The building that is now Anthony's Pizza has a sign that reads, "Pudden Heads, Baseball Cards and Comic Books." The image also shows glimpses of the White Hen Pantry and Doug's Dougout, a popular sports bar in the 1980s. (Courtesy of Northlake City Hall.)

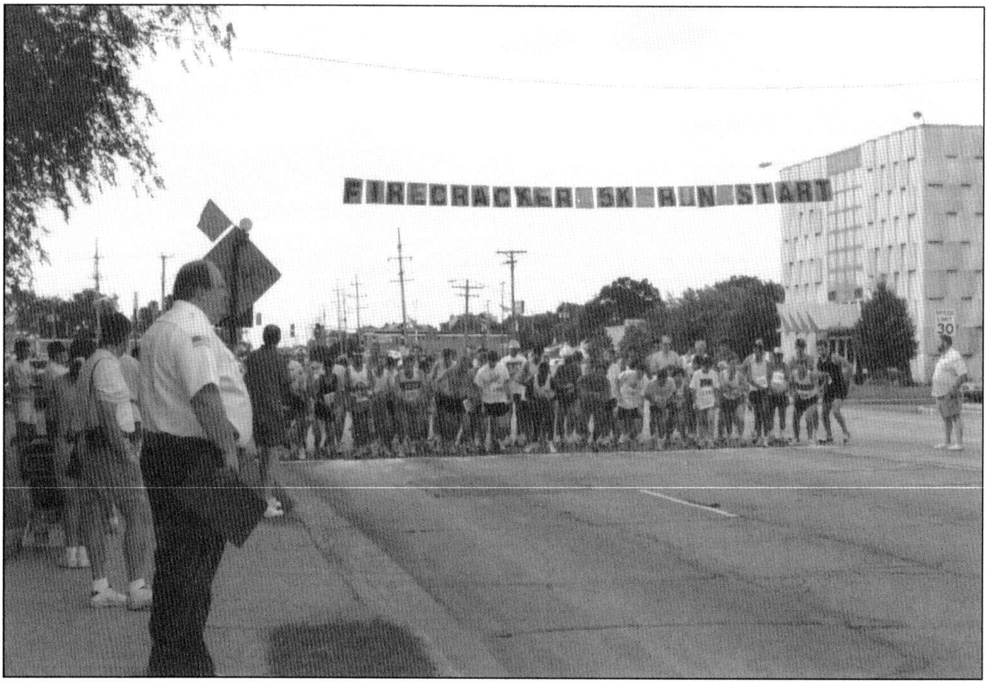

FIRECRACKER 5K RACE. One of the more popular and well-attended events during the festivities was the Northlake Firecracker 5K race, which started on Wolf Road in front of St. John Vianney. After the race, runners would gather in the parking lot of the Northlake Lutheran Church to hydrate themselves (below). The fire truck parked nearby is ready to lend assistance to any runners who may have overextended themselves. (Both, courtesy of Northlake City Hall.)

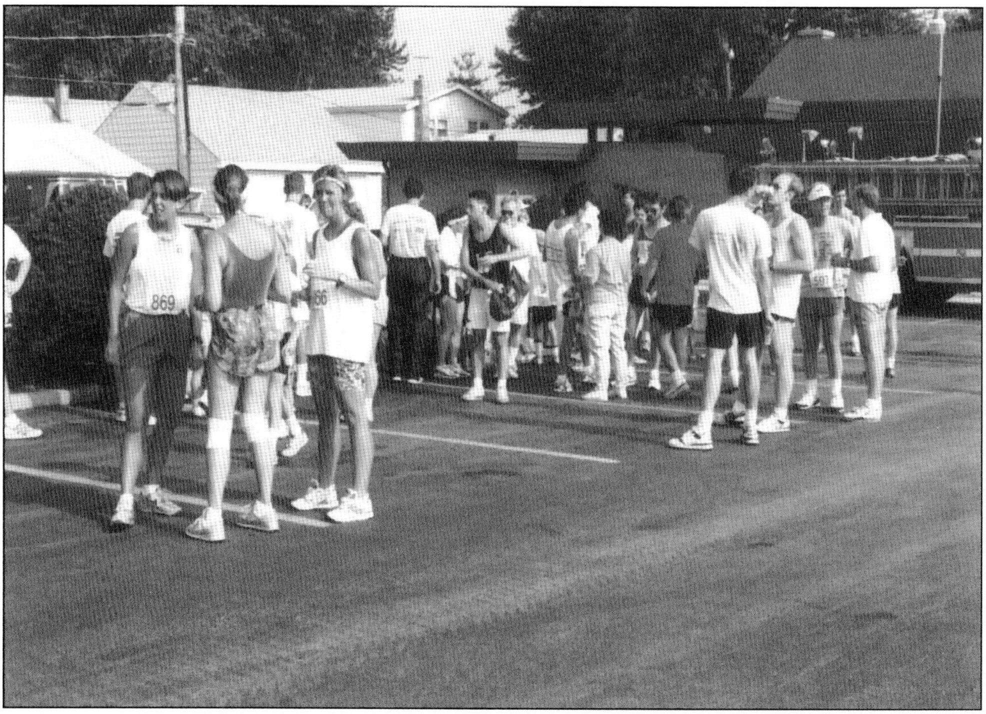

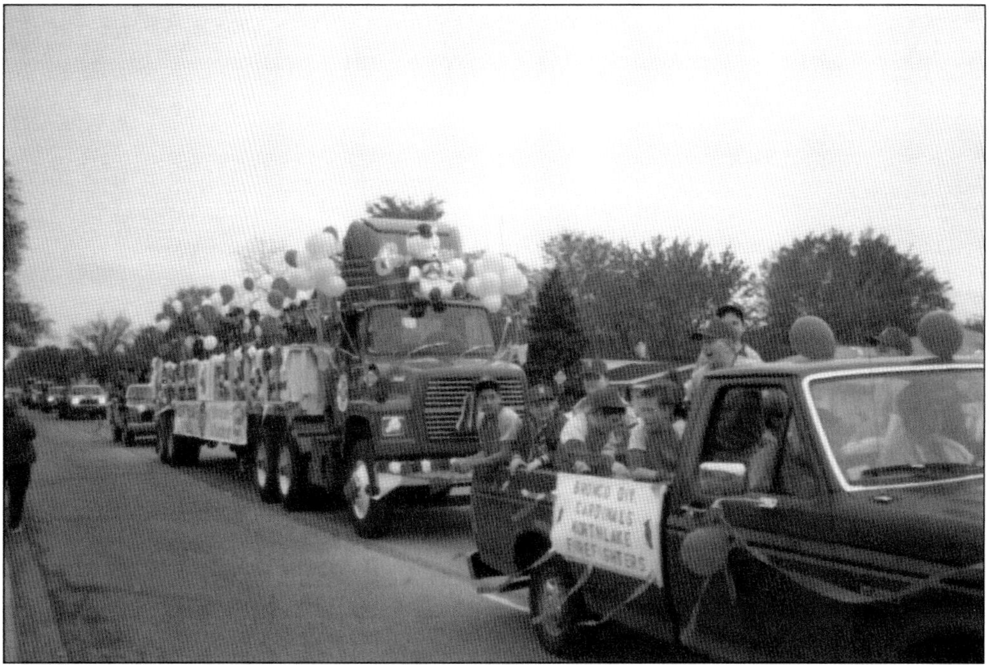

PARADE AND FLOATS. Above, Cardinals baseball players in the Bronco Division ride in the back of this truck, which is followed by a Centrella Grocers truck carrying more players with posters and balloons. Centrella Grocers was a local distributor that employed many workers in the area. Below is a float with Miss Northlake and her court followed by a horse and carriage. (Both, courtesy of Northlake City Hall.)

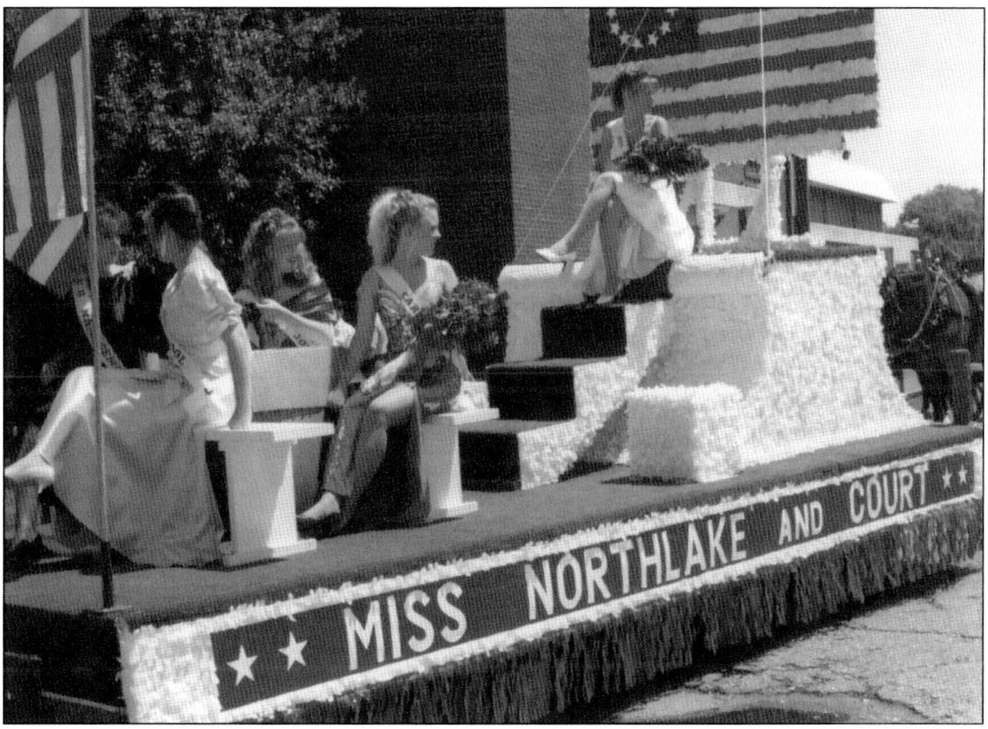

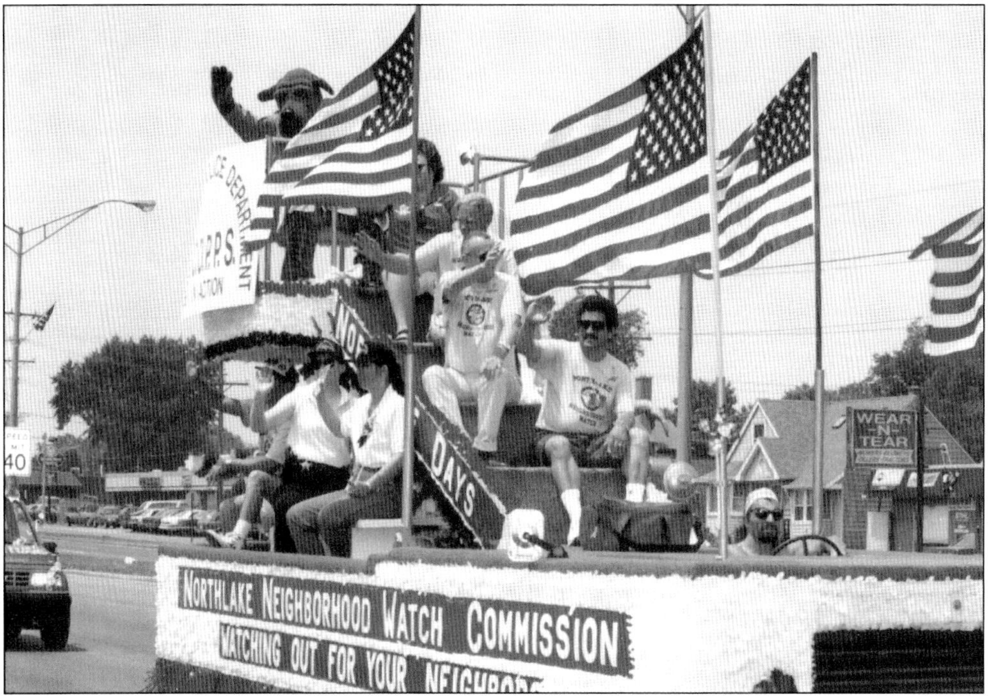

Neighborhood Watch and Official's Floats. One of Northlake's strongest assets has been its long-term stability as a town, which leads to having good neighbors. Above is a float promoting the neighborhood watch commission. Atop the float, McGruff the crime dog waves to onlookers. The float below carried city officials and displayed signs for Mayor Reid Paxson, the city clerk, treasurer, and aldermen. (Both, courtesy of Northlake City Hall.)

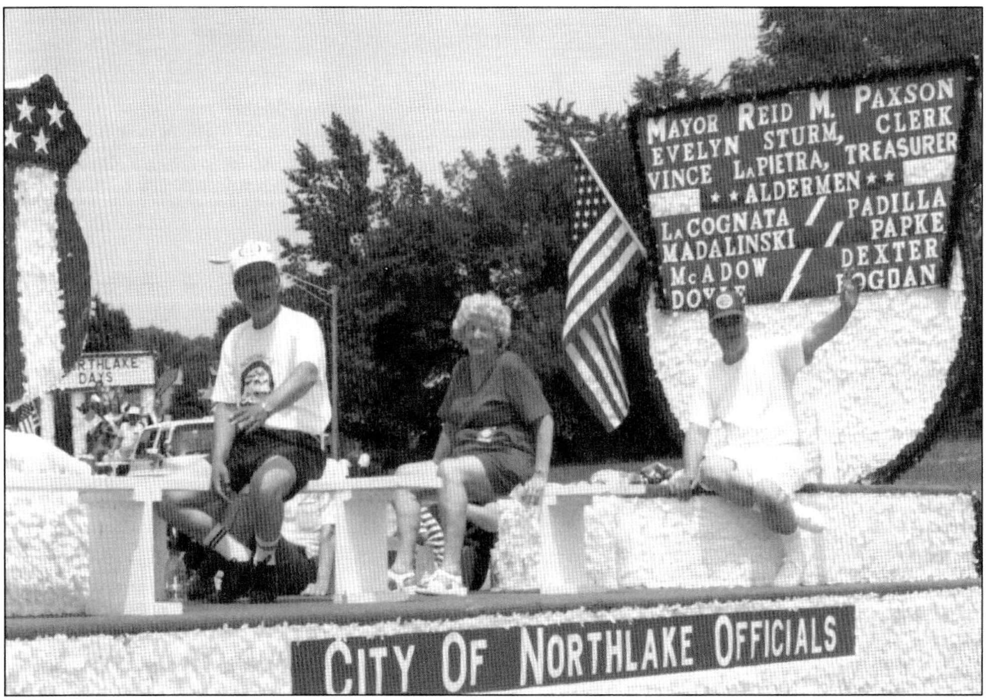

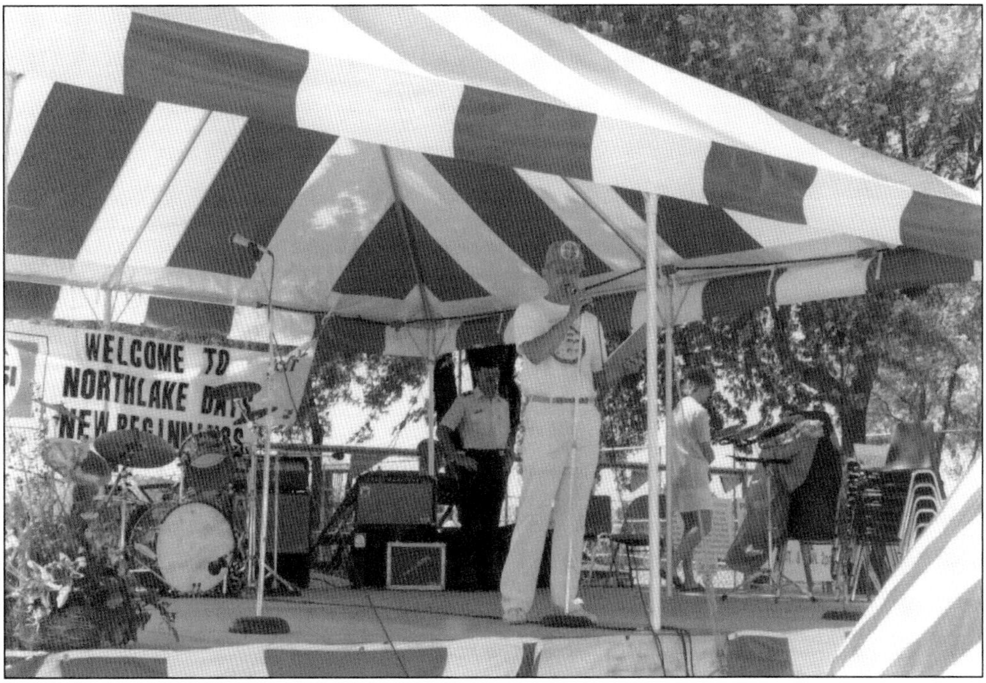

Mayor Paxson Speaks. Here, the mayor gives his annual welcome to the crowd during Northlake Days. (Courtesy of Northlake City Hall.)

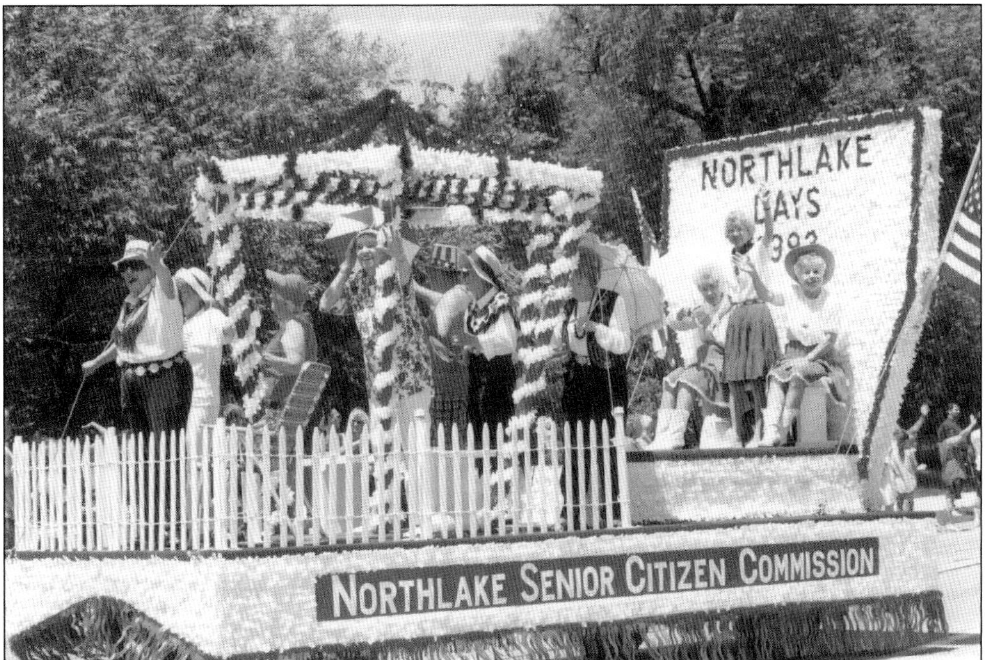

Senior Citizen's Float. Designing floats is a group event for the Northlake Senior Citizen Commission, whose float rumbles through the parade streets with Northlake seniors on board. Northlake values senior citizens highly, offering many services and activities that are tailored to them during Northlake Days. (Courtesy of Northlake City Hall.)

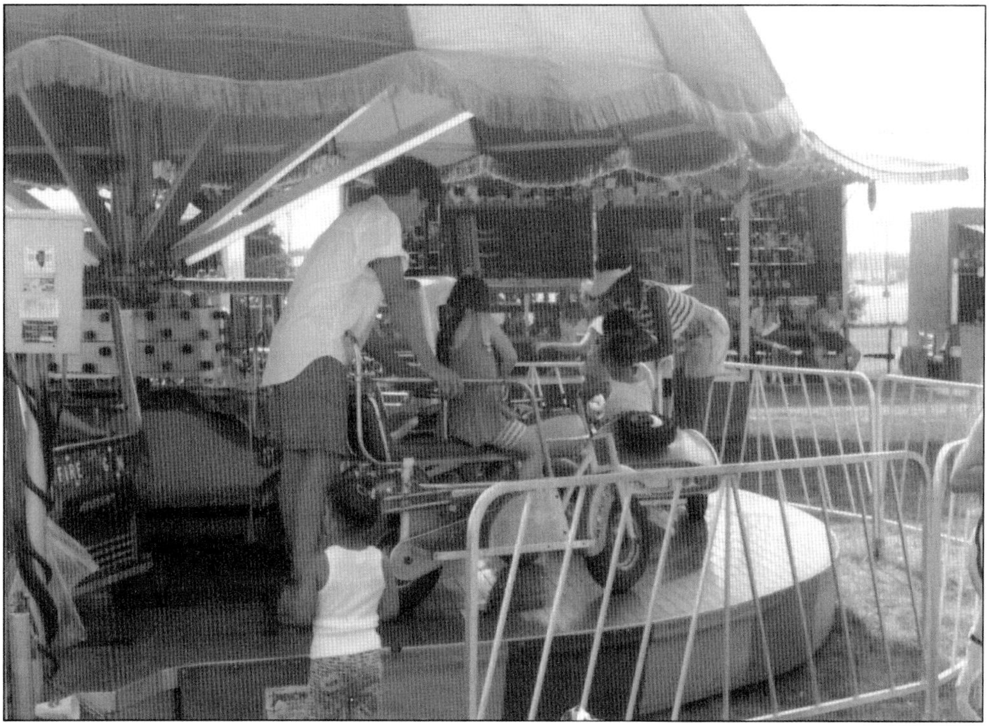

Rides at Northlake Days. Many attractions grab the attention of gatherers at Northlake Days. The most popular attraction for young visitors is the merry-go-round (above). Another popular one is the dragon roller coaster (below), on which some passengers grab tight and some raise their arms, waving to parents. (Both, courtesy of Northlake City Hall.)

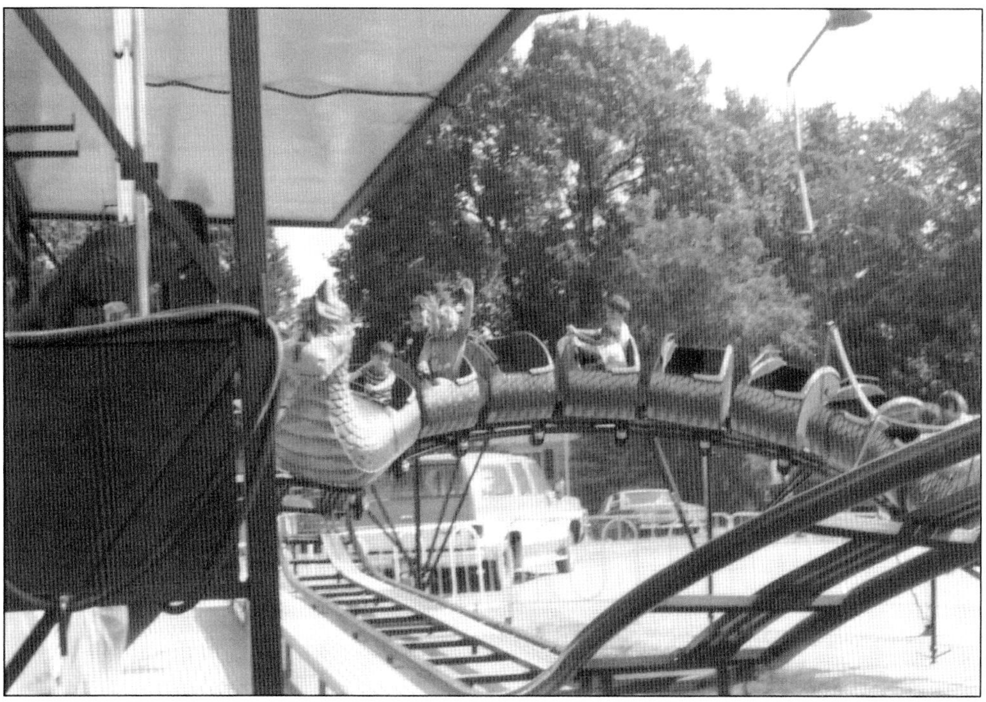

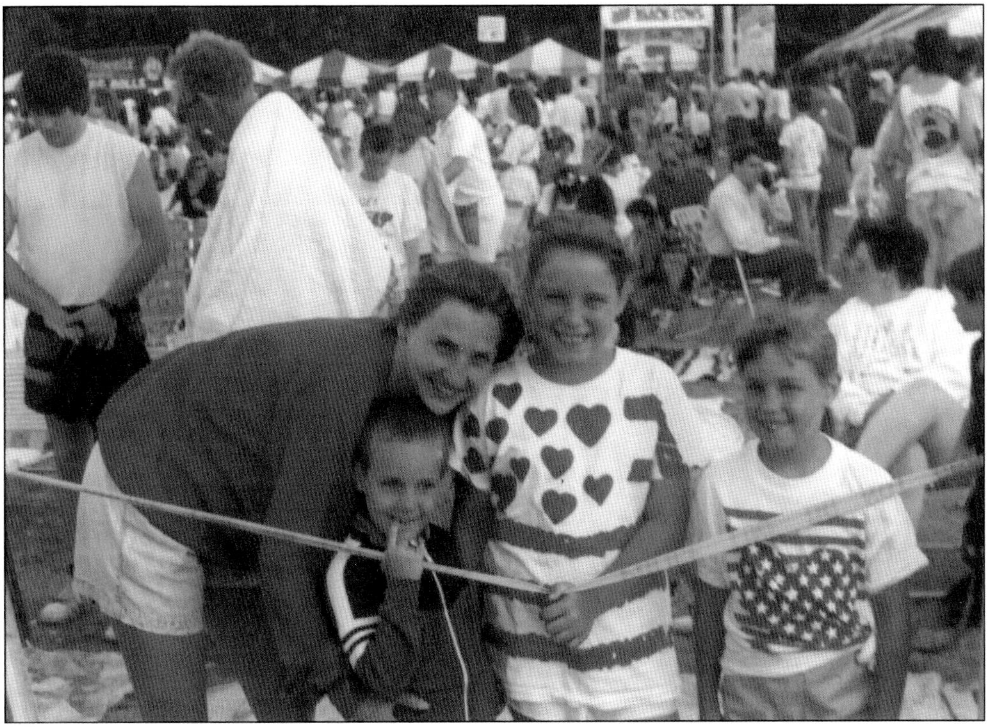

Crowds Gather. For adults, the music is the most popular entertainment. People bring chairs and blankets, as tables are reserved quickly, and wait to listen to the live bands and the event's culmination, the fireworks. Many sponsors take advantage of the crowds with promotions like the giant Coors Light bottle behind the field in the image below. (Both, courtesy of Northlake City Hall.)

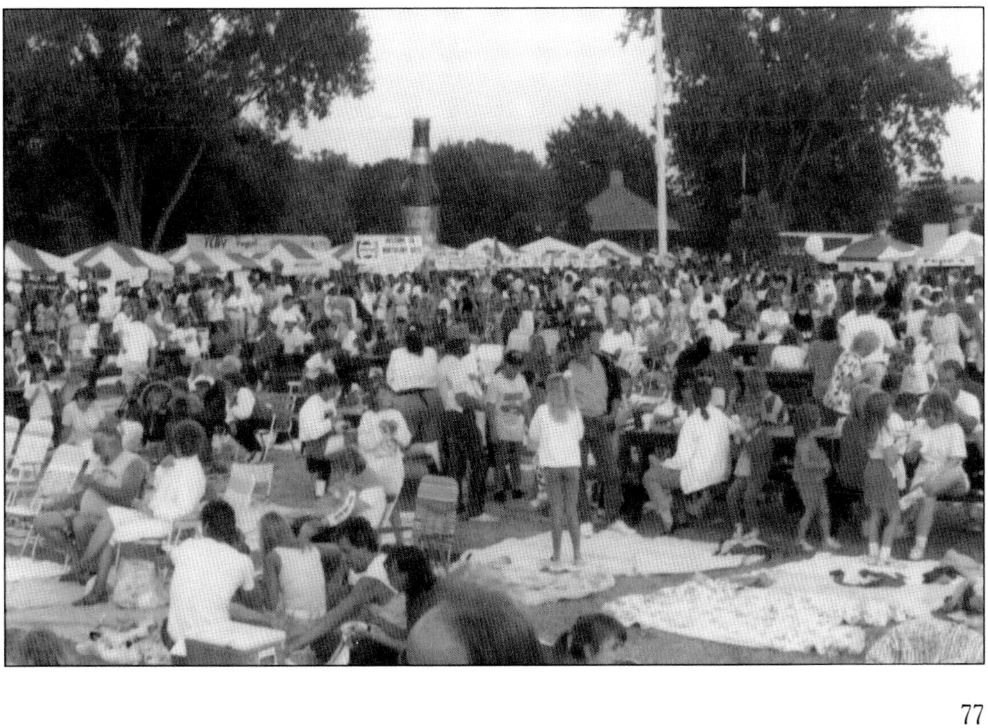

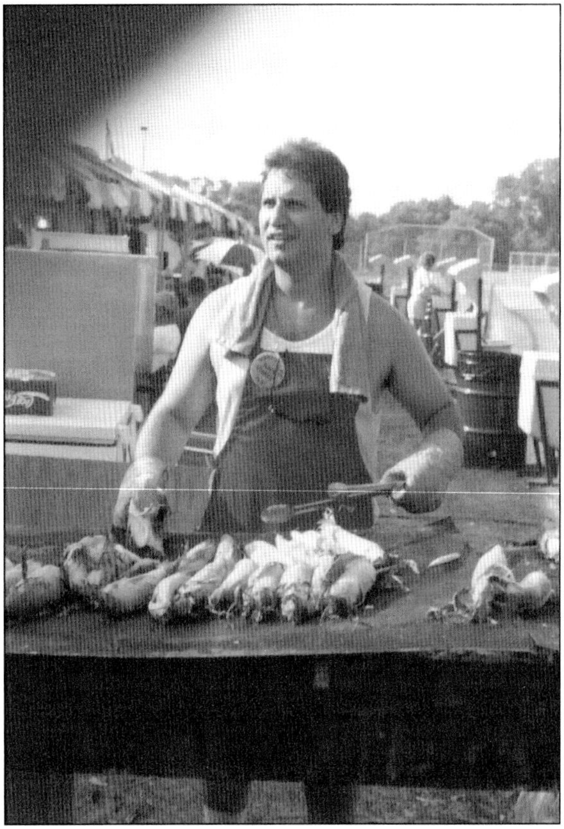

Food Vendors. Many area food vendors reserve spots to sell food weeks in advance. In 1991, the food vendor at left grills corn, battling heat from the grill and from the sun. Below, another vendor sells Glo Sticks to kids for $2 and proudly wears a Northlake shirt with the city logo. (Both, courtesy of Northlake City Hall.)

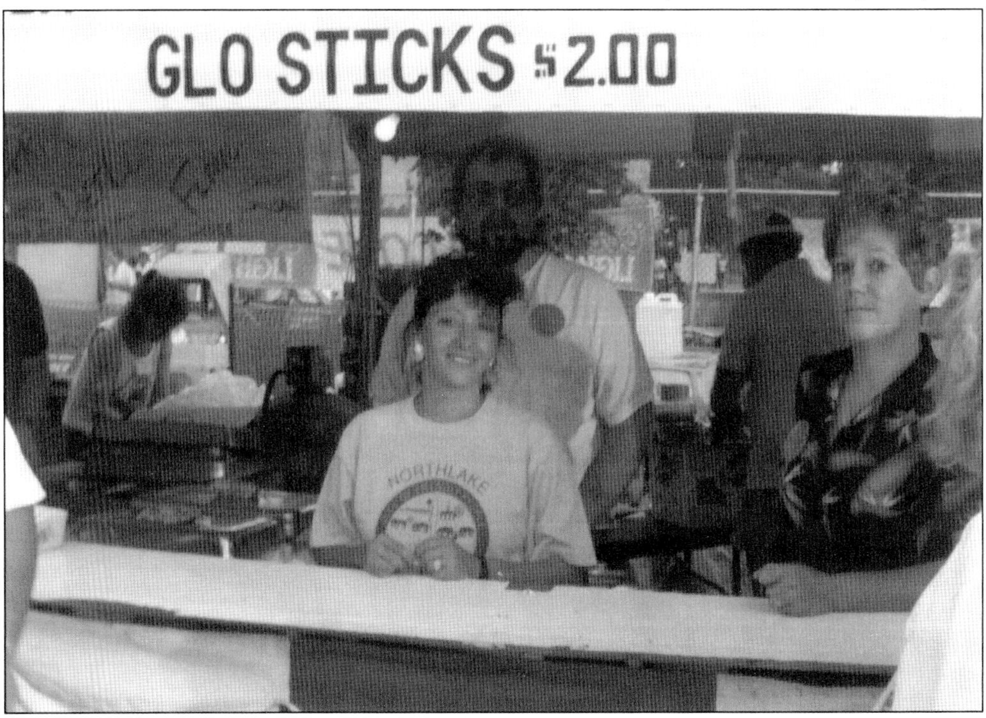

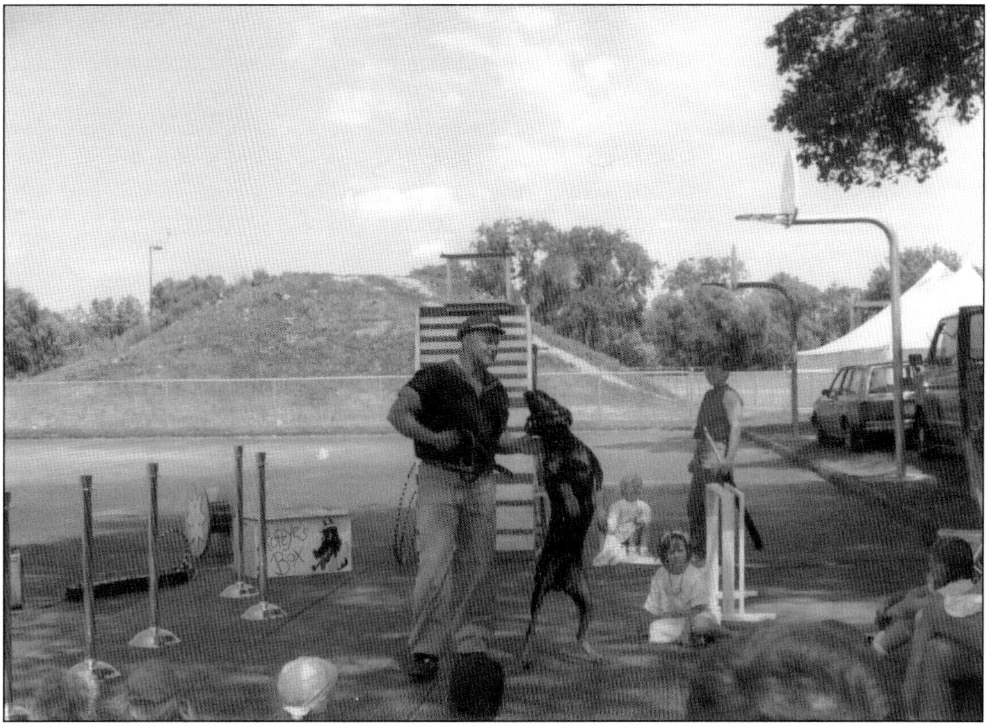

Popeye and Teenage Mutant Ninja Turtles. Above, Popeye entertains onlookers, performing tricks with his dog. Below, a group of children poses with one of the Teenage Mutant Ninja Turtles, which were popular at the time. (Both, courtesy of Northlake City Hall.)

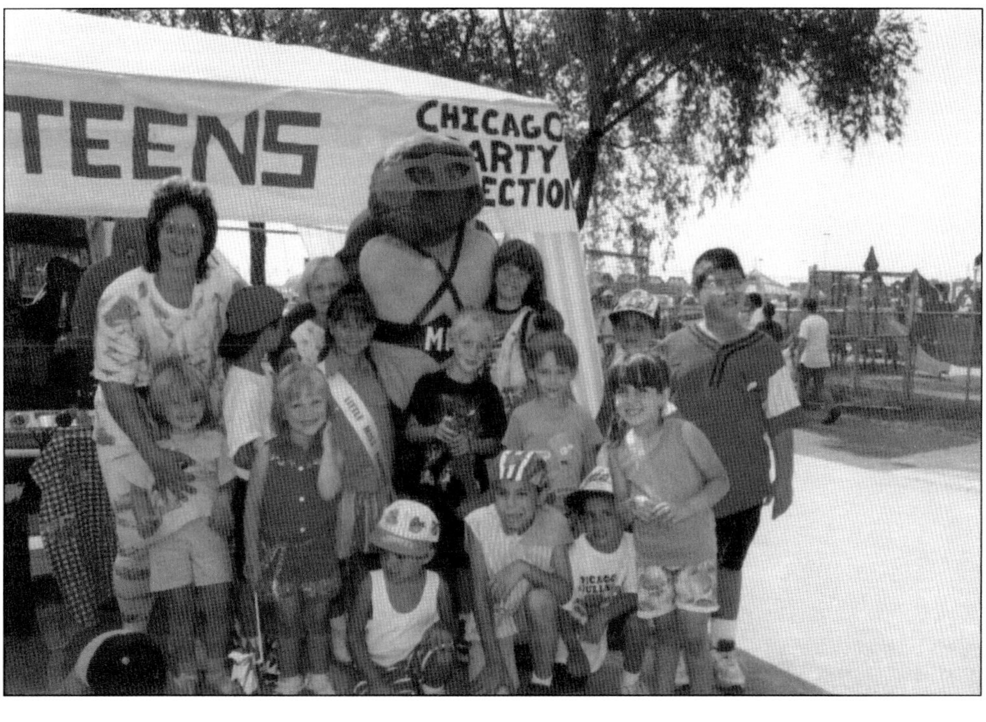

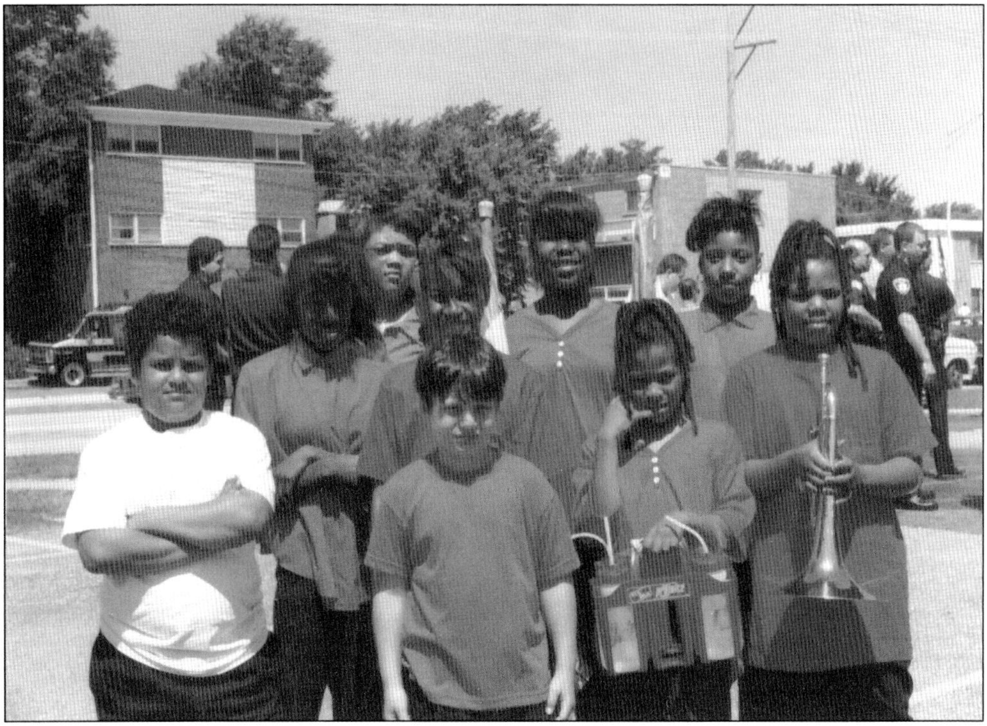

Parade Band Marchers. The above photograph of band marchers at the parade shows the growing diversity of Northlake. Below, other young participants pose in traditional clothing from their native country. (Both, courtesy of Northlake City Hall.)

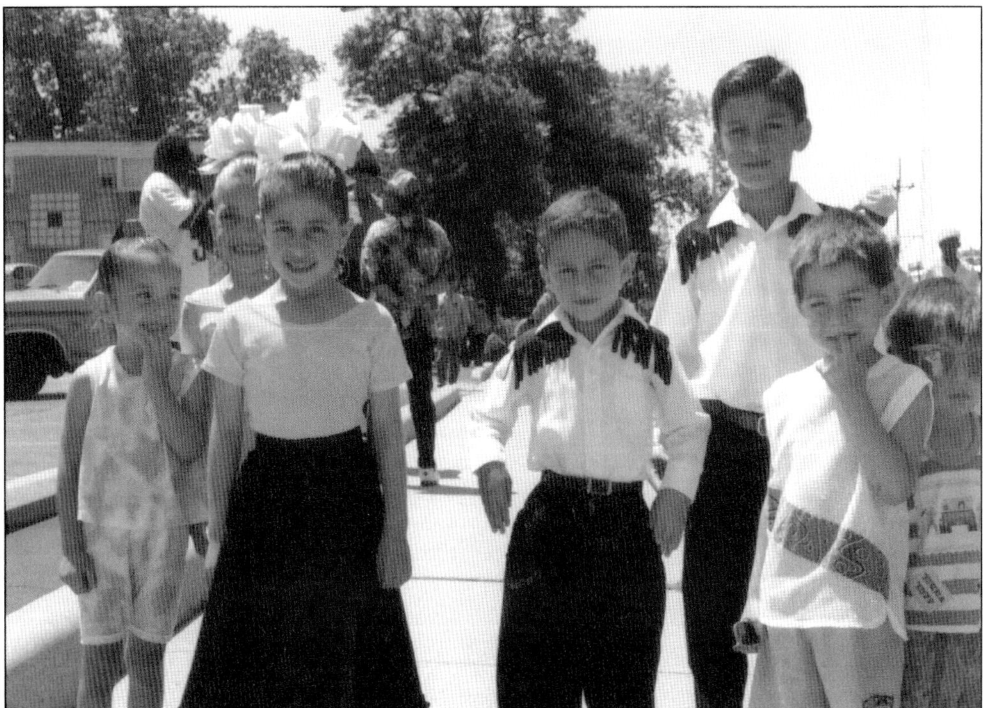

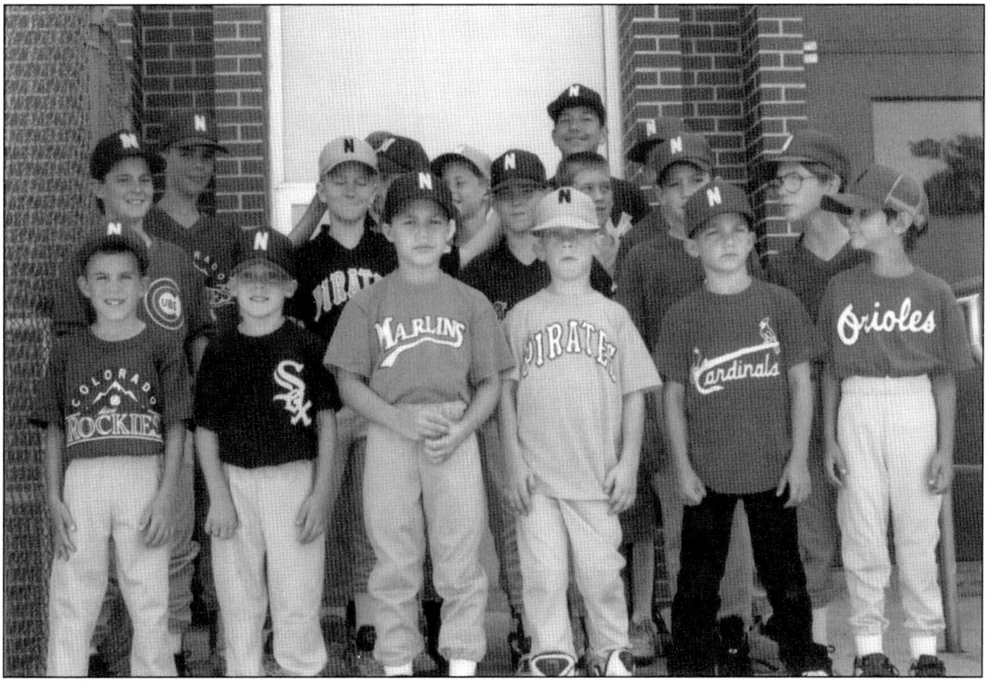

Northlake Days Baseball and Fireworks. Above, members of the local baseball teams participate in the yearly parade. A representative from each team poses for this picture before climbing in the back of trucks and floats. Fireworks on the last night of Northlake Days (below) continues to be one of the best displays around, lighting the sky for miles around. It is common for traffic along the major thoroughfares, specifically North Avenue and Wolf Road, to pull over to the side and admire the wonderful display, which lasts for about 40 minutes. (Both, courtesy of Northlake City Hall.)

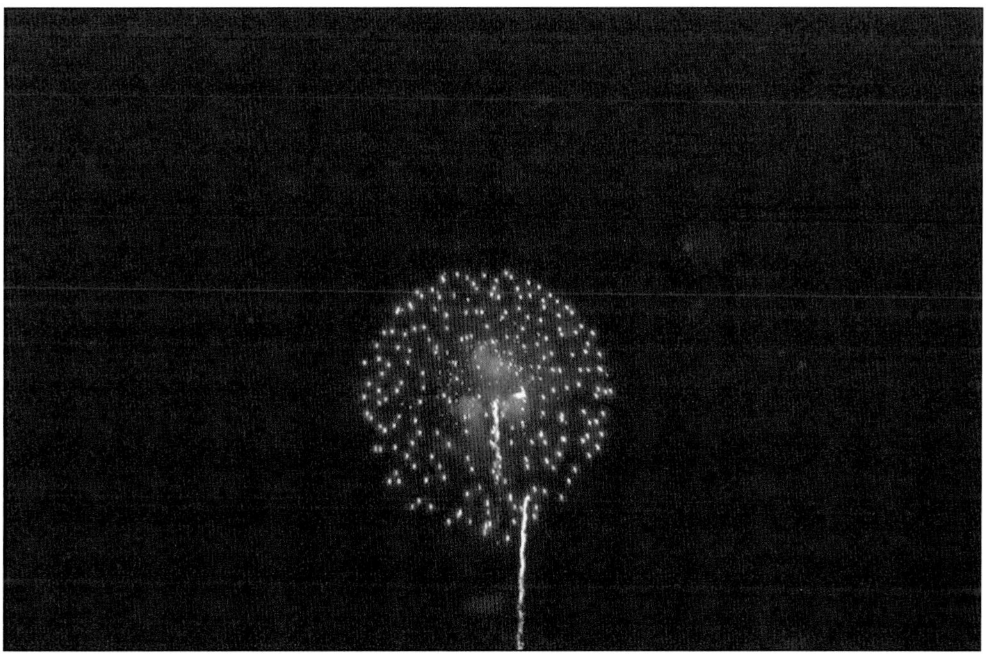

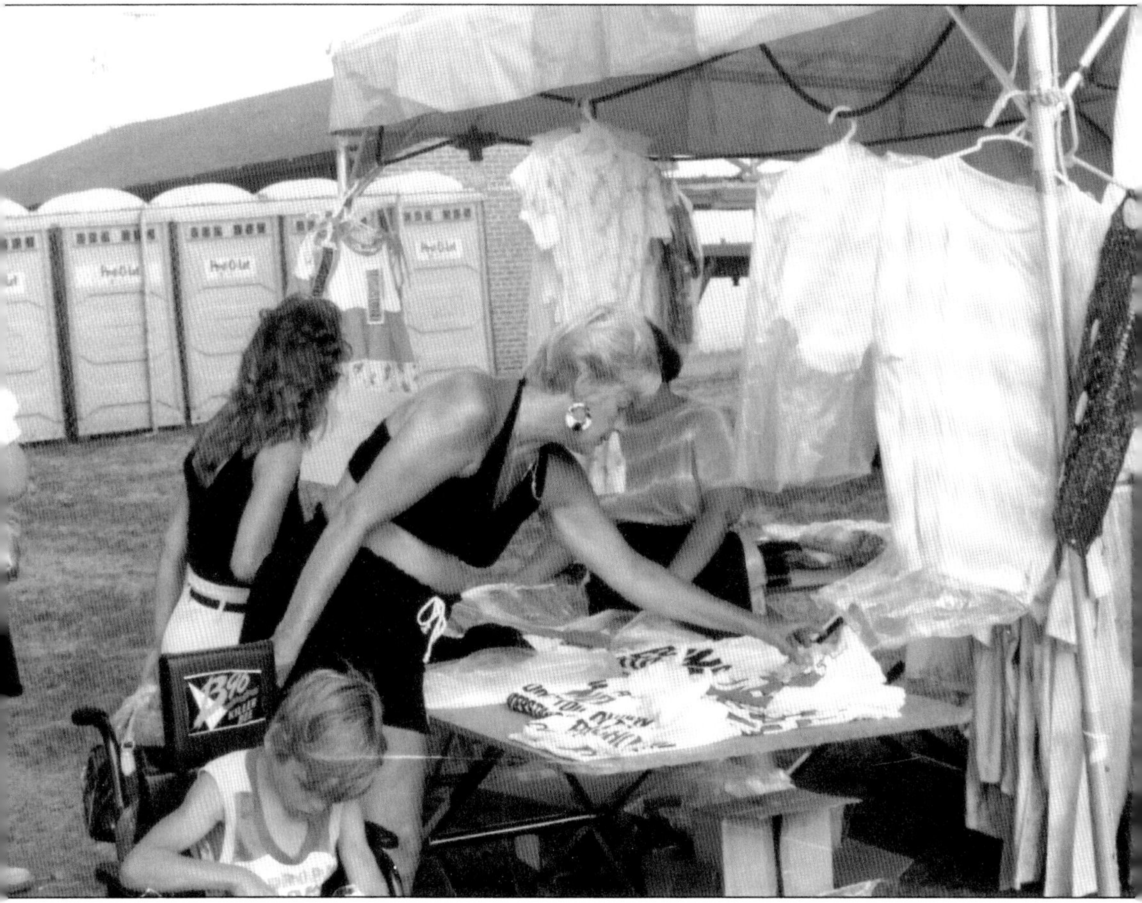

Vendors at Northlake Days. This local resident peruses the shirts being offered by vendors as her son is distracted by another item that has grabbed his attention. The number of portable toilets in the background shows the high attendance at Northlake Days. (Courtesy of Northlake City Hall.)

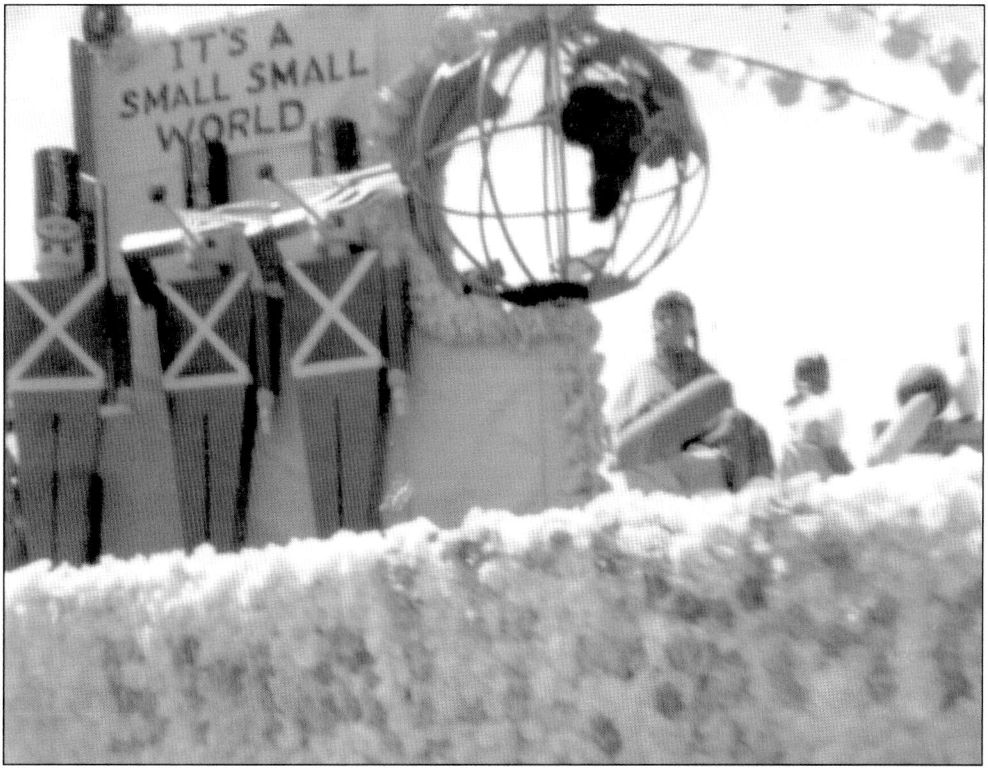

1975 Parade. Above, a float from 1975 celebrates the theme of "It's a Small World After All" with very detailed standing soldiers and a globe. The float marches along Wolf Road entertaining young and old residents alike. The float at right was decorated by members of Saint John Vianney with the same theme. (Both, courtesy of Bob Grenier.)

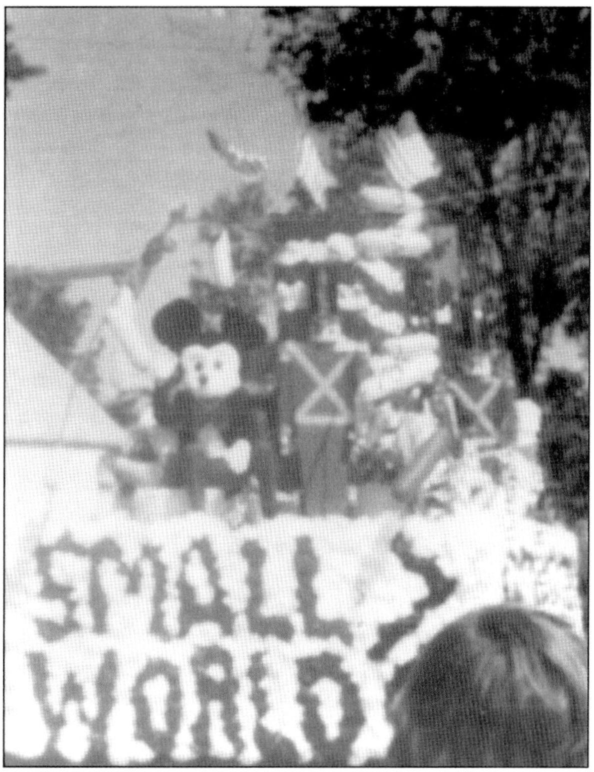

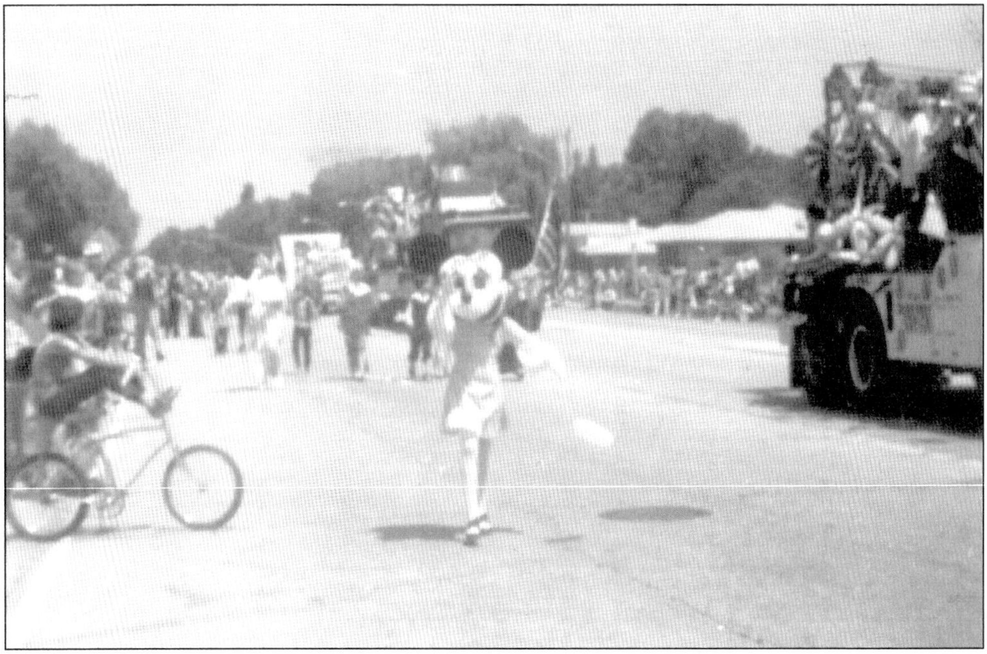

Minnie Mouse Marches. A fully attired Minnie Mouse marches along Wolf Road waving to onlookers as kids with bikes watch the floats and parade marchers going down the street. (Courtesy of Bob Grenier.)

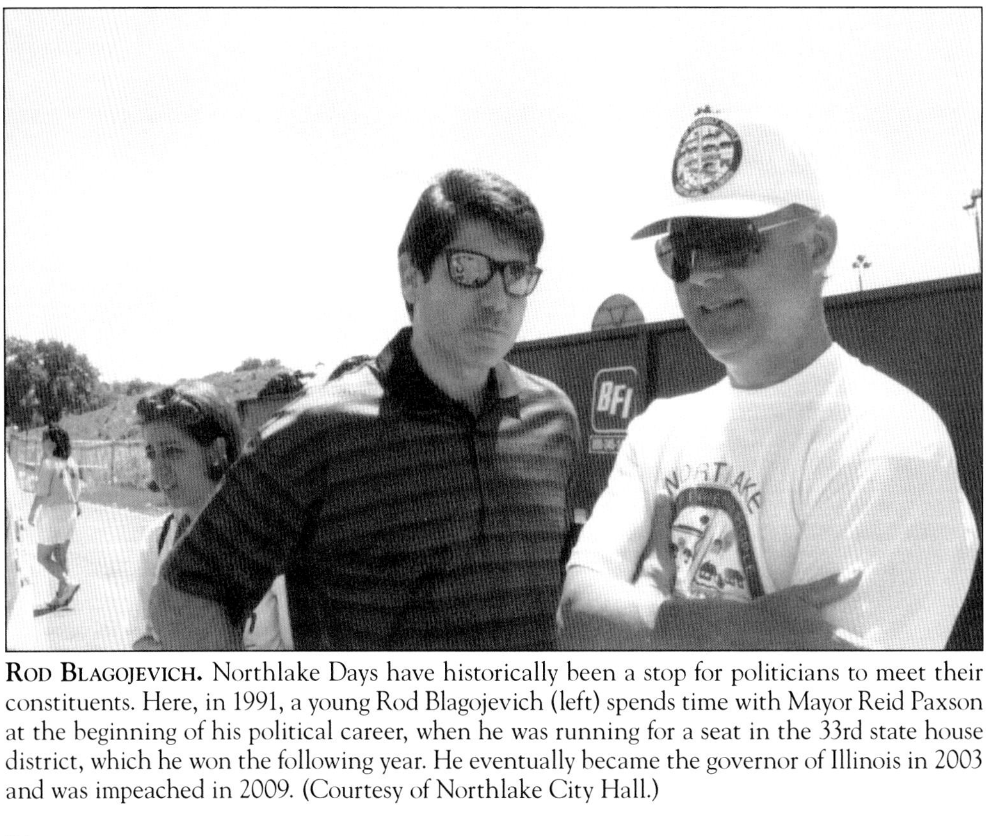

Rod Blagojevich. Northlake Days have historically been a stop for politicians to meet their constituents. Here, in 1991, a young Rod Blagojevich (left) spends time with Mayor Reid Paxson at the beginning of his political career, when he was running for a seat in the 33rd state house district, which he won the following year. He eventually became the governor of Illinois in 2003 and was impeached in 2009. (Courtesy of Northlake City Hall.)

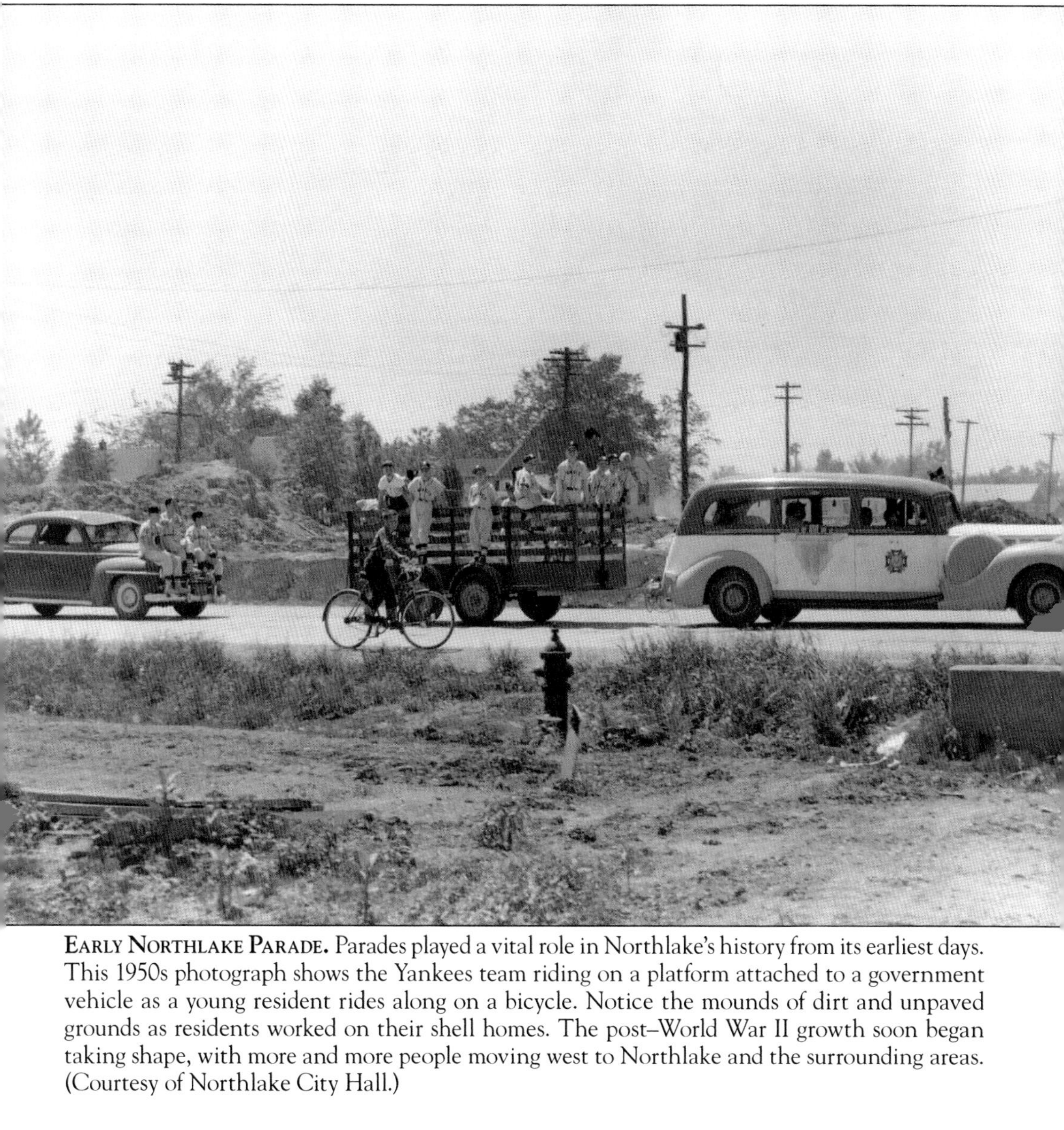

EARLY NORTHLAKE PARADE. Parades played a vital role in Northlake's history from its earliest days. This 1950s photograph shows the Yankees team riding on a platform attached to a government vehicle as a young resident rides along on a bicycle. Notice the mounds of dirt and unpaved grounds as residents worked on their shell homes. The post–World War II growth soon began taking shape, with more and more people moving west to Northlake and the surrounding areas. (Courtesy of Northlake City Hall.)

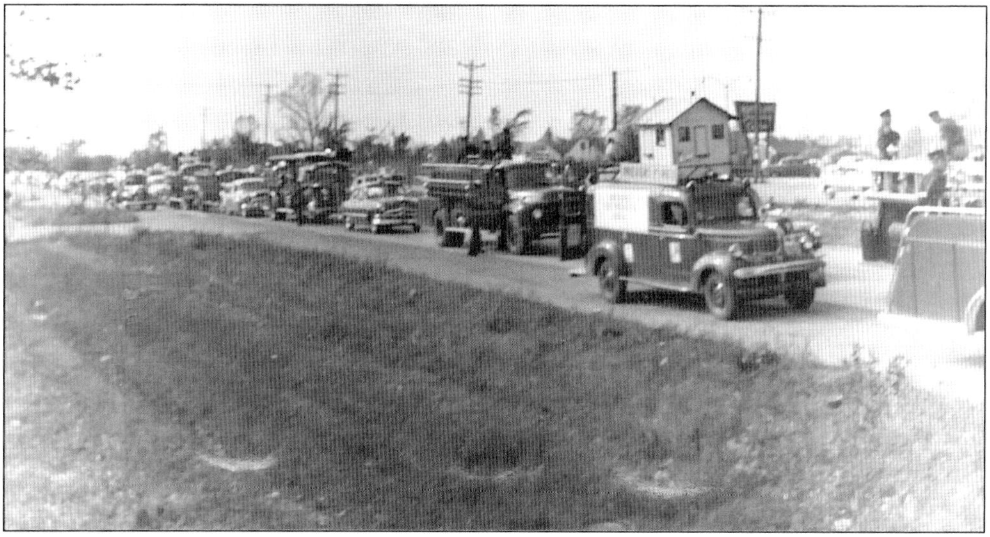

FIRE TRUCK PROCESSION. This procession of fire trucks shows the town's concern for fires, as many have signs warning residents to prevent fires. It was an early Northlake custom to burn grass so that it would grow nice and green the following spring. (Courtesy of Northlake City Hall.)

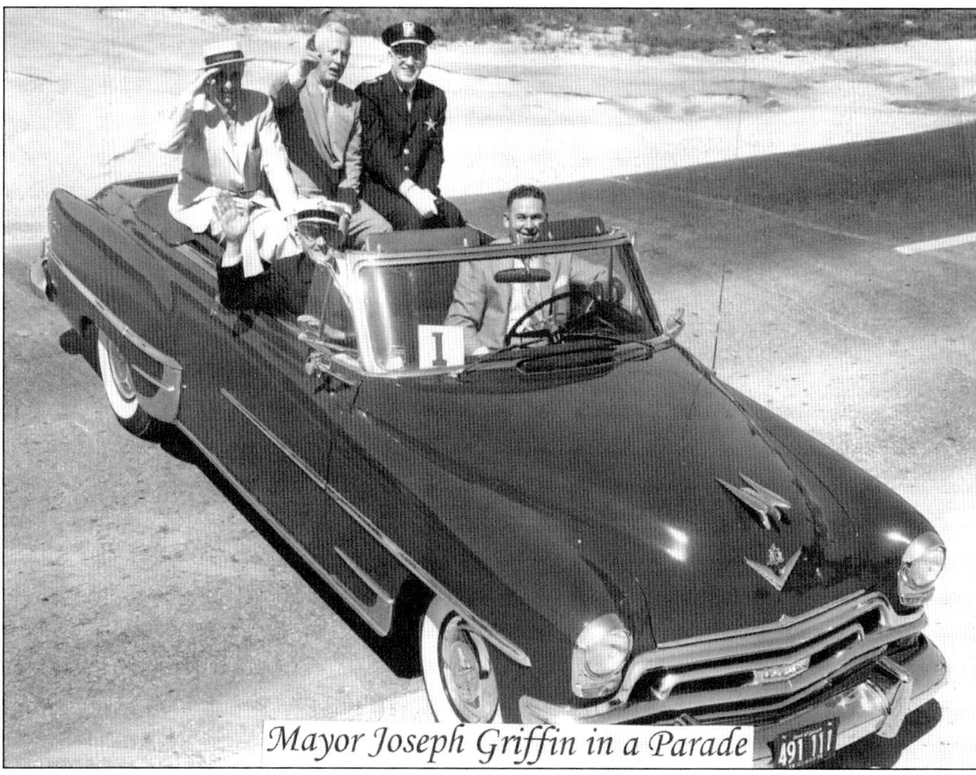

MAYOR GRIFFIN PARADE. Joseph Griffin was elected mayor in 1953. Here, he rides on the back seat of this vehicle during a parade across one of many recently paved roads. During his tenure, the city's three-million-gallon water reservoir and sanitary sewers were built. Just as importantly, West Leyden High School was conceived and construction began on it during his time in office. (Courtesy of Northlake City Hall.)

Five
Religious Life

Faith has always been integral to Northlake. The principal church located near the center of town, St. John Vianney, was founded in 1941 to serve the growing farm community. Ground was broken on August 28, 1941, and eventually Father Robert P. Doyle was called on to serve as the parish's first priest. More than 10 years later, ground was broken again to establish a school, as the Catholic community had grown rapidly in those early years. St. John Vianney parish grew from one service to two and had begun to outgrow its first church building in the late 1950s.

The current church building was erected in the 1960s with stunning architecture. Its exterior is in the shape of a fish, with precast stones creating an appearance of fish scales. On the inside, the pews in all four sections form the shape of a cross, and give a direct view of the altar as the priest celebrates mass. The top section contains tiles depicting various scenes from Jesus's life, the largest in North America when first erected. The church has grown to have a convent and a larger school building. Multiple services are now held and the Spanish-language service continues to grow.

Other local places of worship include Northlake Lutheran Church, founded in 1940 and disbanded in 2012; Northlake Methodist Church, which was on the corner of Belle Drive and Roy Avenue for many years and is now St. Peter Jacobite Syrian Orthodox Church; Trinity Presbyterian Church on Wolf Road and Diversey Street; and a former Lutheran church on South Harold Avenue, which is now occupied by a Hispanic Evangelical congregation.

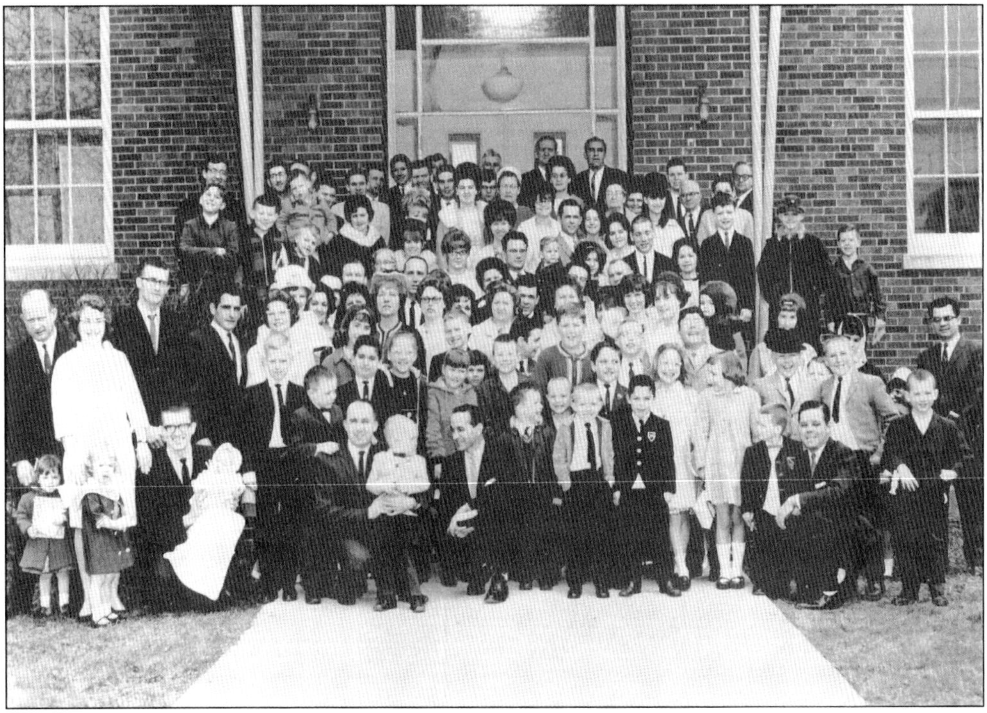

North Avenue Baptist Church. Near city hall and the police station stands a church with a blue cross that states "Jesus Saves." The building was the home of North Avenue Baptist Church for several decades. Prior to building a church on that site, the congregation met at Riley School, as seen here in 1965. The church was founded in 1964 with Bob Kinman as its first pastor; the church's first service was on September 7 of that year. By 1969, the completed building contained a choir section behind the pulpit, which Pastor Kinman stands in front of below. (Both, courtesy of Wanda Rhea.)

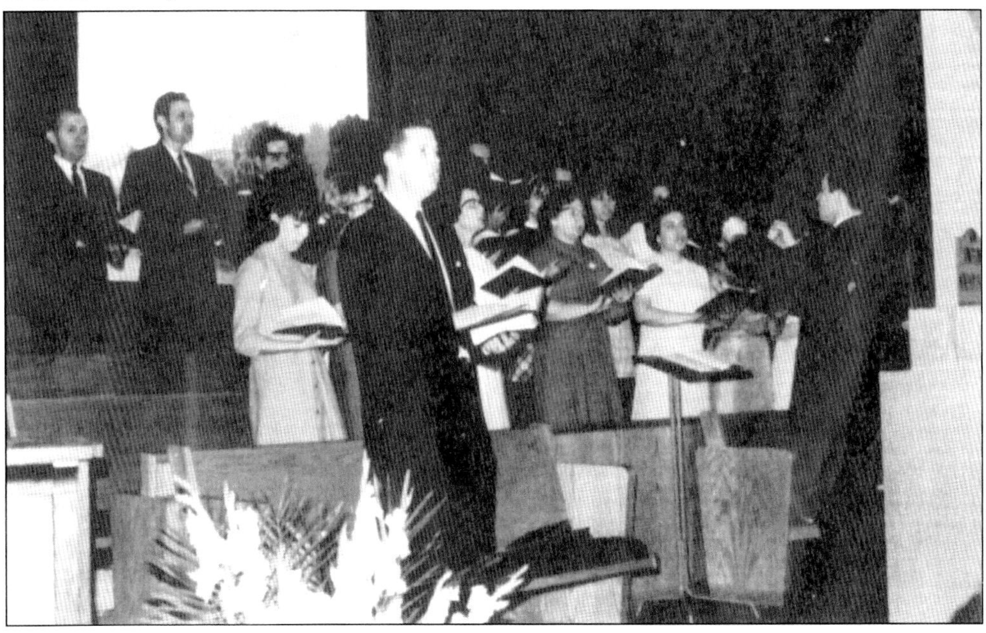

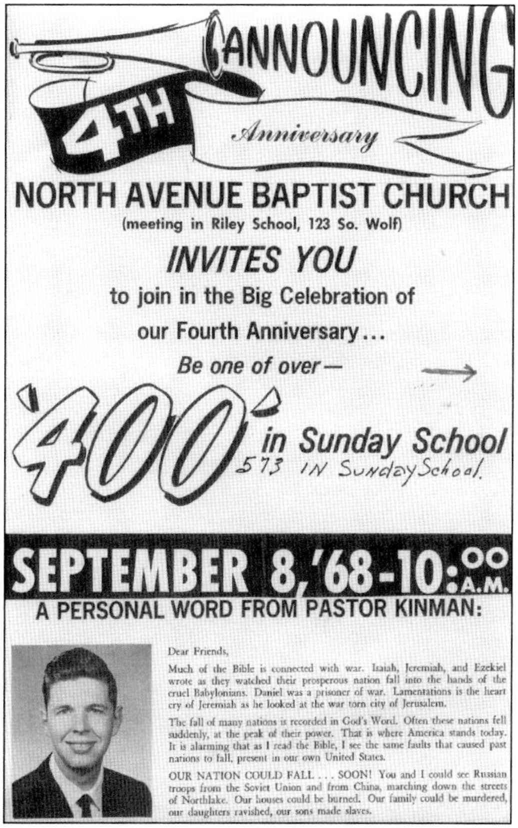

North Avenue Baptist Church. This poster advertises the fourth anniversary celebration of North Avenue Baptist Church on September 8, 1968. The personal message from Pastor Kinman warns of the possibility of Russian and Chinese troops occupying the streets of Northlake. The Cold War was a real threat at the time, and the demonstrations during the Democratic National Convention the previous month were seen by some as prophetic warnings. The luncheon celebrating the fourth anniversary (below) was held in the basement of Riley School. The new building was completed in 1969. (Both, courtesy of Wanda Rhea.)

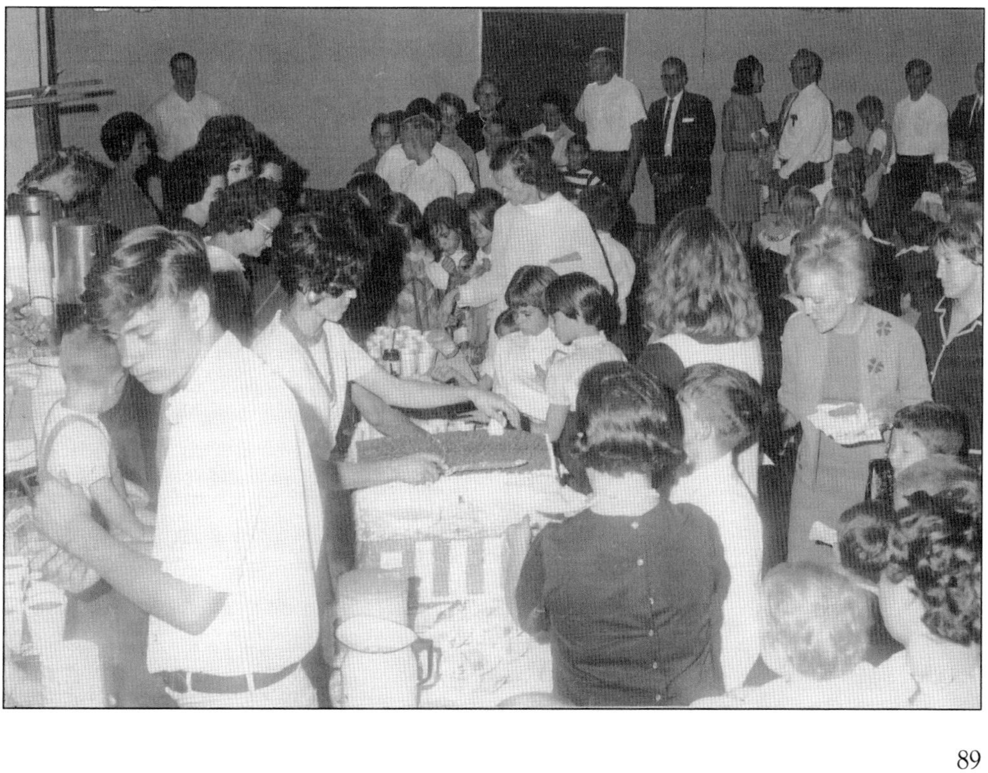

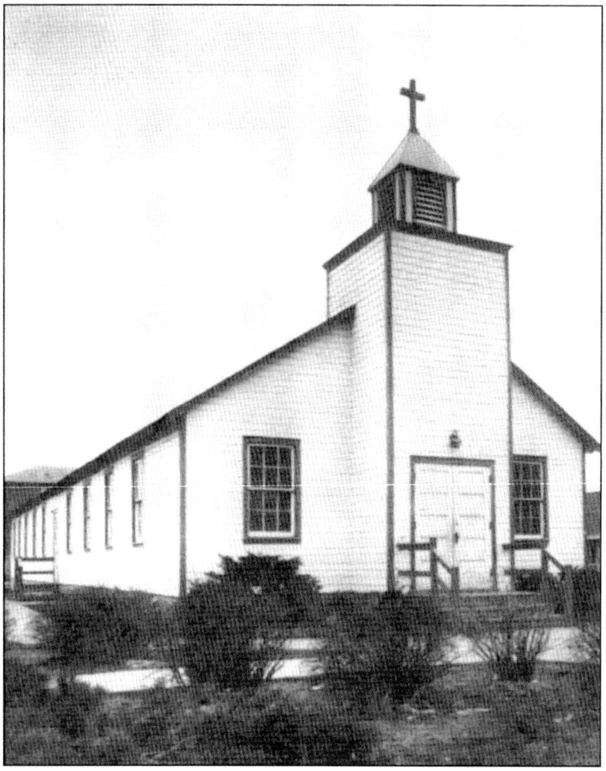

St. John Vianney Church. The original St. John Vianney Church building (left) was the church's home from 1941 to 1954. The church was then relocated to the basement of the newly built school. This building was used for a variety of functions until it was torn down in the 1960s. Below is a view from atop the balcony at the new St. John Vianney Church, which was dedicated on March 7, 1965. Two hands rise from the floor, "lifting" the altar. At the time of its completion, the mosaic tile murals depicting scenes from Jesus's life were the largest of their kind in North America. (Both, courtesy of Northlake City Hall.)

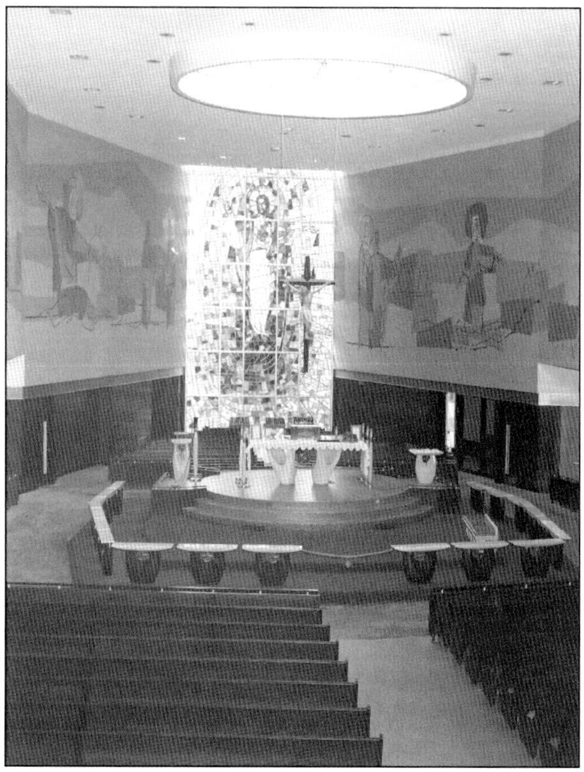

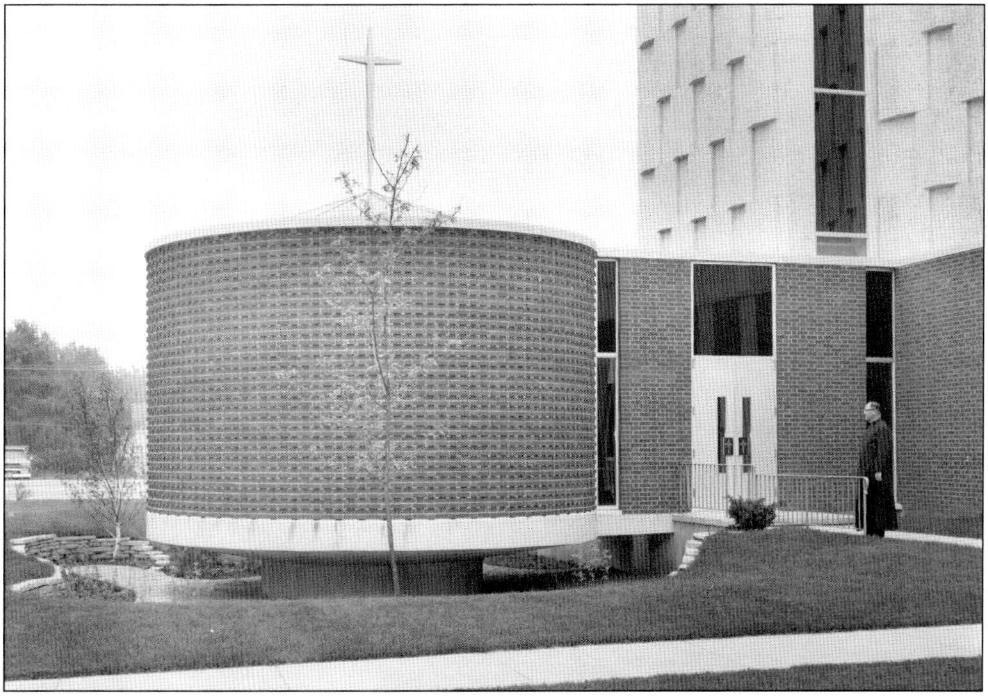

St. John Vianney Baptismal. Pictured is the baptismal that stretches out from the main section of St. John Vianney towards the north side of Wolf Road. Father Boyle stands and looks at the baptismal. (Courtesy of Northlake City Hall.)

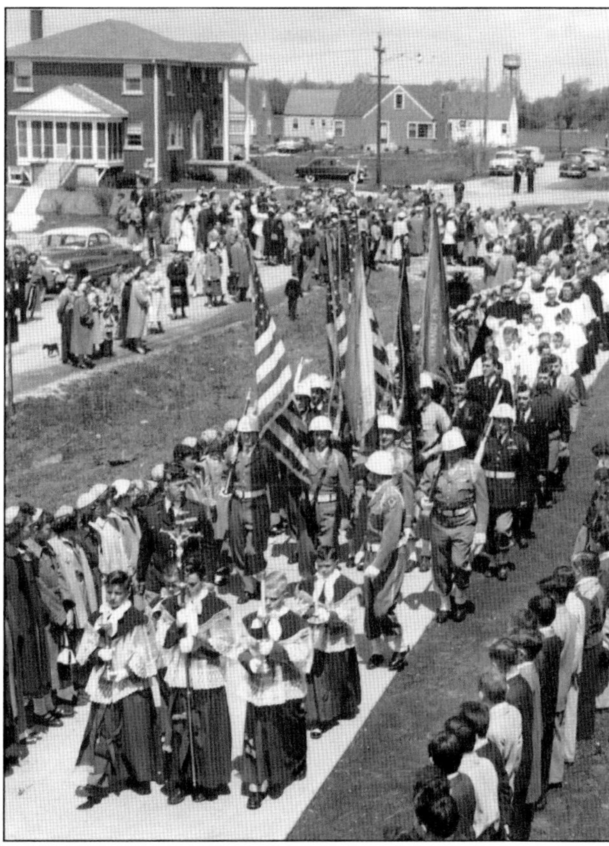

St. John Vianney Procession. Long-standing traditions such as the procession at right continue to this day. Altar boys lead this procession as it winds from near the convent to the church. Military personnel participate in the procession, carrying the American flag and Howard H. Rohde Post flag. Policemen block certain streets, preventing cars from entering the area. Many of the modern-day processions are led by Spanish-speaking priests and congregations. Notice the open space, as there were still many vacant lots, which are now occupied by homes. (Courtesy of Northlake City Hall.)

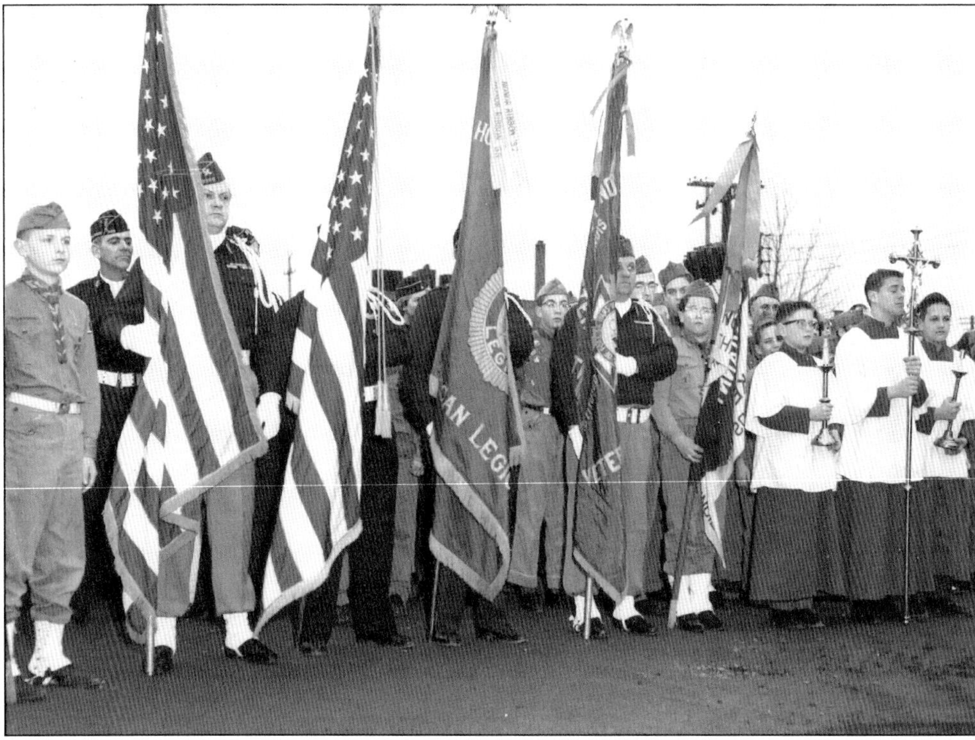

St. John Vianney Procession. The American Legion guard is joined by altar boys from St. John Vianney. Prior to the founding of St. John Vianney, the only congregation in close proximity to Northlake was St. Gertrude's, in the neighboring town of Franklin Park. (Courtesy of Northlake City Hall.)

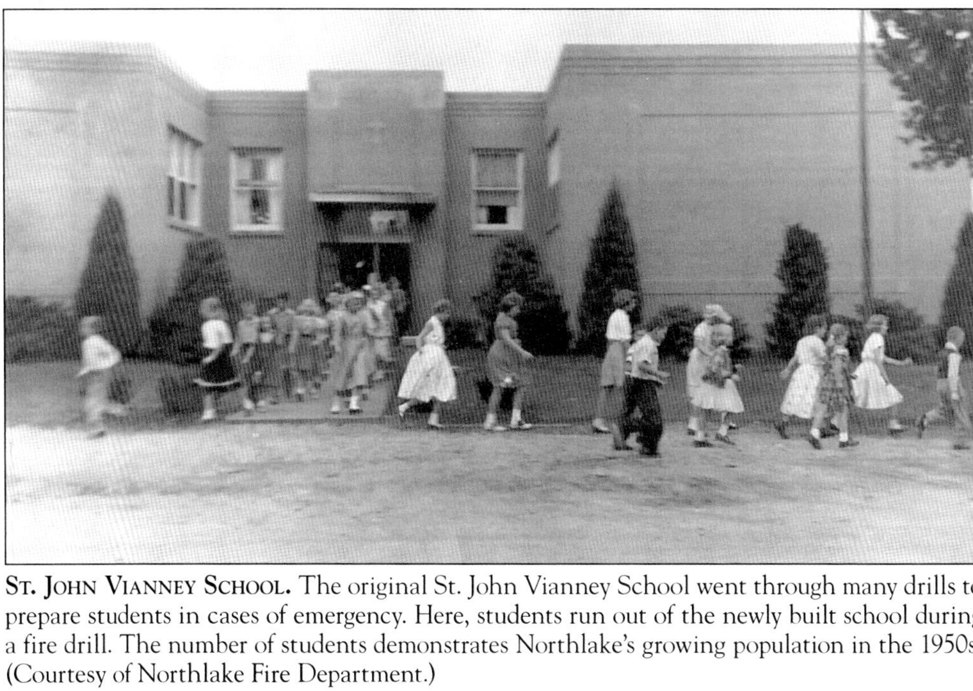

St. John Vianney School. The original St. John Vianney School went through many drills to prepare students in cases of emergency. Here, students run out of the newly built school during a fire drill. The number of students demonstrates Northlake's growing population in the 1950s. (Courtesy of Northlake Fire Department.)

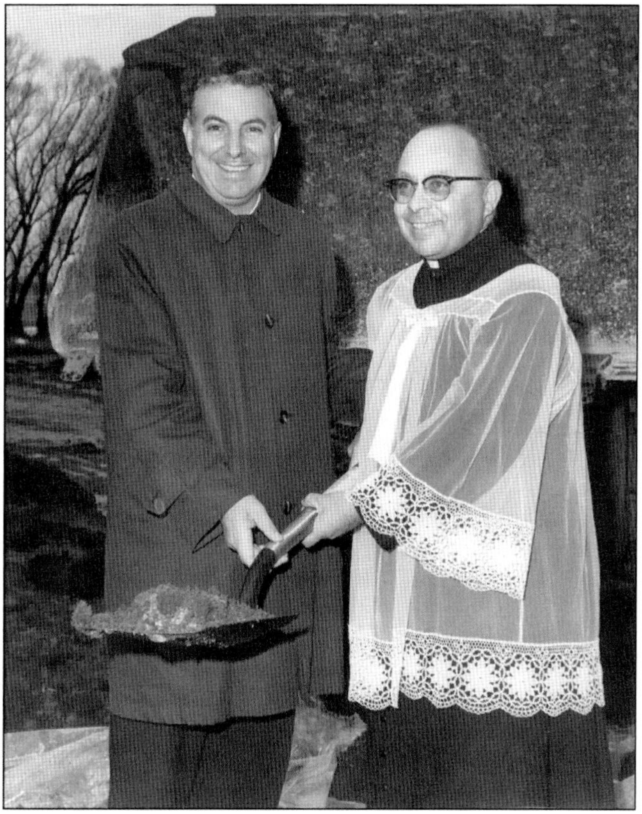

ST. JOHN VIANNEY DEDICATION. At right, Mayor Neri (left) poses with Father Armando Pierini at the St. John Vianney School dedication on May 9, 1954. Both men were hugely influential in the growth of Northlake. On the dedication program below, the original name of the school, St. John Baptist Vianney Grade School, is seen on the side of the building. (Both, courtesy of Northlake City Hall.)

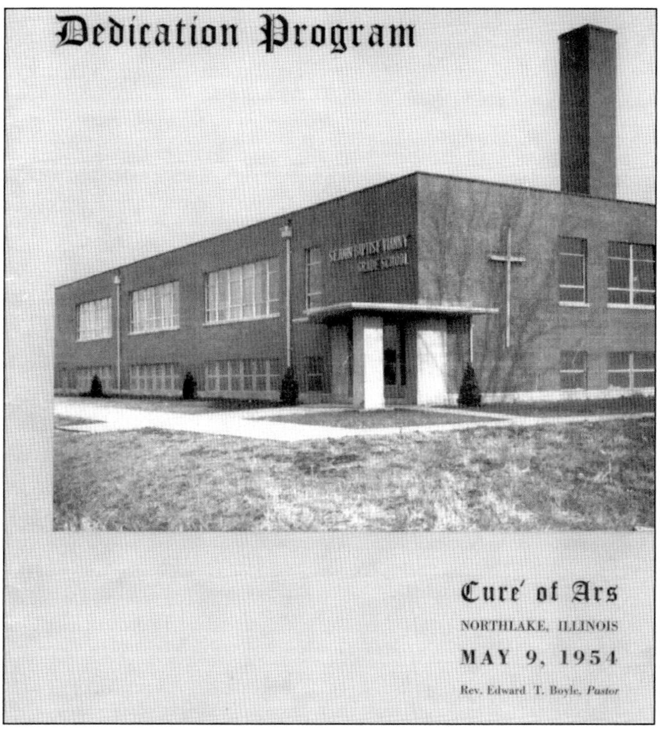

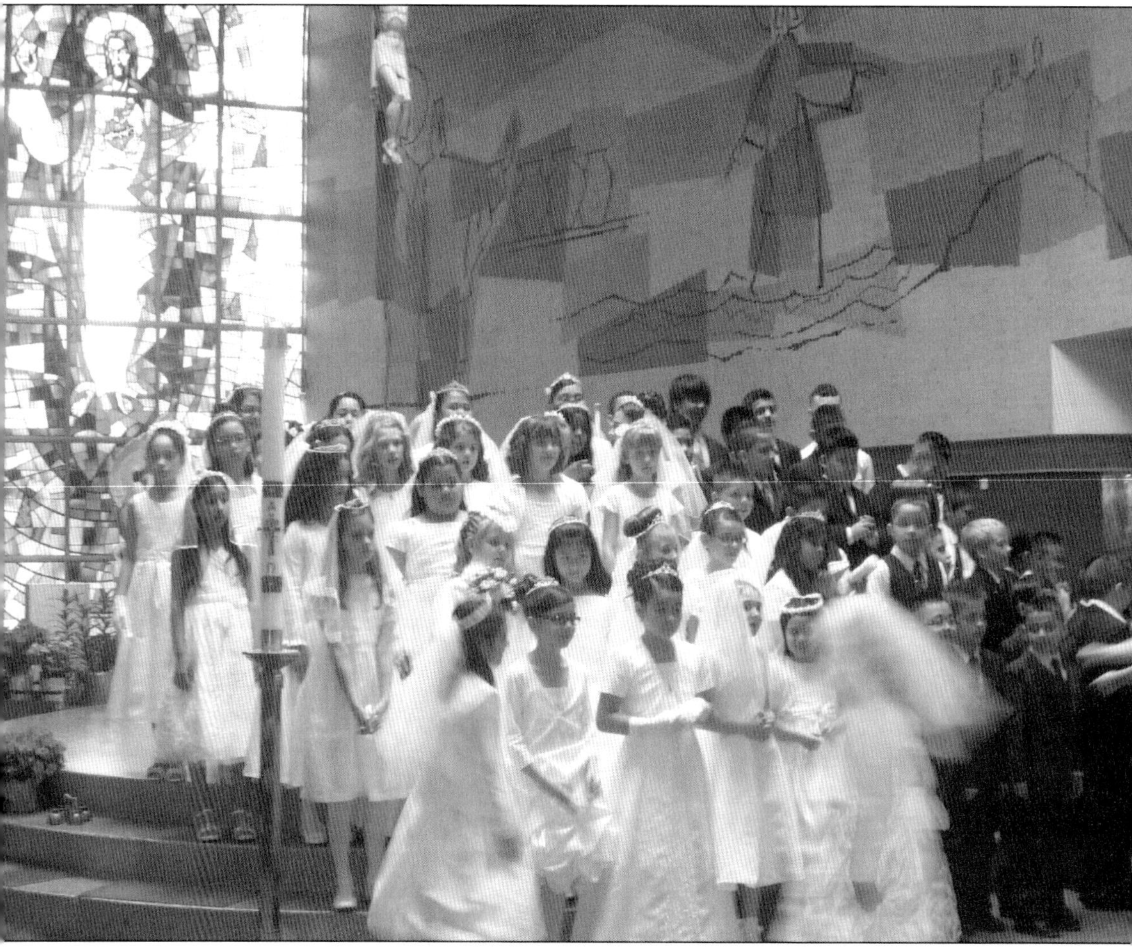

First Communion. This recent St. John Vianney first communion ceremony demonstrates the more diverse population now attending the churches in the area. Children of Mexican and Polish descent are greater in number than in the past. The background provides a close view of the mural depicting the different scenes of Jesus's life, which has captured the attention of parishioners for more than 50 years. (Author's collection.)

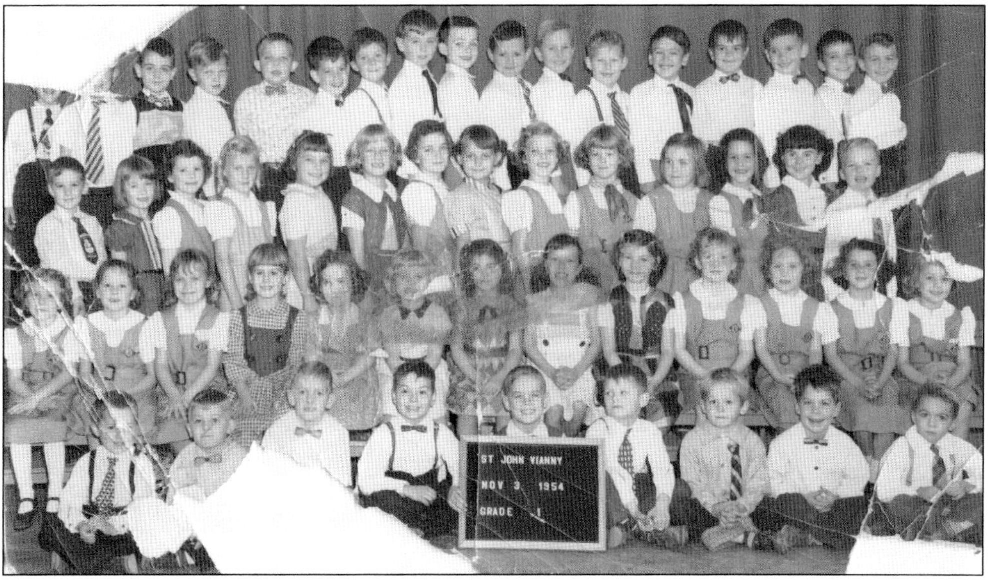

St. John Vianney Original Class. This first-grade class was the first complete class that graduated from St. John Vianney School, in 1961. Although here the boys were wearing shirts and ties and many of the girls were wearing skirts, a standard uniform was later set in place. (Courtesy of Pam Crow.)

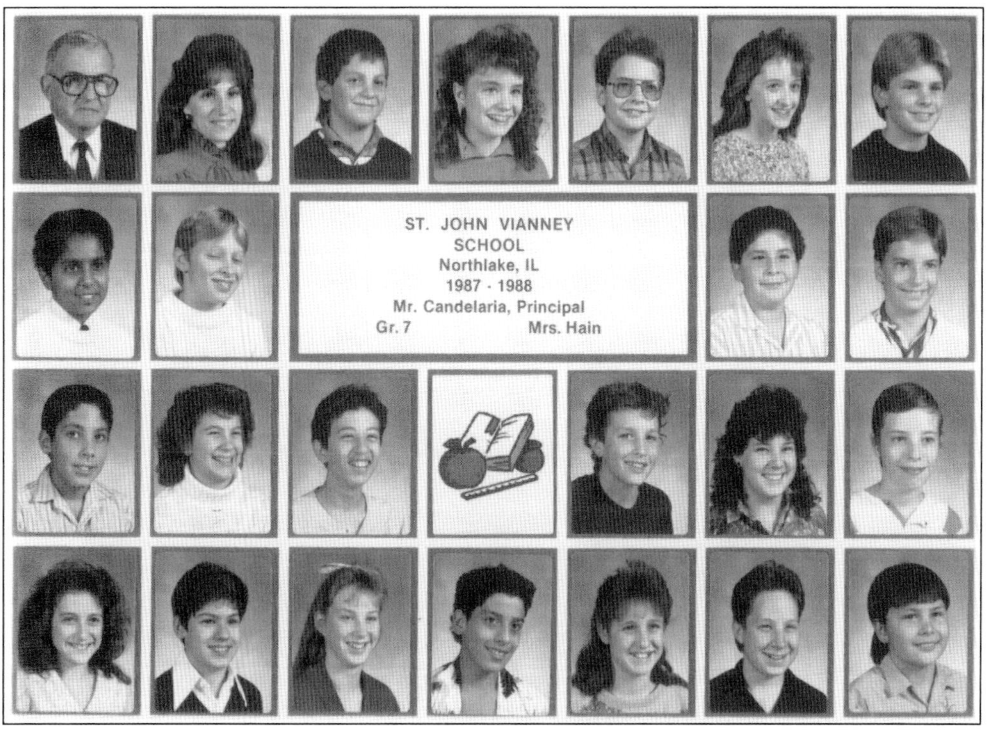

1987–1988 Class Picture. In the 1980s, St. John Vianney's student body grew more diverse as people from different nationalities started moving into the area. Some of those nationalities included Indian, Mexican, Puerto Rican, Filipino, and Ukrainian. (Author's collection.)

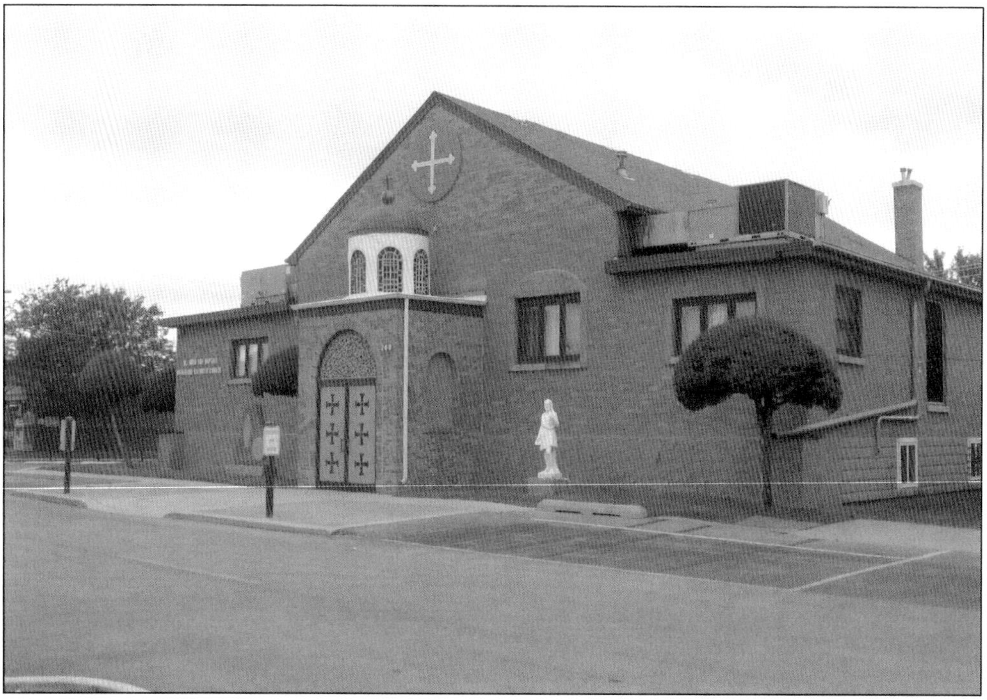

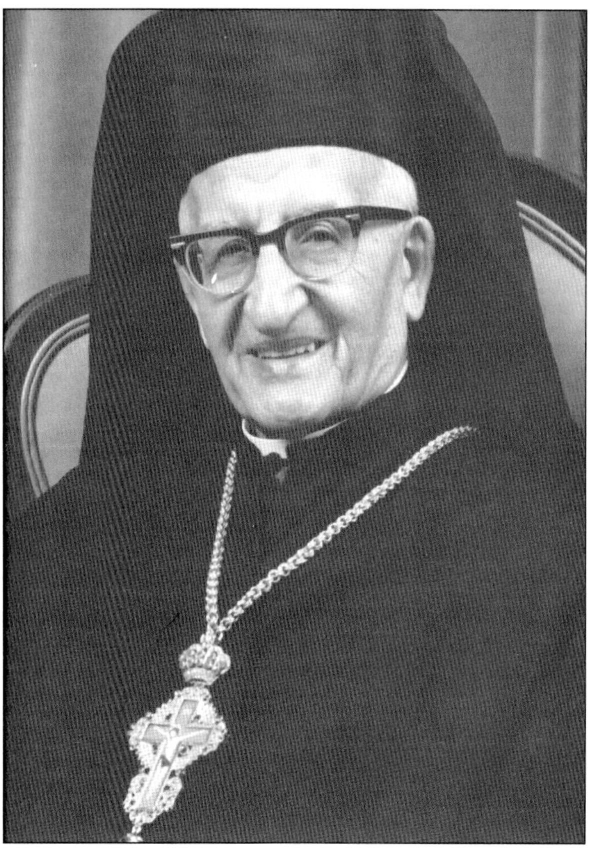

St. John the Baptist Melkite Catholic Church. St. John the Baptist Melkite Catholic Church, on the corner of North Avenue and Roy Street, initially formed in 1966. They purchased this building in 1969 under their second pastor, Father Cyril Haddad (left). (Both, courtesy of St. John Melkite Catholic Church.)

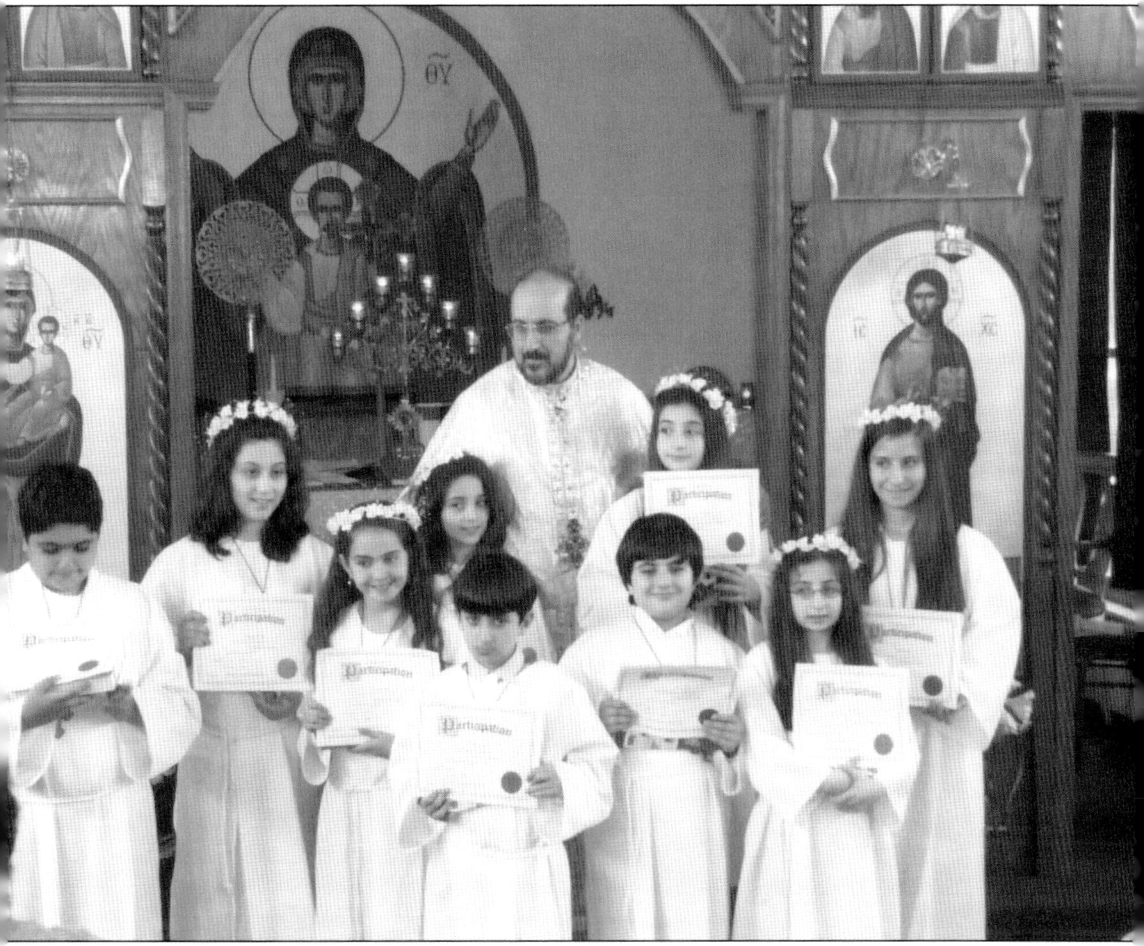

SERVICE OF FIRST RECONCILIATION. Above, current pastor Father Fouad Sayegh is surrounded by children as he leads the Service of First Reconciliation. Father Sayegh has been serving this congregation and the surrounding communities since September 2006. The congregation currently includes more than 200 families, with Syrian, Lebanese, Palestinian, Jordanian, Egyptian, and Iraqi backgrounds. (Courtesy of St. John the Baptist Melkite Church.)

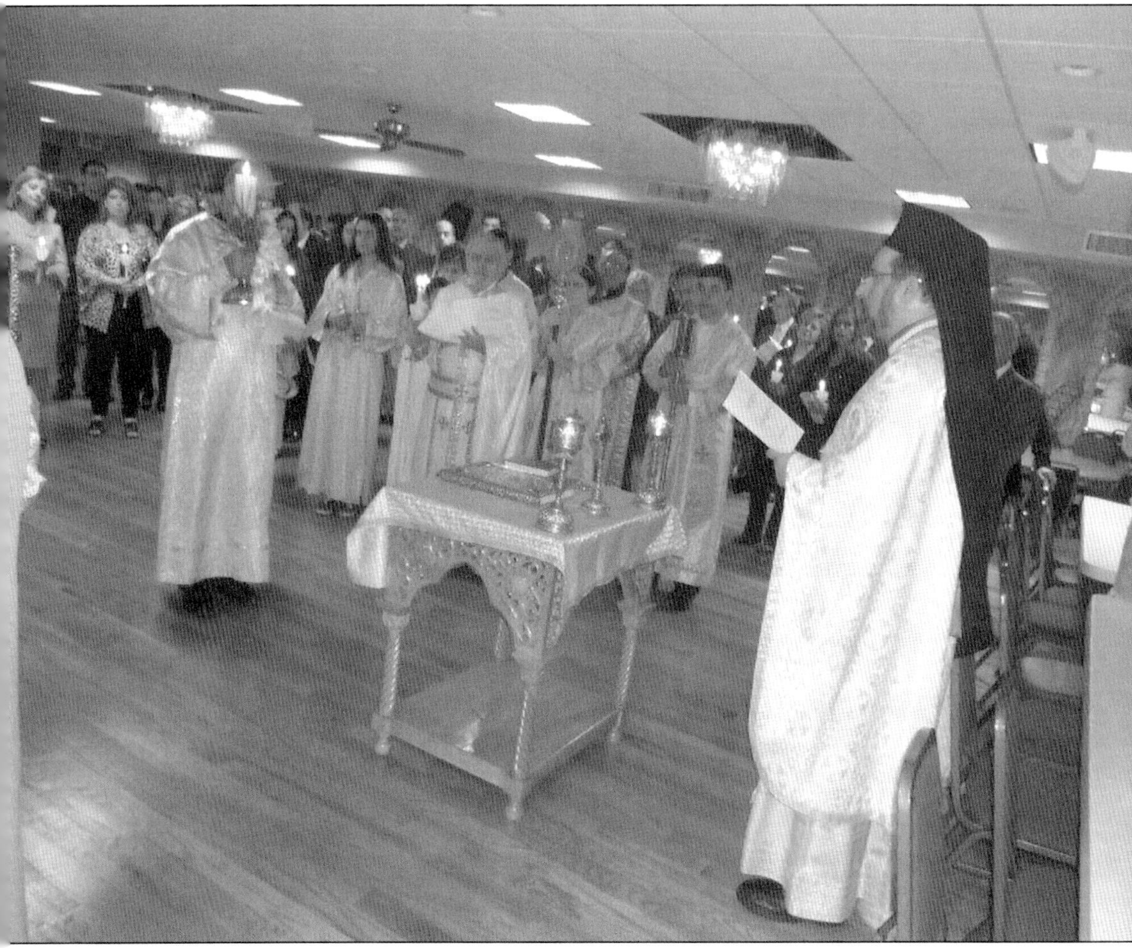

St. John the Baptist Melkite Church Service. Father Fouad Sayegh leads this service at St. John's Hall next to the church as the congregation shows signs of strength after struggling several decades ago. The first part of the Pascha (Easter) celebration, called Hajmeh, starts outside St. John's Hall. (Courtesy of St. John the Baptist Melkite Church.)

Six

A Great Education

Four schools were founded for the earliest Northlake residents: Roy, Whittier, Westdale, and Riley Schools. Roy School served students from kindergarten through eighth grade. Whittier School had a curriculum for children through the fourth grade, later expanding to eighth grade. Riley School taught students until sixth grade.

After Riley, kids would commute via the school bus to Sunnyside Junior High School on Wolf and St. Charles Roads, providing excitement as the ride took them on a two-lane wooden bridge over the Proviso railroad yards on Mannheim Road. This circuitous route was necessary because the old burned-out bridge on Wolf Road was never rebuilt.

In 1971, Northlake Junior High was founded next to Riley School. This led to a consolidation, as more schools had recently opened to serve the baby boom population. Students from Mark Twain and Ben Franklin Schools were also now required to attend the new Northlake Junior High.

Unfortunately for many friendships nurtured in grade school, North Avenue has always served as the dividing line between the districts for West Leyden High School and Proviso High School. Residents living north of North Avenue attended West Leyden, just over a mile north on Wolf Road, and those living south of North Avenue were in the Proviso school district.

The sole high school in Northlake, West Leyden High School, continues to be a microcosm of America, with Anglo, Latino, Polish, and African American students. With an unwavering commitment to the arts, students' abilities are frequently showcased with drawings, paintings, ceramics, and murals. For those ready to put their hands to work, courses continue to be offered in such fields as construction/woods, autos, metals, and printing, proving that as technology continues to shift and change, industrial skills are still in demand.

In athletics, West Leyden High School has fielded competitive teams on the baseball diamond, basketball court, and football field. The school has also always had tough wrestlers, sending many to state competitions over the years. Some graduates have gone on to compete in college and at all levels of athletic competition, representing the school well.

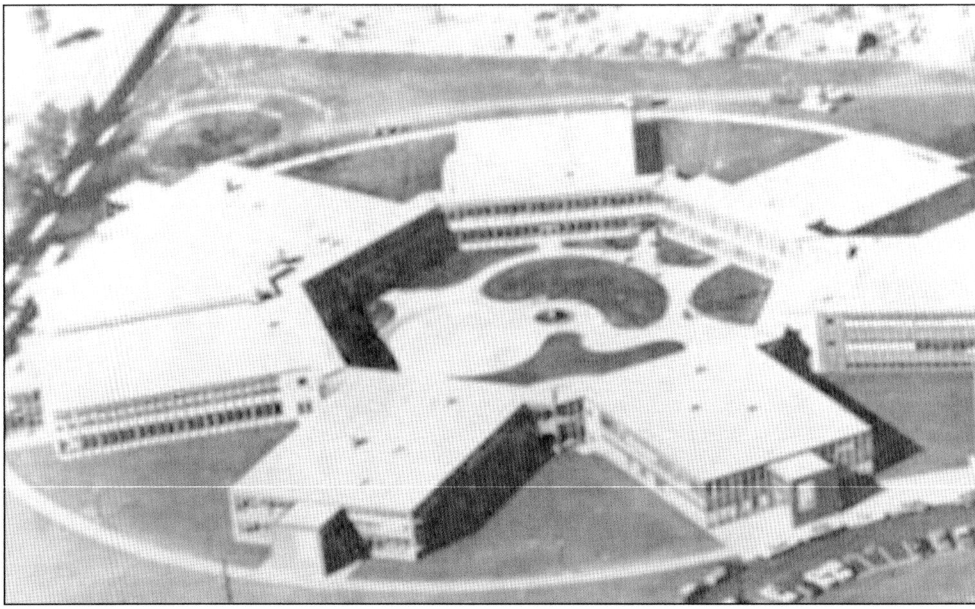

West Leyden High School. West Leyden High School, which opened in 1958, was originally constructed in the form of a wheel with spokes. The inner courtyard provided well-landscaped grounds with places to sit. The athletic fields are behind the school. (Both, courtesy of Franklin Park Library.)

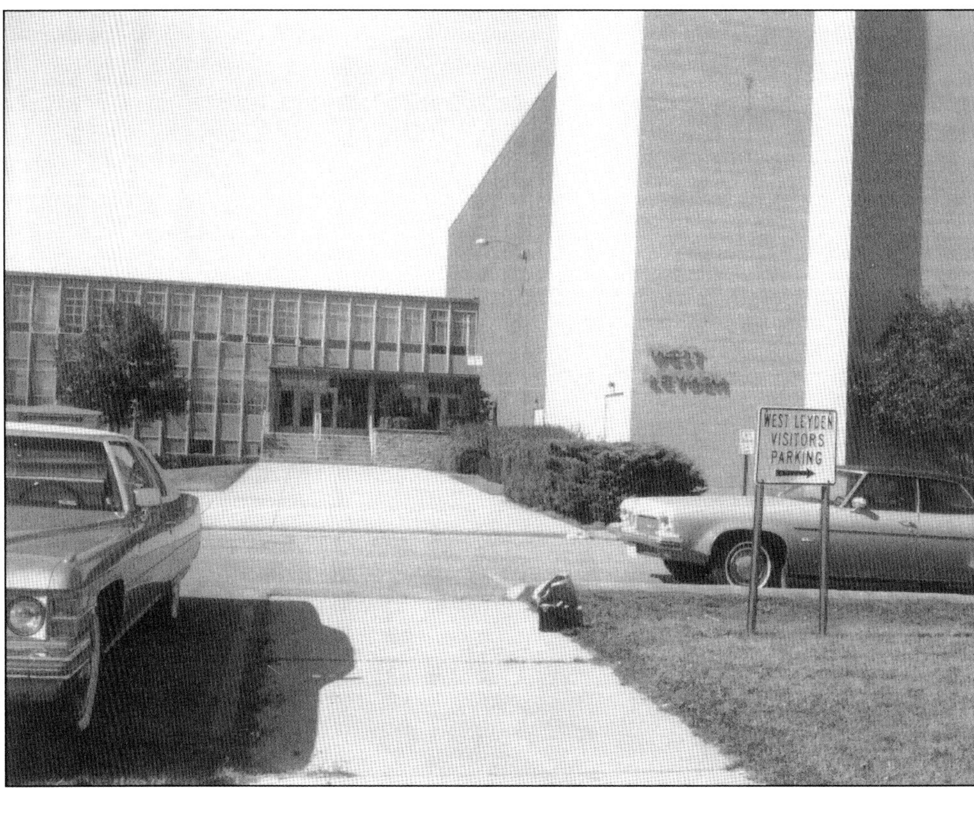

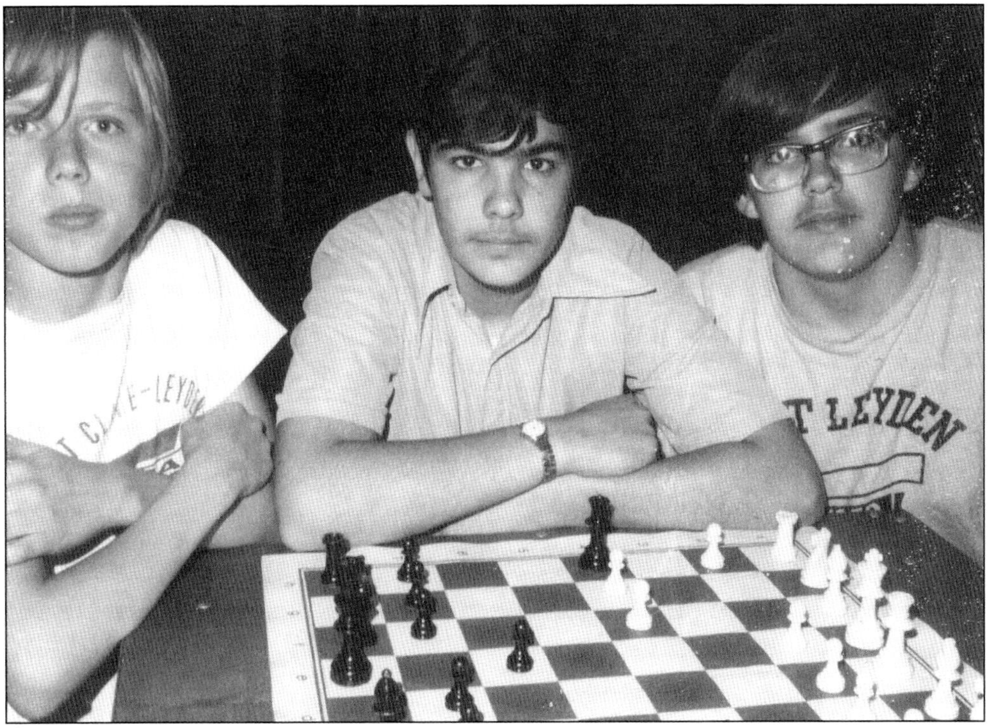

West Leyden Knights Chess Team. From West Leyden's founding up until its 1981 merger with East Leyden, the West Leyden Knights excelled in many athletic competitions. The wrestling team placed fourth in the 1968–1969 state finals and the chess team placed second in the 1975–1976 state finals. (Courtesy of Northlake City Hall.)

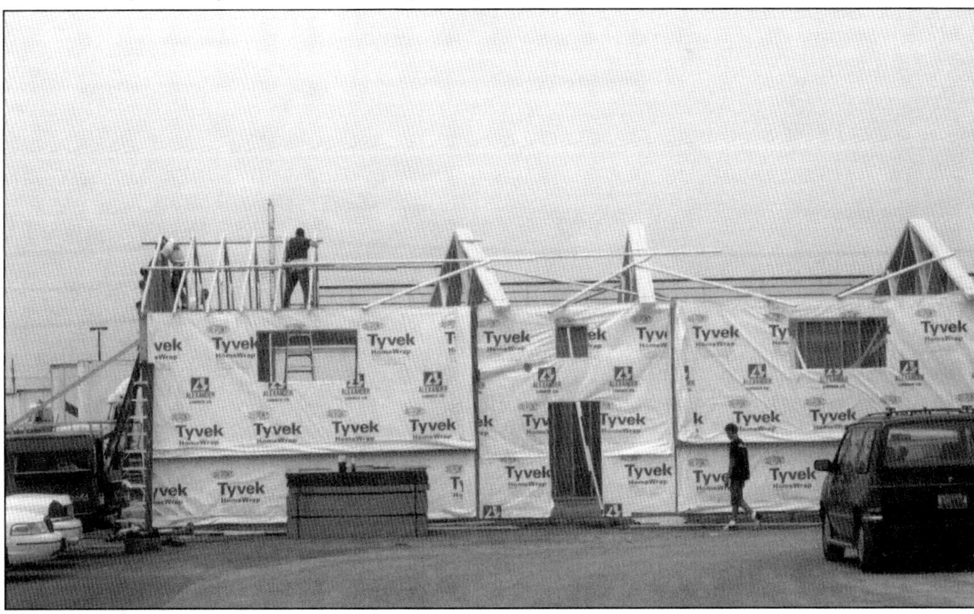

West Leyden Workshop. One of the West Leyden's strengths has been its construction and woods courses, which provide students the opportunity to work with their hands. Students built this Public Works storage building in 2001. (Courtesy of Northlake City Hall.)

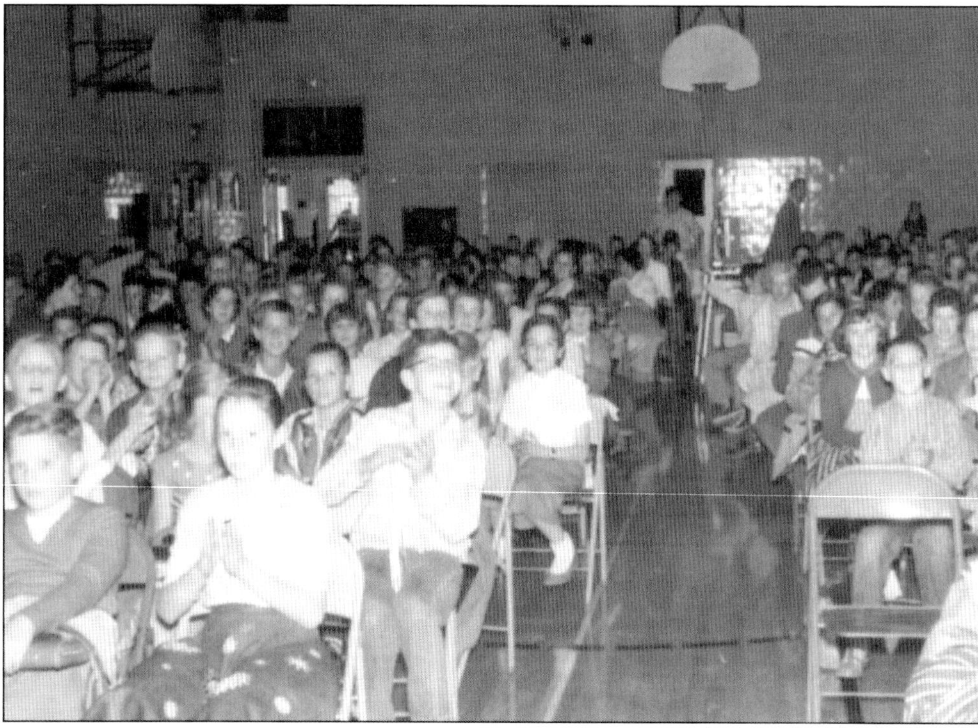

Roy School Fire Prevention. In the 1950s, fire prevention education was important. Here, Roy School students listen intently as they are taught about preventing fires. (Courtesy of Northlake Fire Department.)

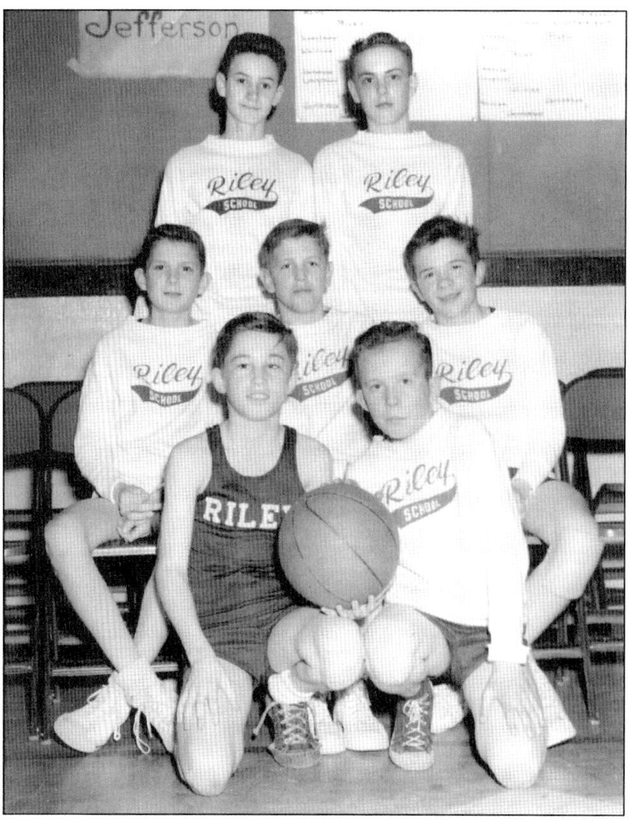

Riley School Basketball Team. Athletics were integral at Riley. One of this basketball team's heated rivalries was with the Jefferson School. (Courtesy of Northlake City Hall.)

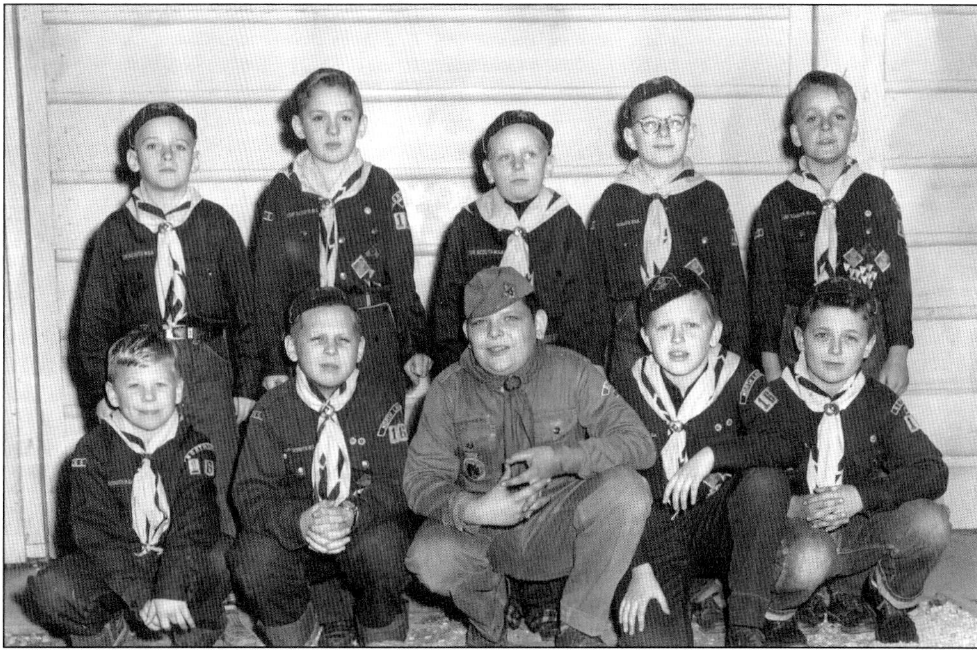

Roy School Cub Scouts. Roy School Cub Scouts have been an active part of community life. These 10 Cub Scouts posed for this photograph in 1950. Ken Murawaski is second from the left in the second row. (Courtesy of Northlake City Hall.)

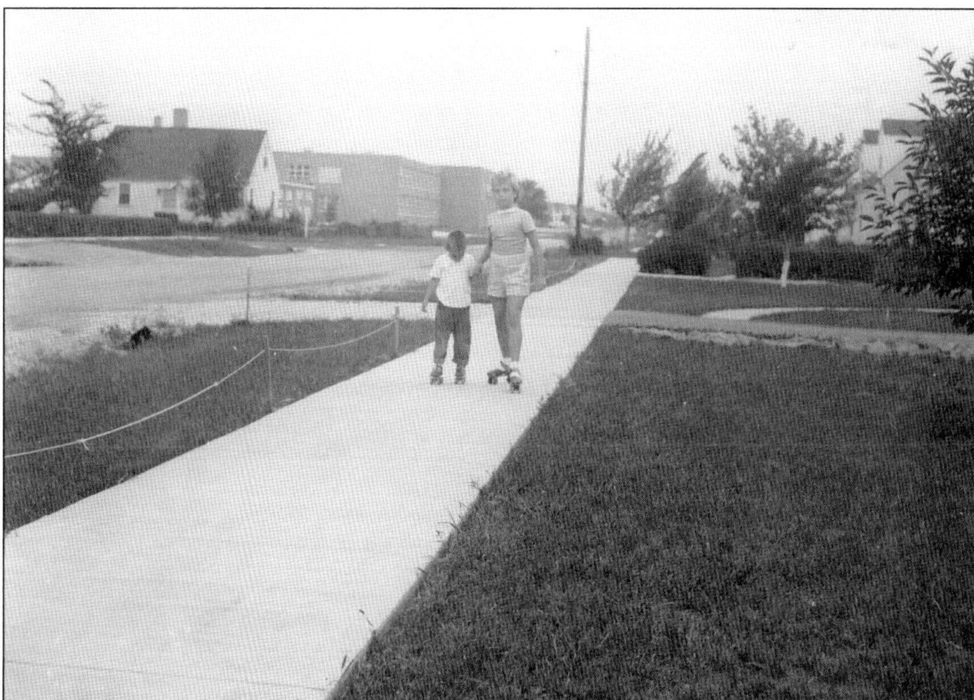

Rollerskating Near Roy School. These two young residents hold hands as they rollerskate on the freshly built sidewalks with Roy School in the background. (Courtesy of Northlake City Hall.)

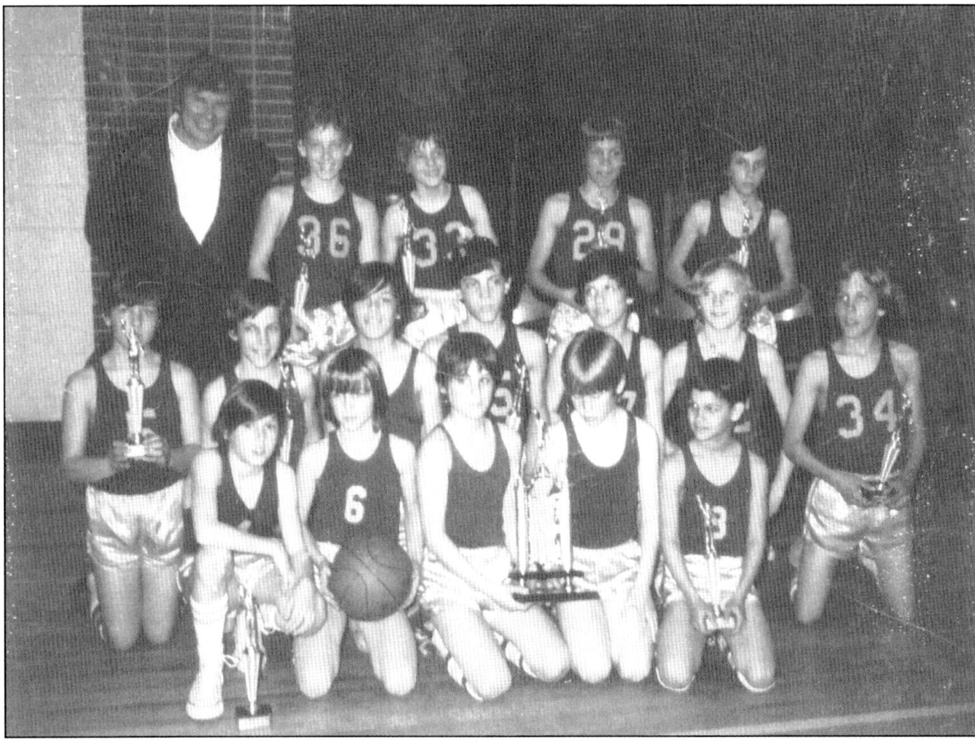

ROY SCHOOL BASKETBALL. Roy School also had a strong athletic program. Here, the school basketball team poses with trophies. (Courtesy of Northlake City Hall).

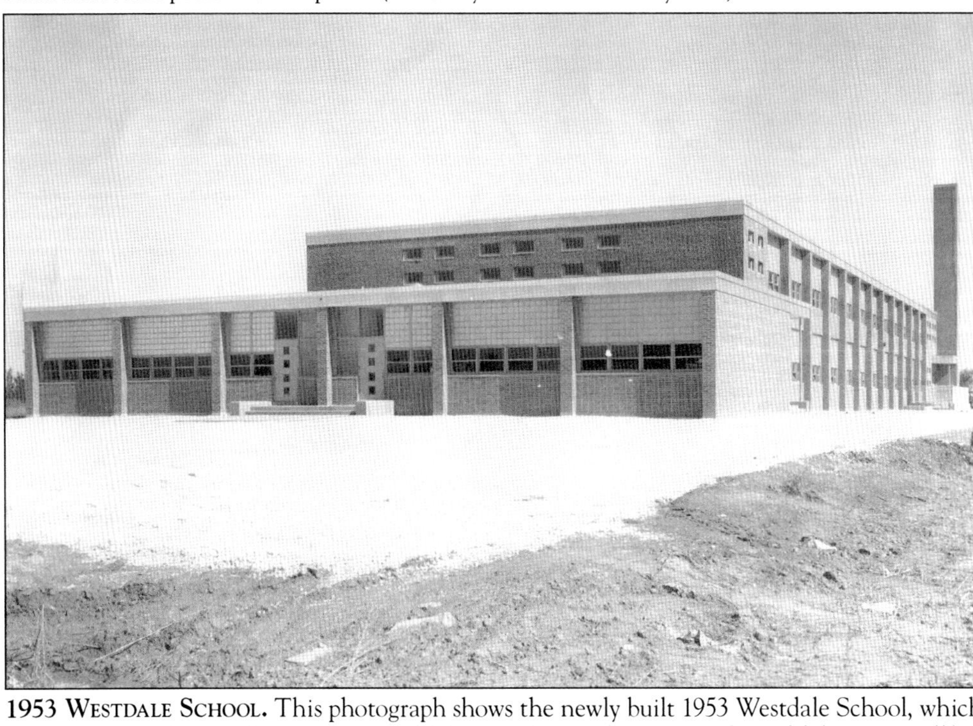

1953 WESTDALE SCHOOL. This photograph shows the newly built 1953 Westdale School, which served parts of the rapidly growing Northlake population. (Courtesy of Northlake City Hall.)

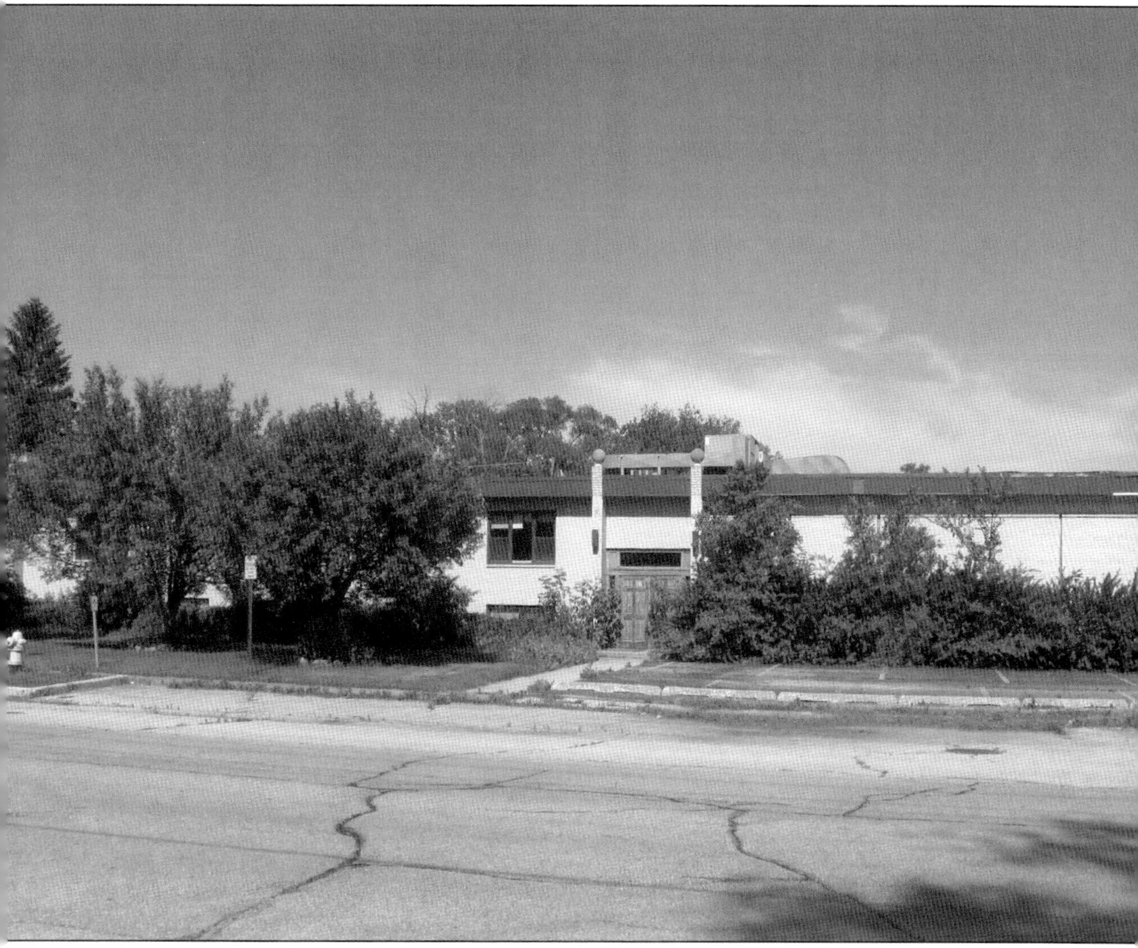

Mark Twain School. One of the earliest schools in Northlake was the Mark Twain School, seen here in its current empty state. Many of the students who would have attended Mark Twain in the past now attend Northlake Junior High on Wolf Road. (Author's collection.)

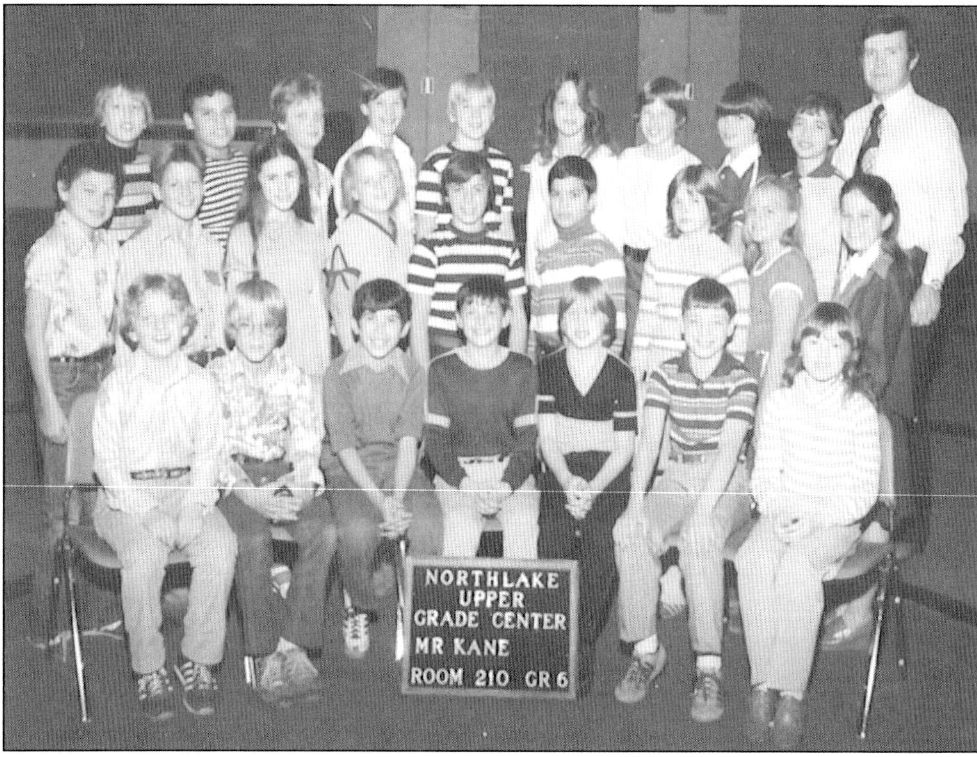

CLASS PICTURES. These two class pictures show students from Northlake (above) and Whittier (below) in decades past. These two schools have greater diversity today. (Both, courtesy of Northlake City Hall.)

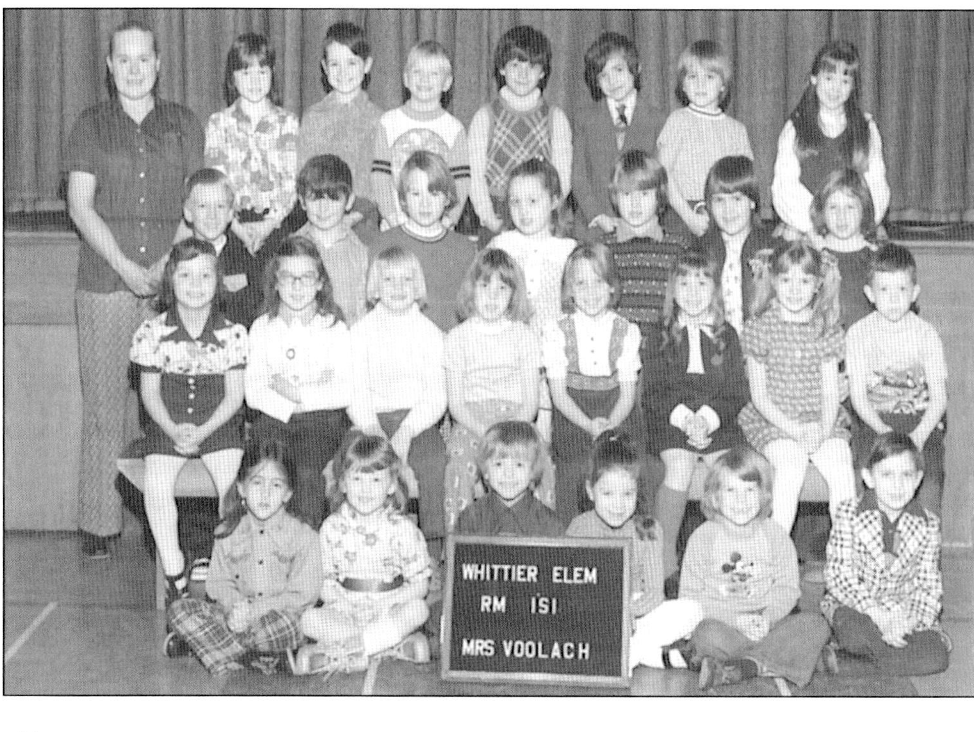

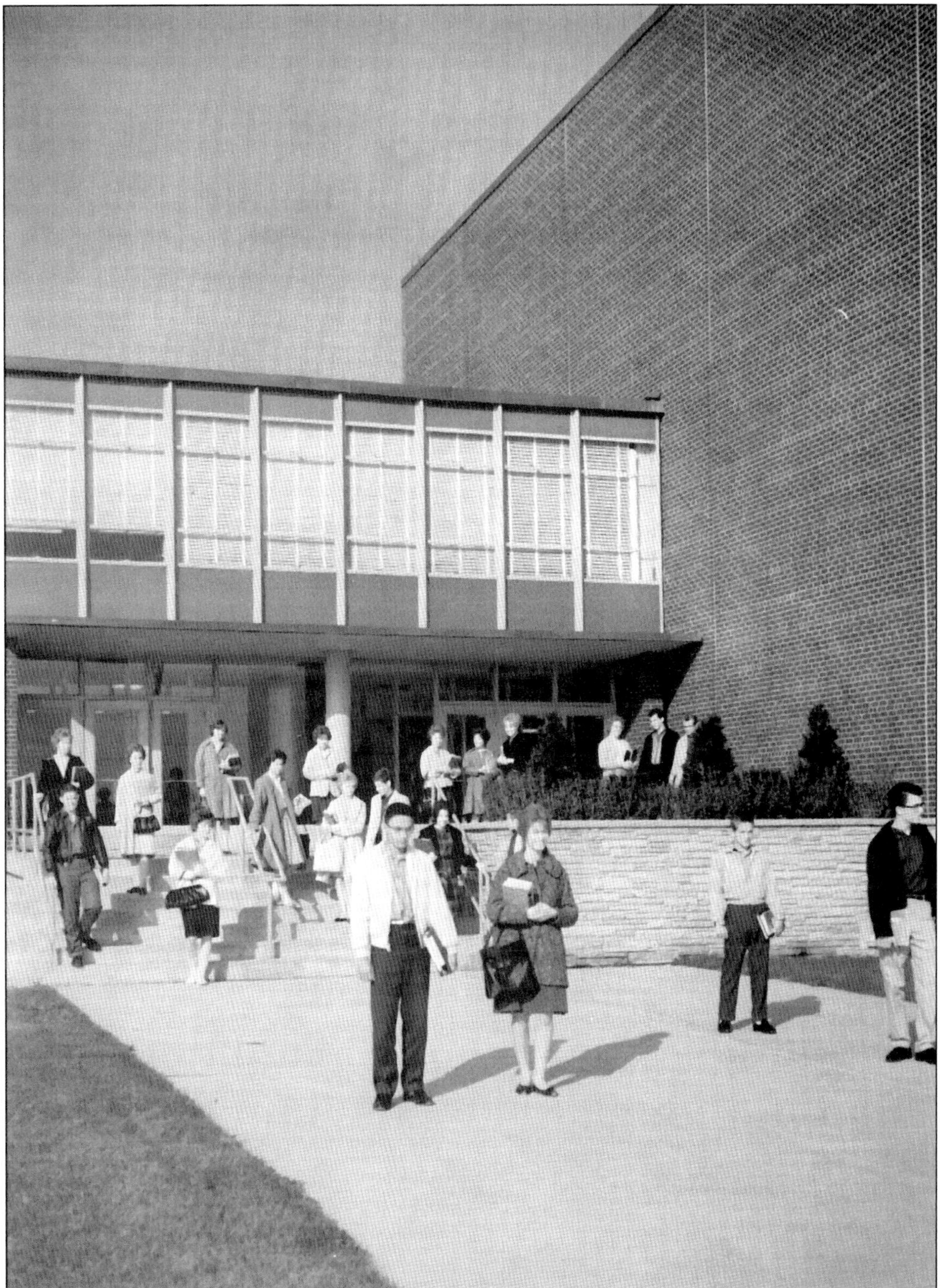

West Leyden Students. Students walk out of West Leyden High School in the early 1960s, when the school was about 10 years old. The school eventually underwent extensive renovations because of the noise from O'Hare Airport. (Courtesy of Northlake Public Library.)

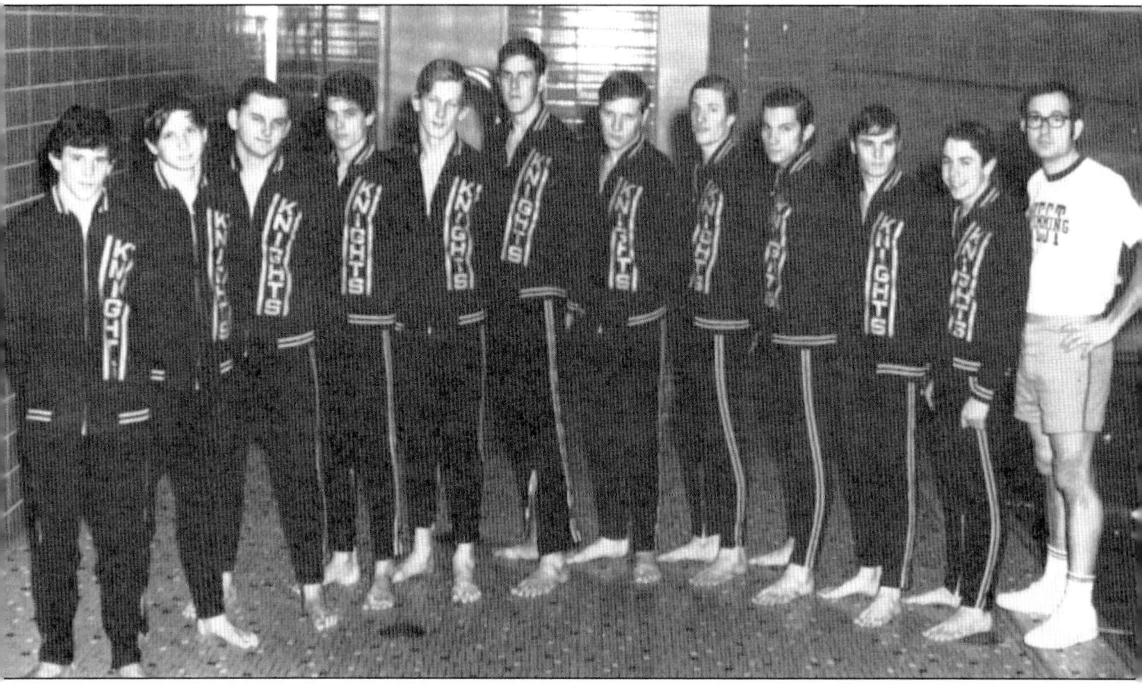

WEST LEYDEN KNIGHTS SWIM TEAM. This West Leyden High School swim team included, from left to right, R. Lobe, F. Hilgenberg, K. Howard, R. Davies, D. Dickens, J. Davies, B. Korzenksi, F. Jahnke, R. Tolomei, K. McPhillips, K. Paulsen, and Coach R.B. Russell. (Courtesy of Northlake Public Library.)

Seven

Moving Forward in Changing Times

Many of the original business establishments in the community—the taverns frequented by industrial workers and the mom-and-pop stores—have given way to chain stores that provide everything a homeowner could want. Nothing remains of Northlake Hardware, with its personal attention to detail and its many electrical boxes for homeowners to do their own electrical wiring. Today, a Home Depot employs many local residents.

Spata's Shoes and Goodwill Barber Shop have long since left us. Hair stylists have filled that void, and today, Wal-Mart provides more than enough shoes and other products. The building that housed Gray's Drug Store still stands, but half of it is a medical clinic and the other half is a Subway sandwich shop.

Technology continues to shape the way things are done around here. The police department no longer uses typewriters and a basic phone system; it now relies on state-of-the-art equipment and a dedicated 911 emergency service line. The fire department's original emergency response vehicle is now equipped with the latest technology to provide residents with everything from basic first-aid treatment to booster shots for diabetic shock and a 12-lead EKG machine for heart attack victims.

Our library has expanded multiple times to best serve Northlake and the surrounding community. Books remain on the shelves, but e-readers are also available for patrons. It is not uncommon today to hear other languages spoken and taught at the library; in fact, staff members learn Spanish and Polish to best reach the community.

Although Northlake's motto, "City of Friendly People," remains the same, this city of former shell homes has adapted and thrived in many ways. Northlake baseball continues to be popular with kids, but Leyden Bears football is now just as popular. And the high school soccer team has had much success in recent years. In many ways, this chapter, with all the contrasts it shows, demonstrates that Northlake continues true to form.

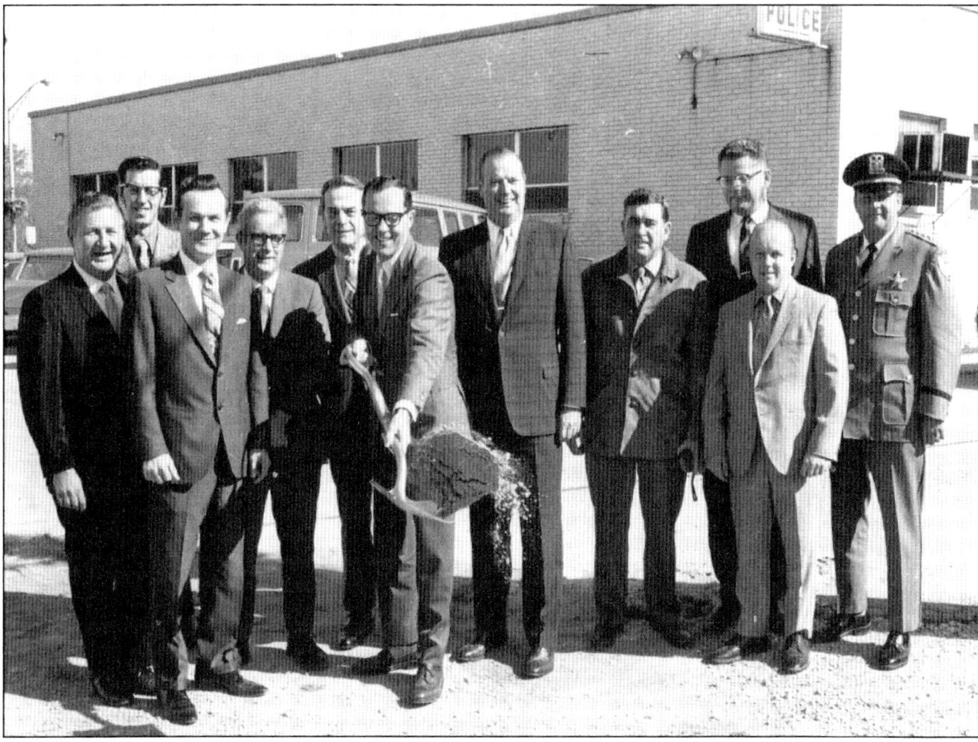

Police Department Growth Annex and New Police Station. As a result of the growing population, there was a need for an additional police building. The image above shows the ground breaking for the new Police Building Annex, presided over by, from left to right, Jack Schultz, city manager; William Miller, alderman; Ralph Sievert, alderman; Robert LaBeau, alderman; Bruce Quisenberry of Northlake Industrial Council; Eugene Doyle, mayor; Robert Wallace, president of Zenith Radio Distributing Corporation; John Lesher, alderman; John Lawrisuk, president of Northlake Kiwanis; Frank Sullivan, alderman; and Lee Gehrke, police chief. The modern police station is below. (Above, courtesy of Northlake City Hall; below, author's collection.)

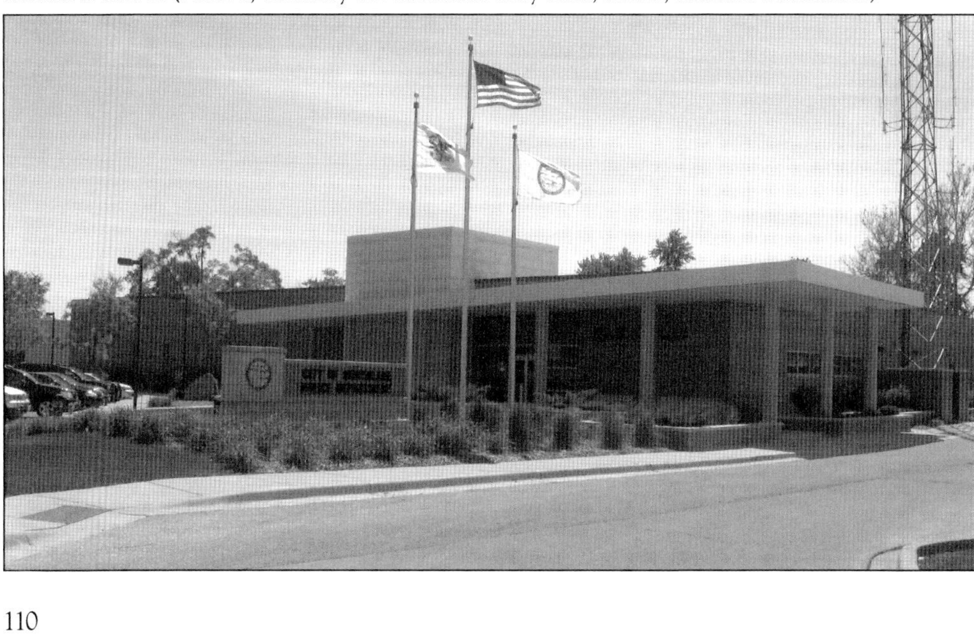

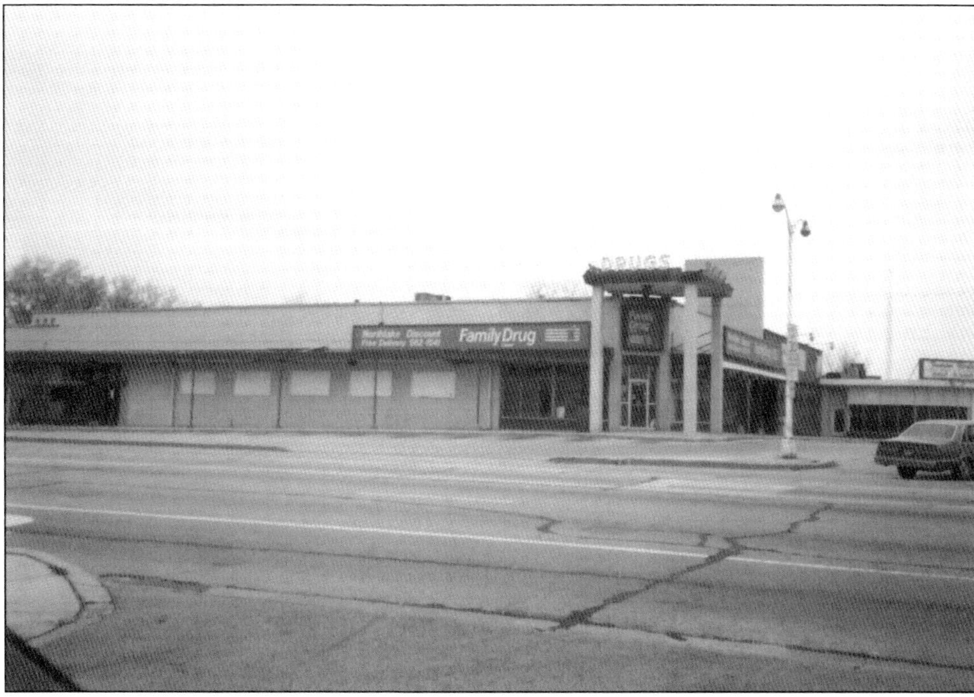

Family Drug and Walgreen's. Prior to the rise of corporate pharmacies, Northlake's Family Drug remained strong. After a Walgreen's moved into the building across the street, it was vacant for a short time, but eventually Walgreen's moved into it, remodeling and expanding it because its business had outgrown the facility across the street. Walgreen's remains open 24 hours a day and provides vaccinations, prescriptions, and other services that are vital to the community. (Above, courtesy of Northlake City Hall; below, author's collection.)

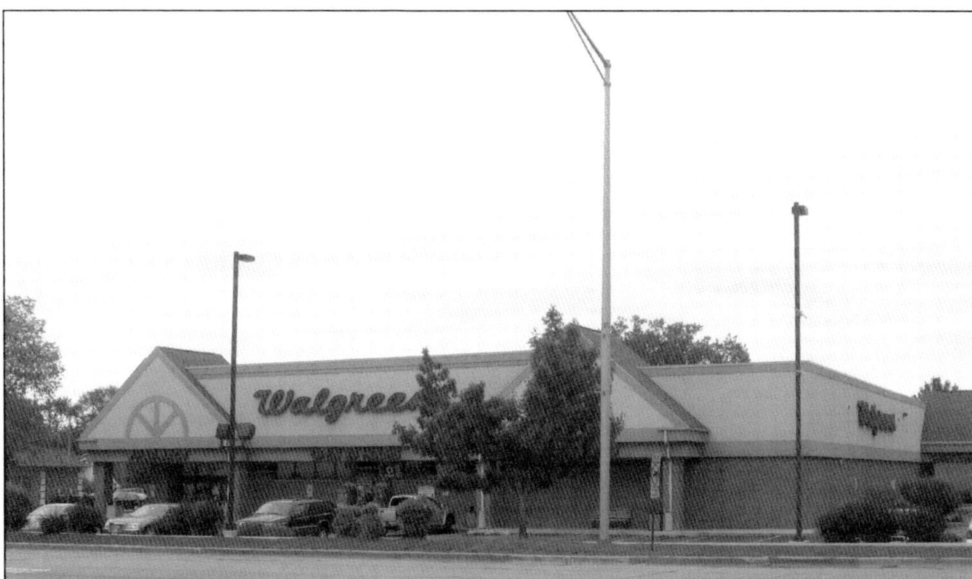

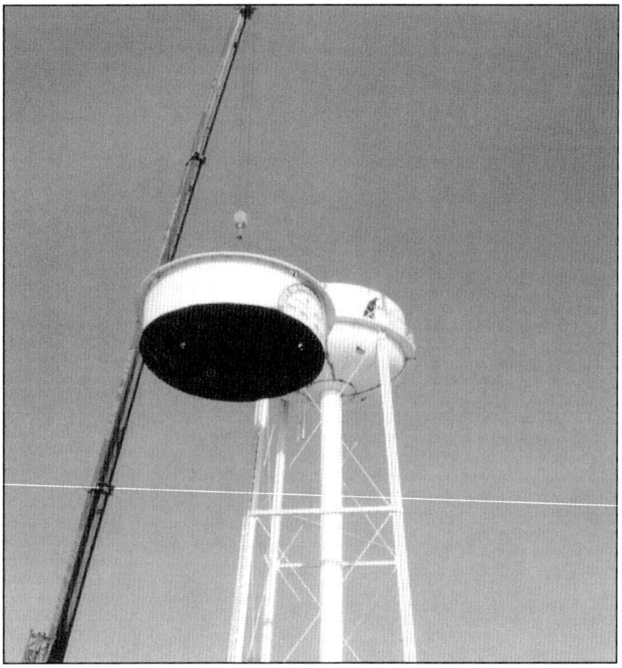

NORTHLAKE WATER TOWER, THEN AND NOW. The original water tower, which has served as a landmark since Northlake was incorporated in the early 1940s, was finally replaced in 2002. Into the 1950s, the tower's water was still primarily well water supplied from the base of the tower. The new water tower holds many more gallons and has a better design. (Left, courtesy of Northlake City Hall; below, author's collection.)

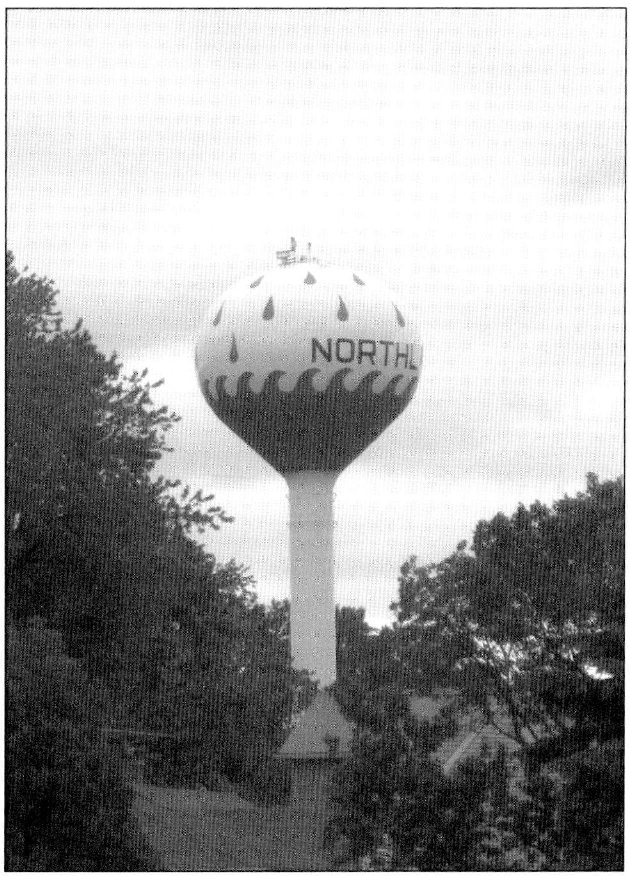

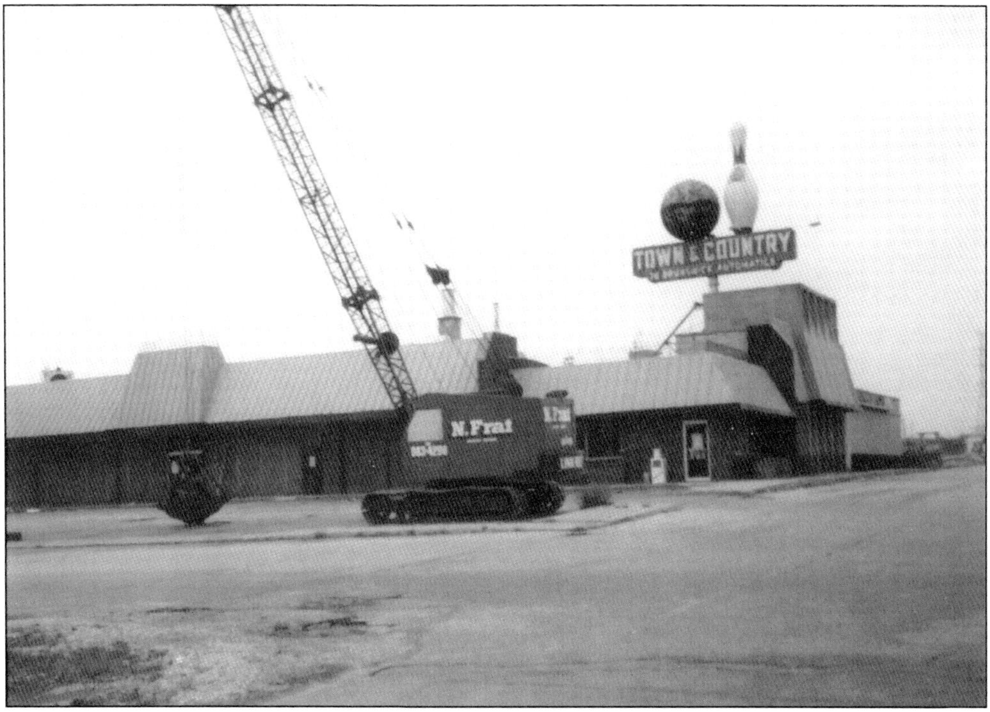

Town and Country Bowl and Home Depot. The Town and Country bowling alley that entertained locals until 1991 was torn down, along with many homes, to make way for the Wal-Mart, Sam's Club, and Home Depot. (Above, courtesy of Northlake City Hall; below, author's collection.)

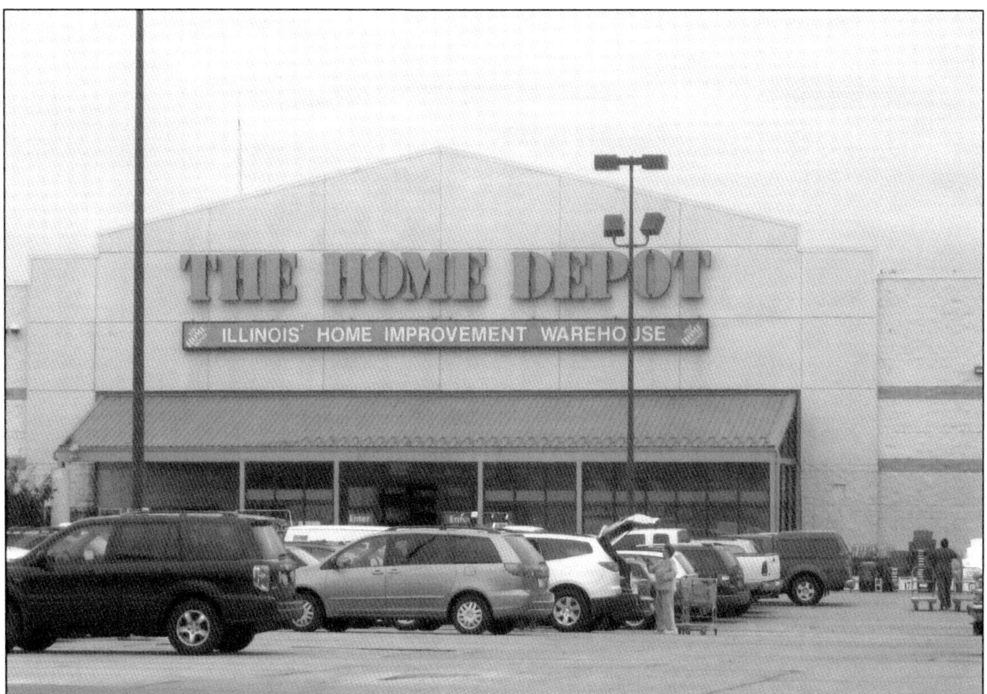

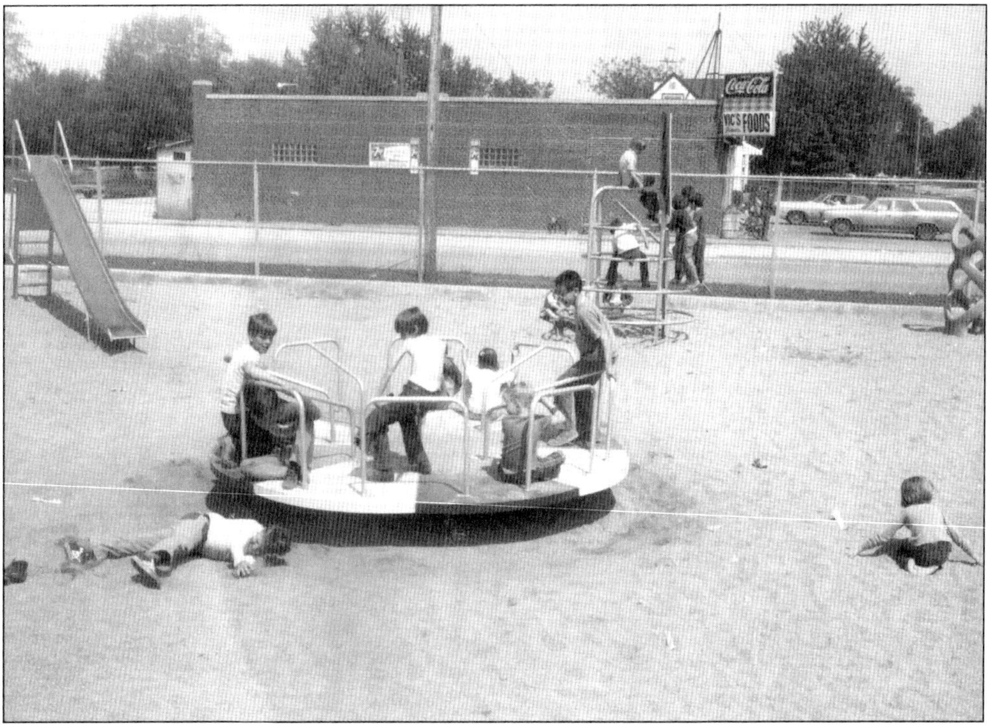

FUL-ROY PARK, THEN AND NOW. The playground at the corner of Fullerton Avenue and Roy Street is still a park with rides and sand, but today, the slides are weatherproof and there is a sand volleyball court for older kids and adults. (Above, courtesy of Northlake City Hall; below, author's collection.)

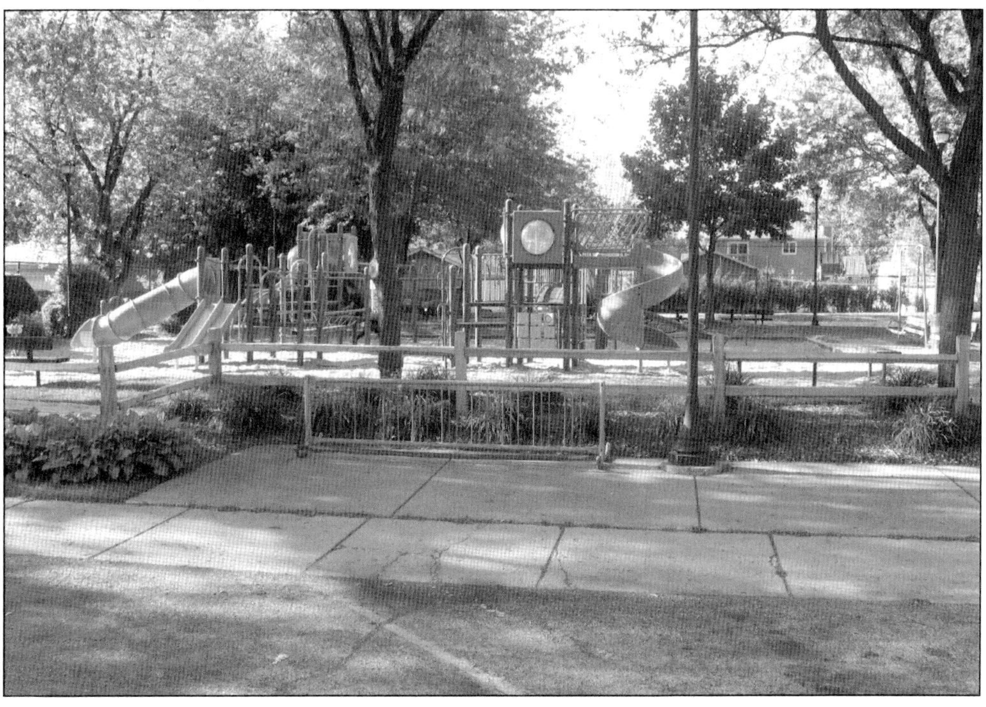

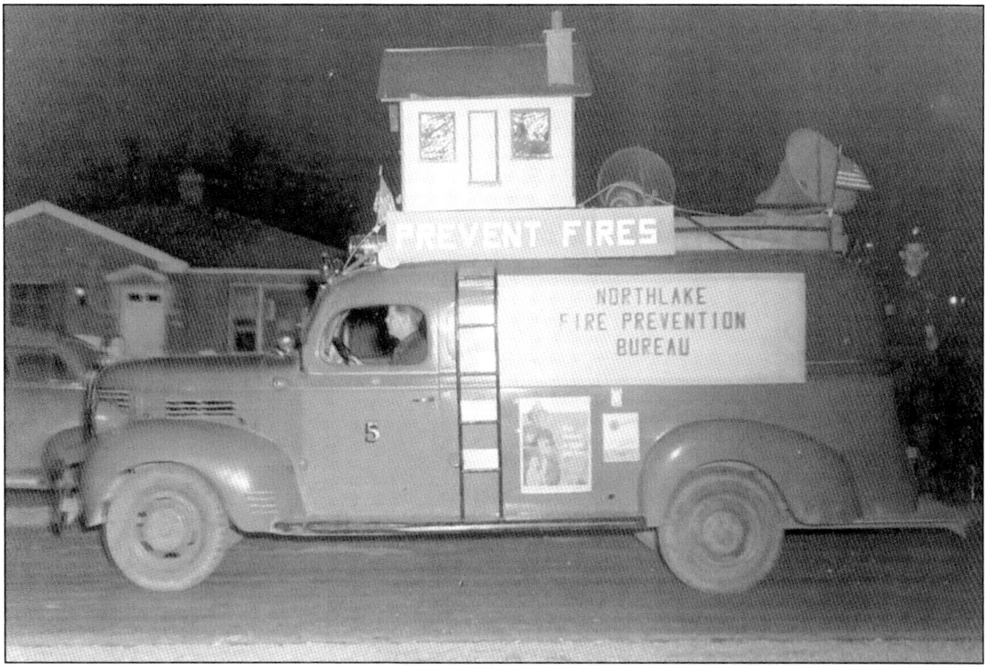

Ambulances, Then and Now. Northlake's Oxygen and Light unit, seen above in 1952 warning residents to prevent fires, served as the town's emergency medical response vehicle until 1964. The current ambulance (below) is equipped with the latest technology and notifies the hospital of a patient's condition ahead of time. It also has a 12-lead EKG machine. (Both, courtesy of Northlake Fire Department.)

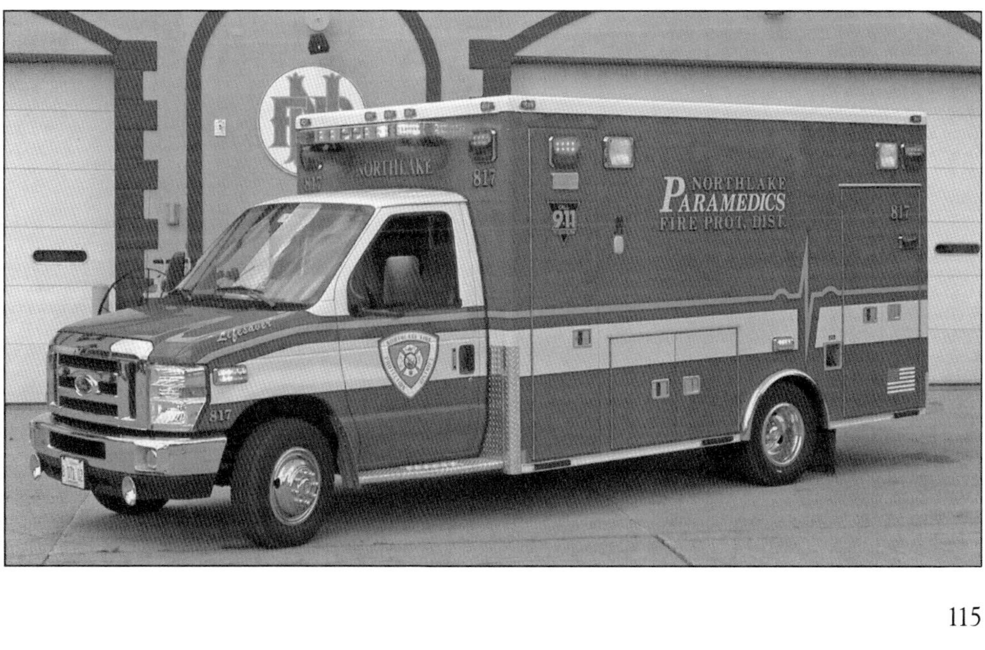

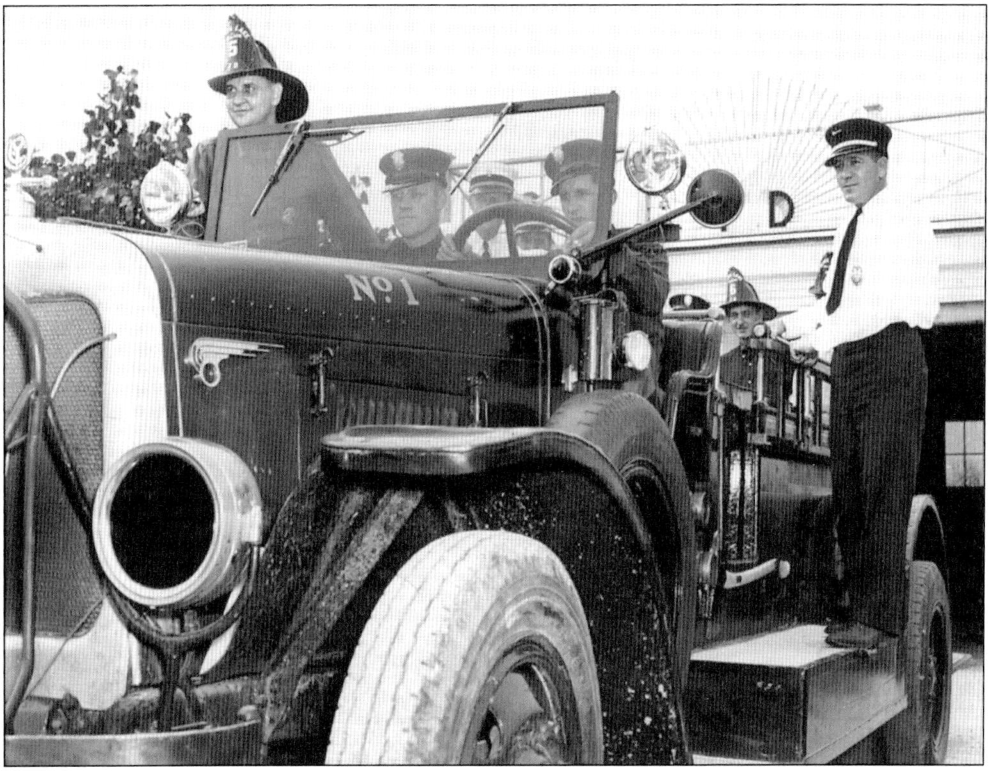

NORTHLAKE FIRE TRUCK. The Northlake Fire Department purchased the 1940 Engine No. 1, seen here, from the Lombard Fire Department for $500 and subsequently sold it to the River Forest Fire Department in 1947. A close look at the fireman standing on the passenger side shows the town was not yet incorporated at the time of this photograph, as the two-word name "North Lake" is printed on his helmet. (Courtesy of Northlake Fire Department.)

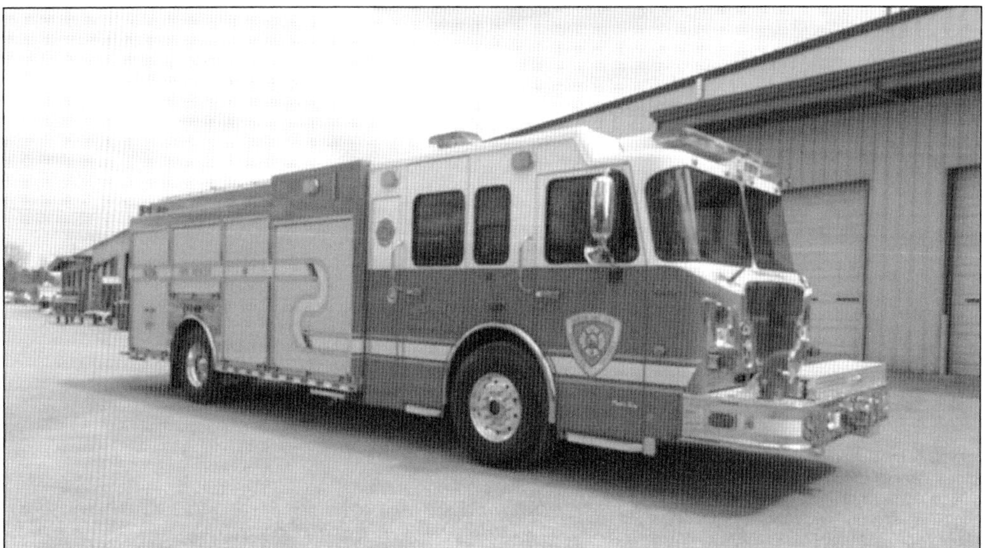

NORTHLAKE'S LATEST TRUCK. The newest Northlake fire truck has all the equipment needed to fight fires and respond to other emergencies. (Courtesy of Northlake Fire Department.)

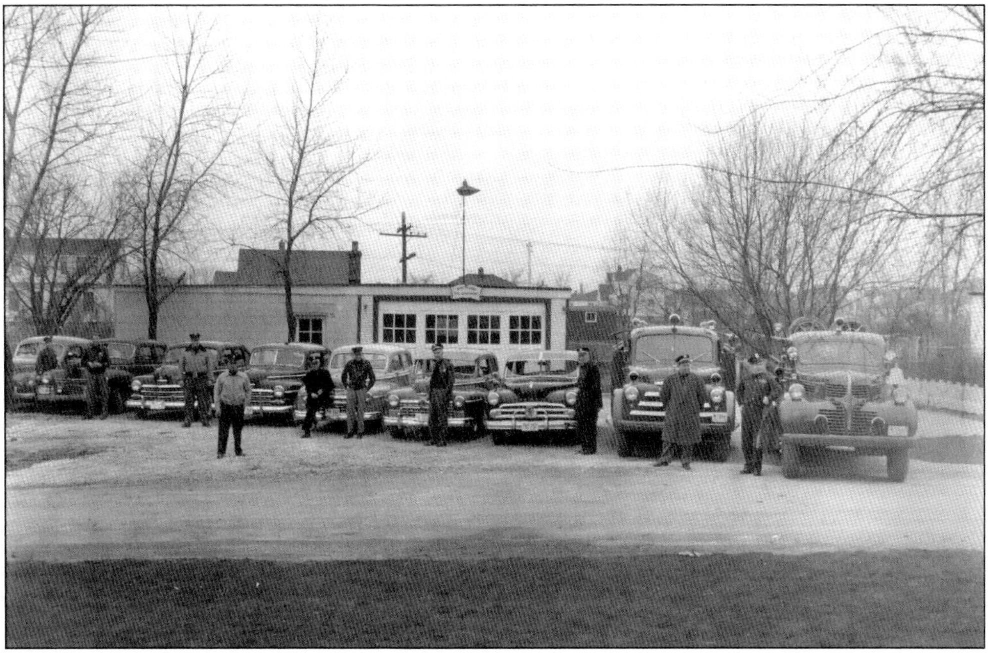

NORTHLAKE FIRE STATION, THEN AND NOW. The original two-bay fire station (pictured above in 1953) now has four bays. The original volunteer fire fighters are no more, as full-time, well-equipped men and women handle all types of fires and emergencies today. (Above, courtesy of Northlake City Hall; below, author's collection.)

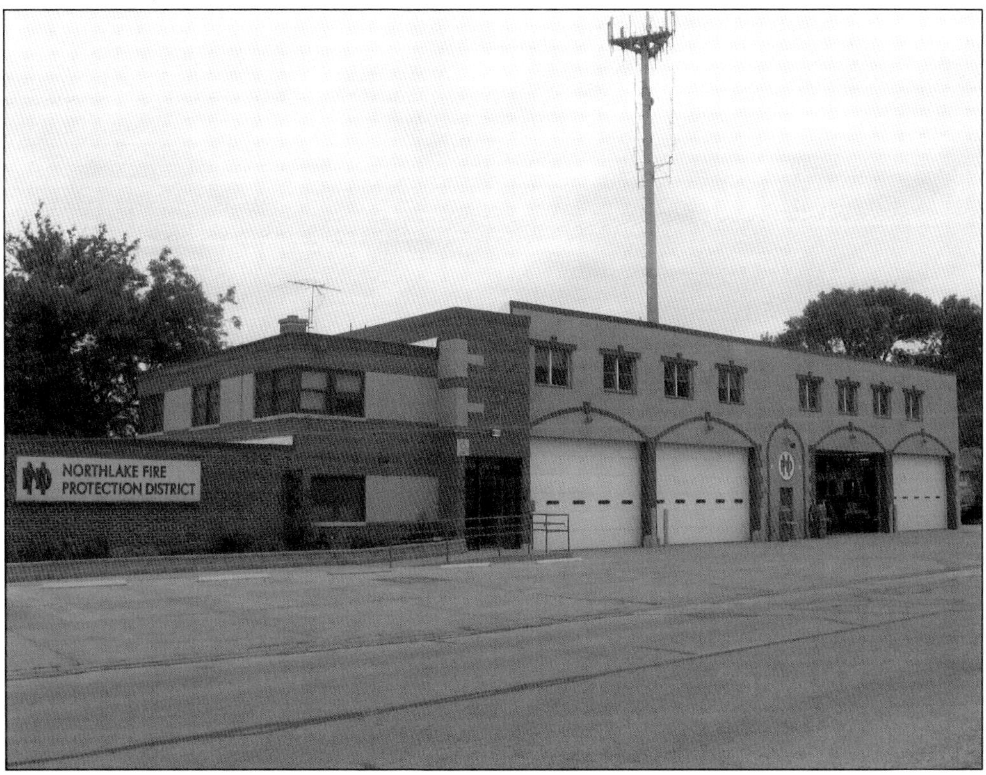

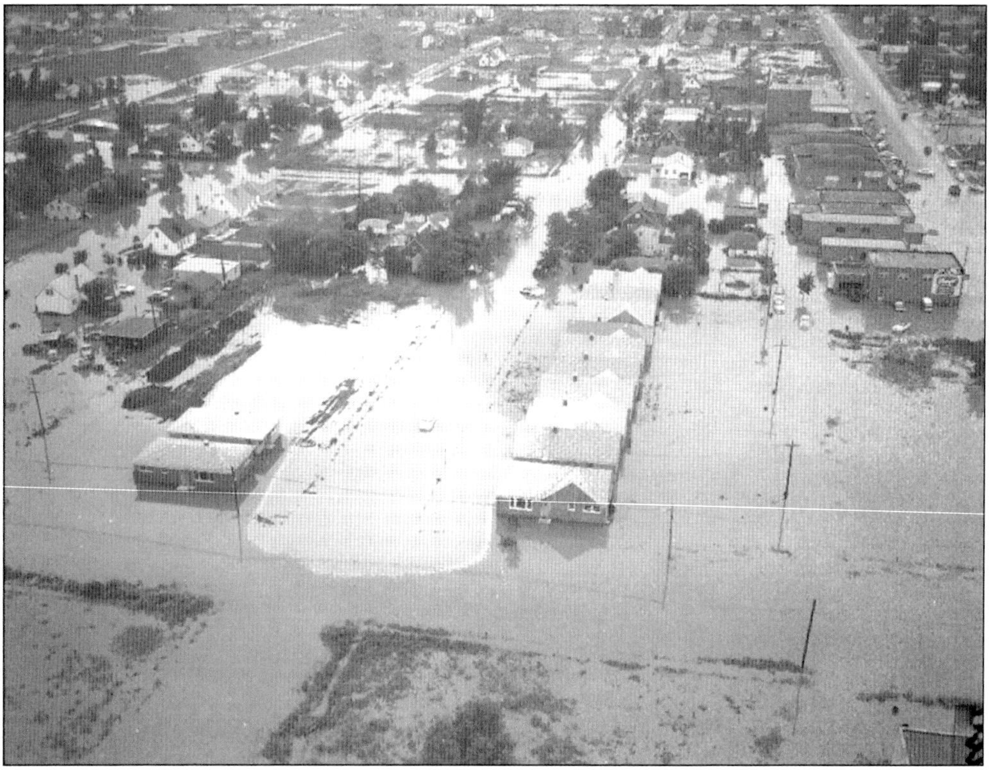

1957 Flooding. This aerial photograph shows extensive flooding in parts of Northlake. Flooding was a common problem for the growing community. (Courtesy of William Piper.)

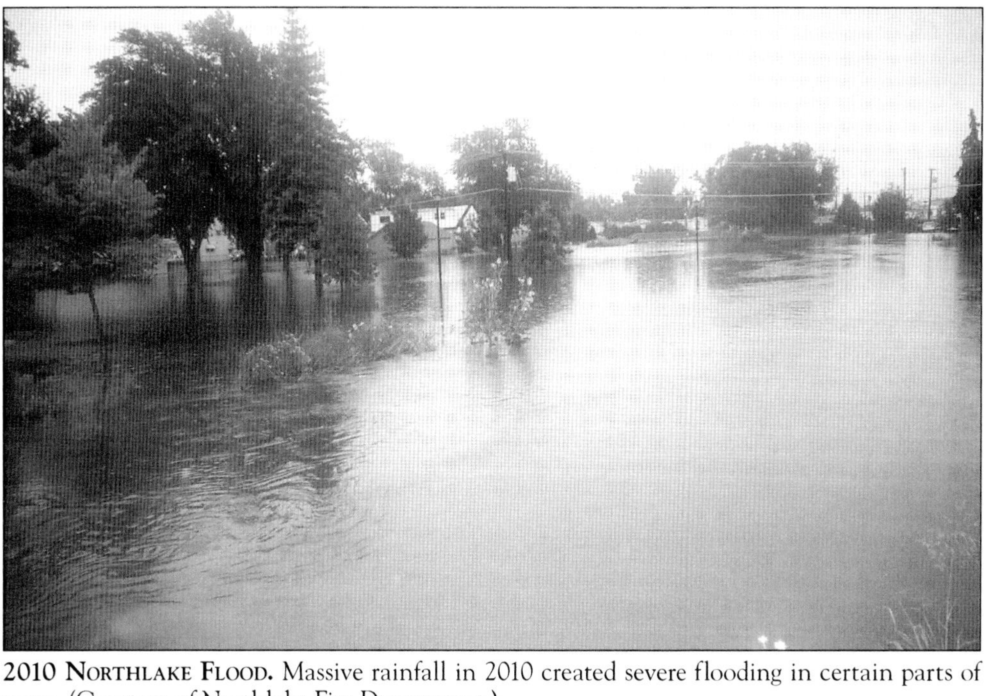

2010 Northlake Flood. Massive rainfall in 2010 created severe flooding in certain parts of town. (Courtesy of Northlake Fire Department.)

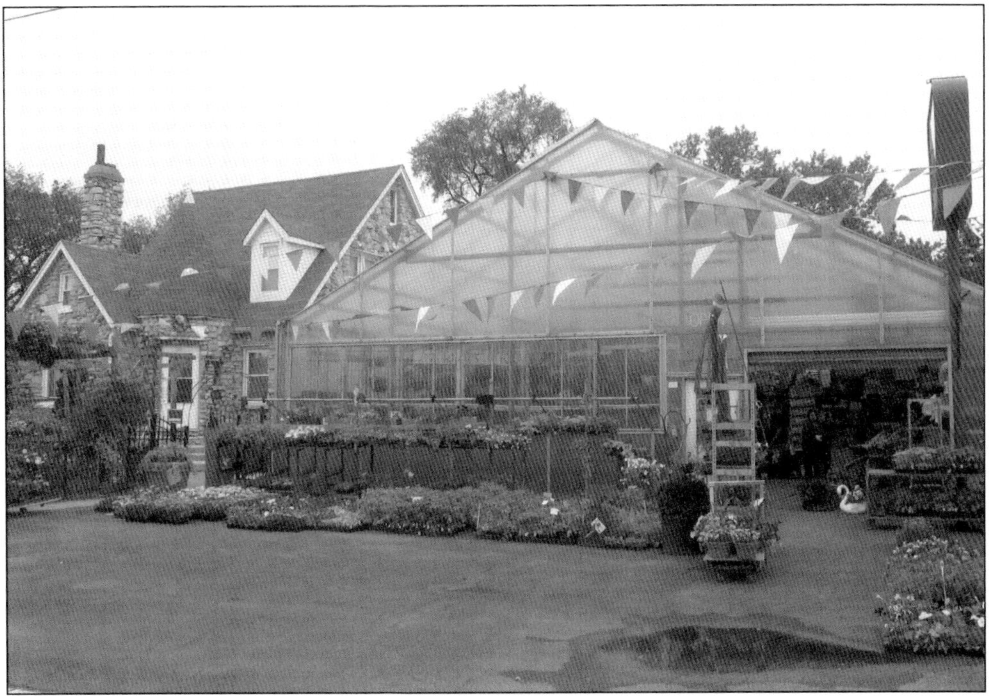

Lou's Garden Center and Alejandra's Restaurant. One of the first homes built along North Avenue was this one, which now serves as Lou's Garden Center, which also includes a greenhouse to grow plants, herbs, and vegetables. This business is one of the oldest still open in Northlake and always participates in parades and other community events. Directly across the street, the popular Alejandra's Restaurant (below) provides excellent Mexican food and outdoor seating. (Both, author's collection.)

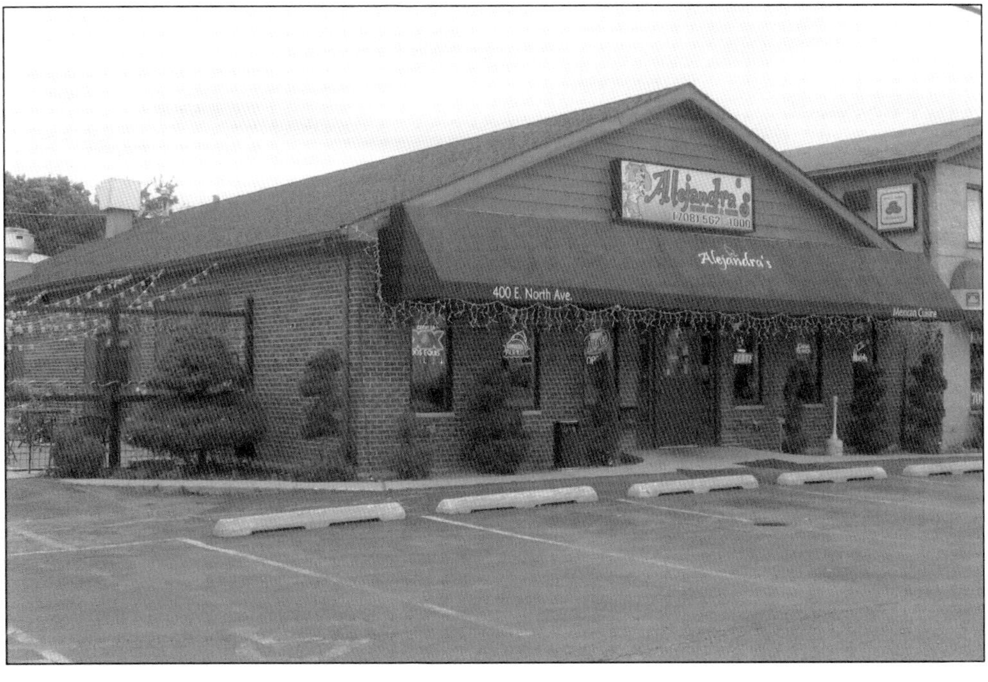

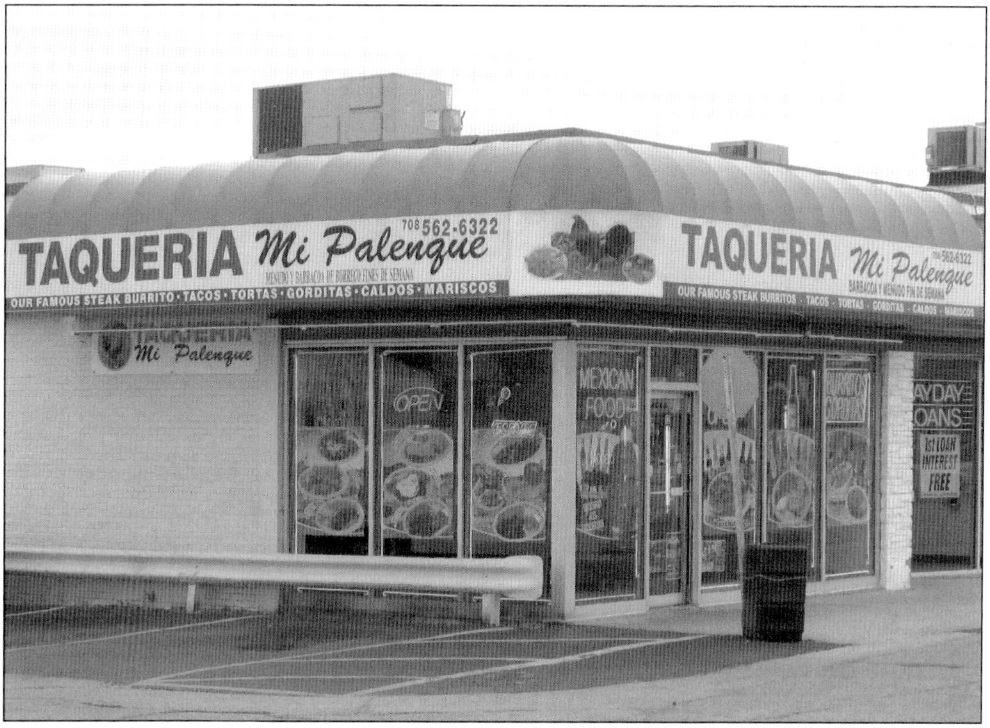

Mi Palenque. Along the strip that used to house Pan's Foods, on the northwest corner of North Avenue and Wolf Road, this Mexican taqueria now serves locals tacos, tortas, and other Mexican dishes. (Author's collection.)

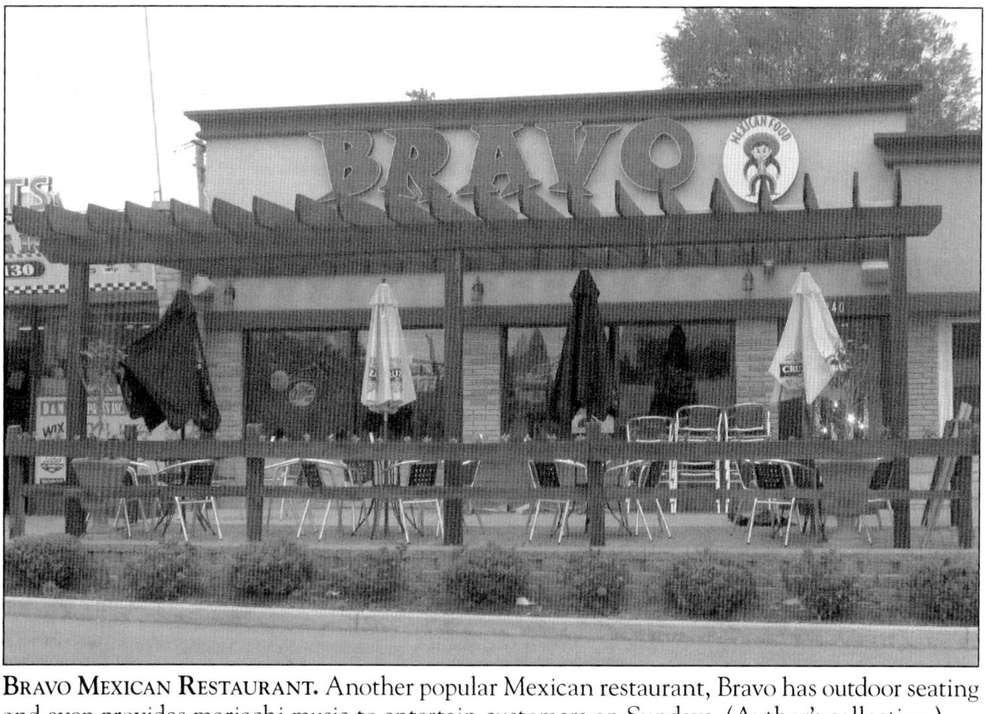

Bravo Mexican Restaurant. Another popular Mexican restaurant, Bravo has outdoor seating and even provides mariachi music to entertain customers on Sundays. (Author's collection.)

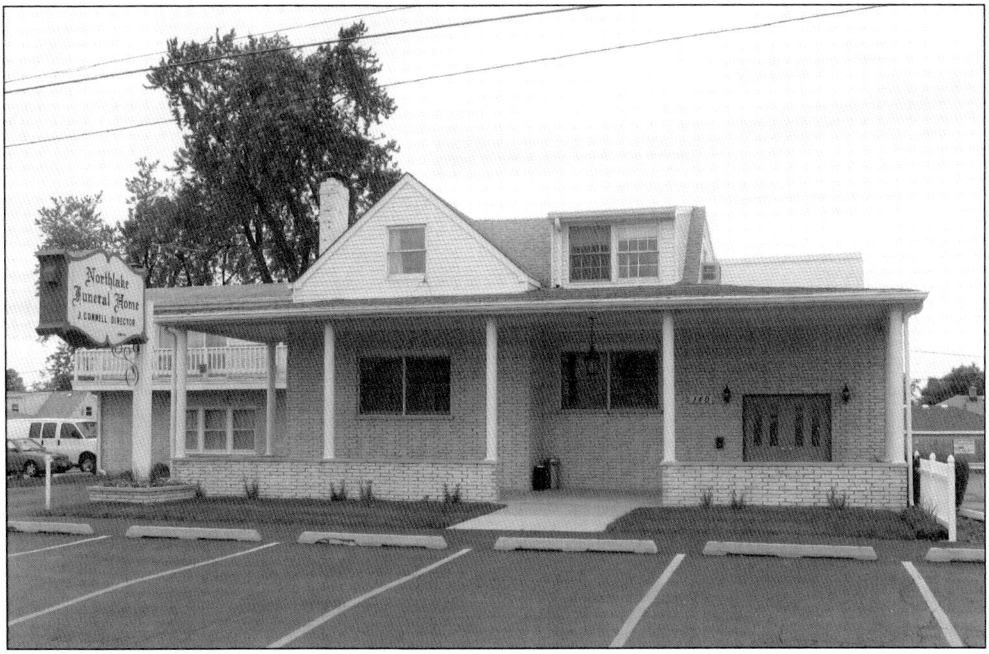

NORTHLAKE FUNERAL HOME. Northlake Funeral Home was started by John and Juanita Connell out of a tiny home in 1965. It has since grown to include multiple rooms, giving more space for grieving families. The original owner's daughter continues to manage the family business to this day. (Author's collection.)

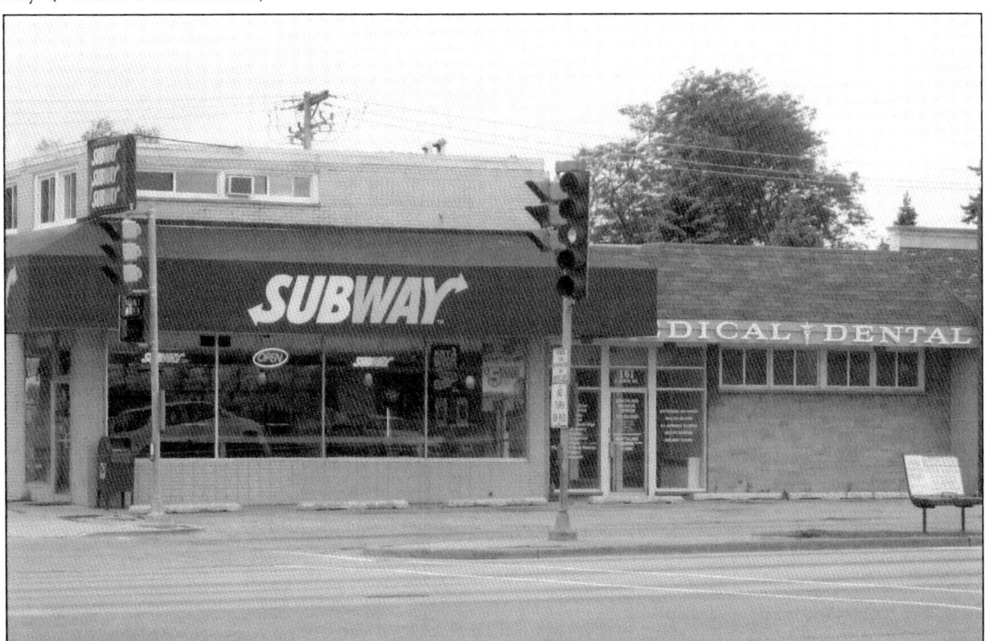

SITE OF GRAY'S DRUG STORE. The original Gray's Drug Store, which served the community well into the 1980s, has since been remodeled into a Subway and a medical and dental center. In the 1980s, it was common to see children ride their bicycles to Gray's Drug Store to purchase comic books and baseball cards. (Author's collection.)

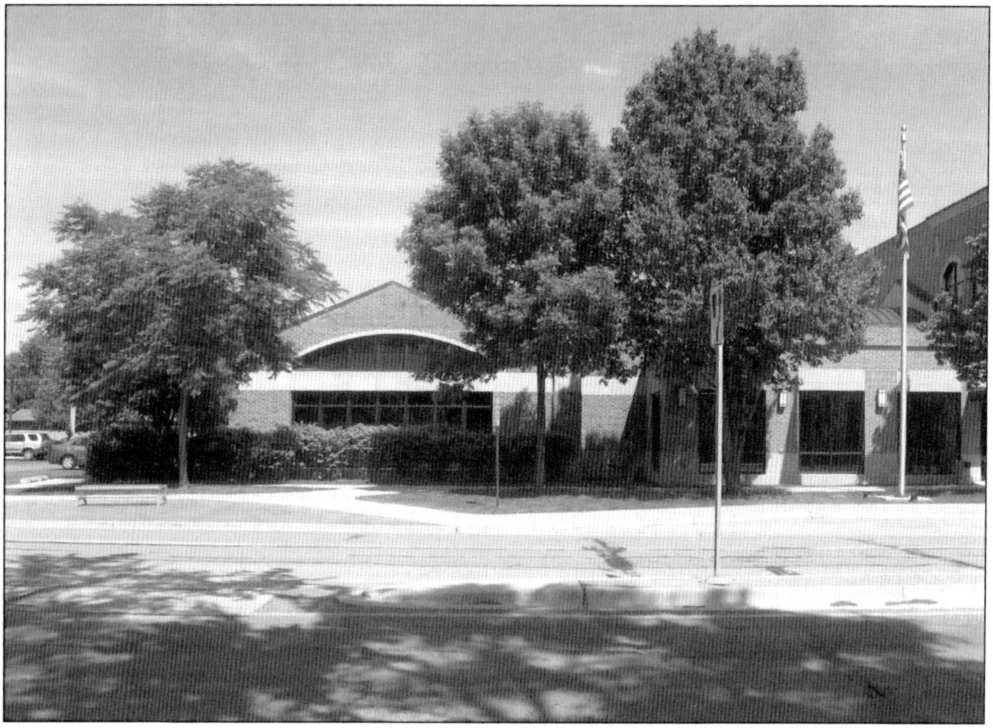

Library. The original library on Wolf Road was dedicated on October 25, 1964. The new library building was built 29 years later, in 1993, and still stands. In 2007, a Prairie-style addition provided more room for programs serving the community. Today, there are approximately 30 staff positions and multiple languages are spoken. (Both, author's collection.)

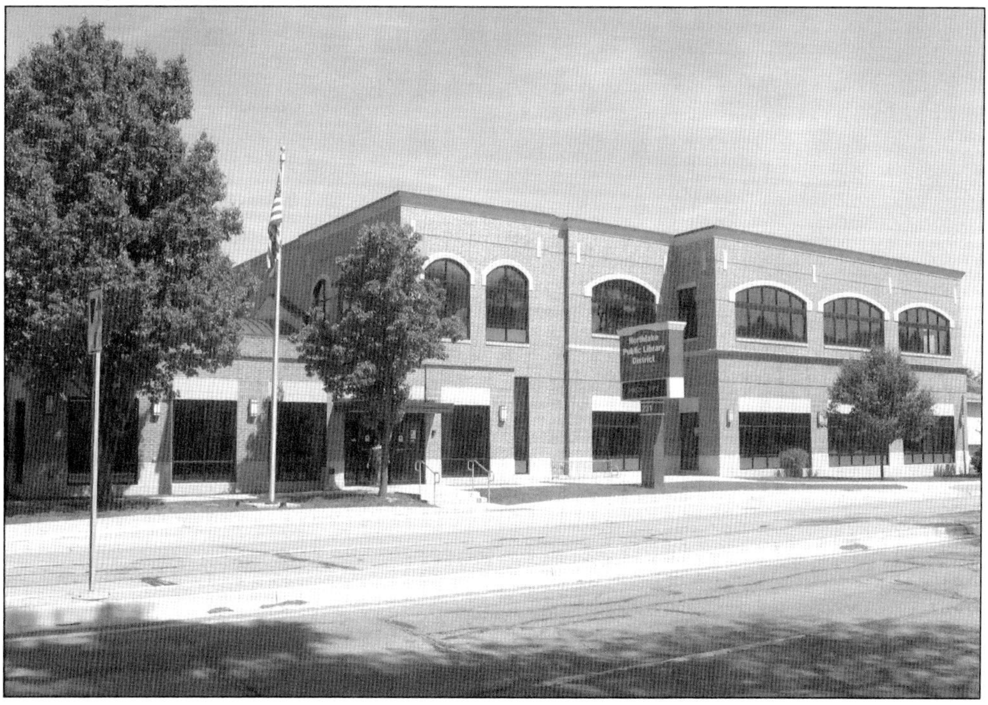

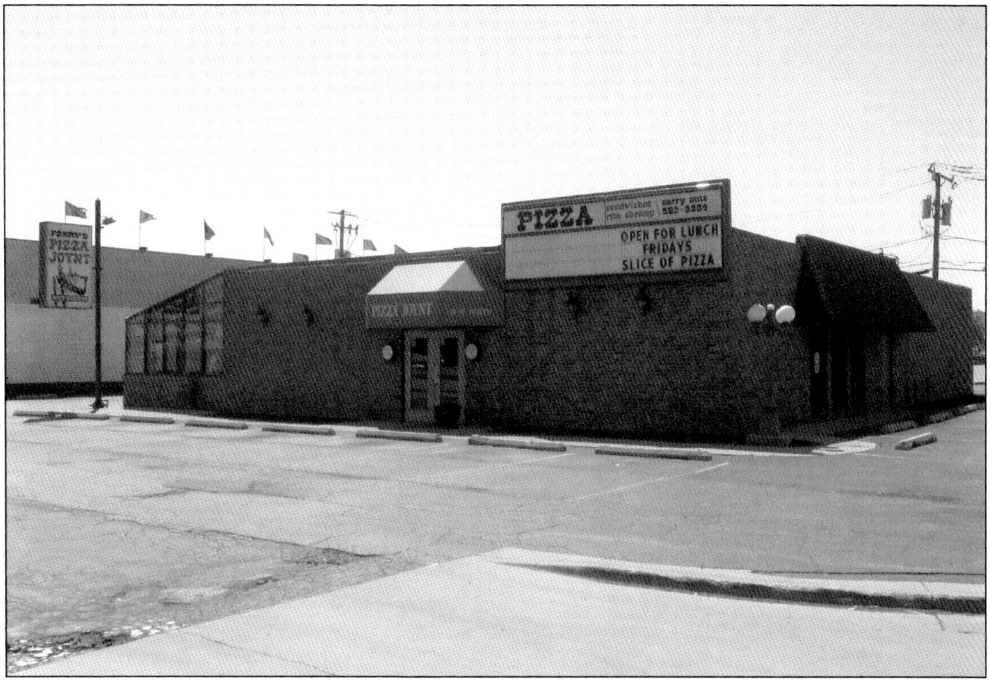

Perry's Pizza Joynt. Perry's Pizza Joynt has been a mainstay in Northlake since it was established in the late 1970s. It later moved to its current location on North Avenue, but Jack Perry continues to run it the same way he did decades ago. (Author's collection.)

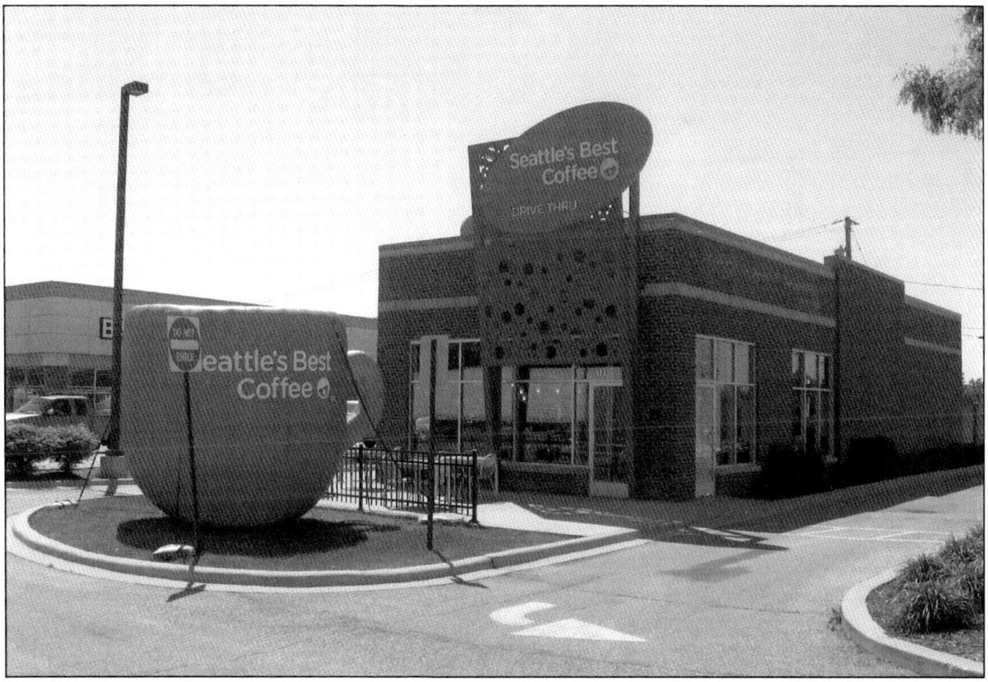

Seattle's Best Coffee. Because of the diversification of the population in recent years, Northlake was selected as the site of a Seattle's Best Coffee concept store, which includes drive-through service. (Author's collection.)

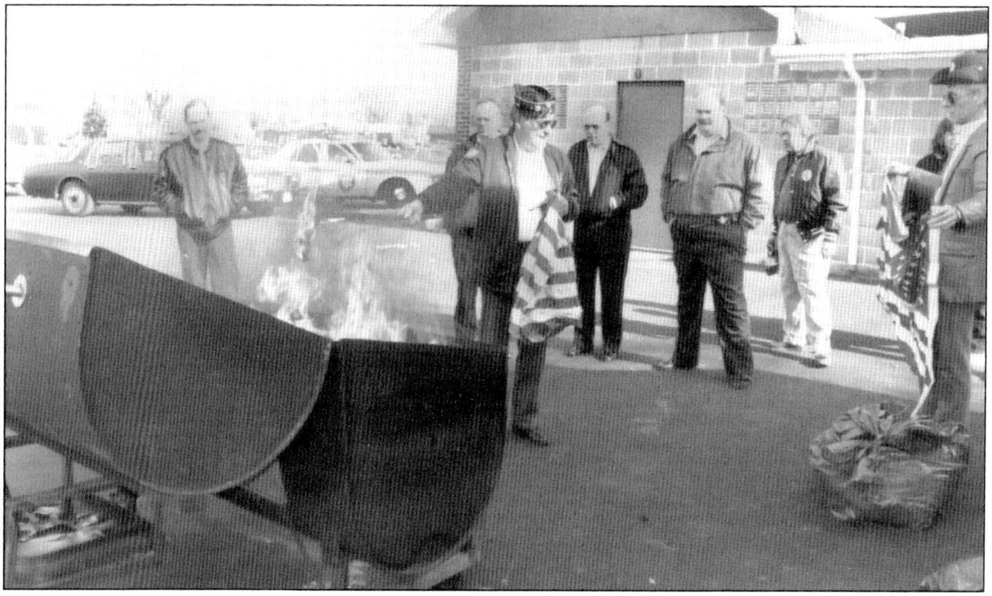

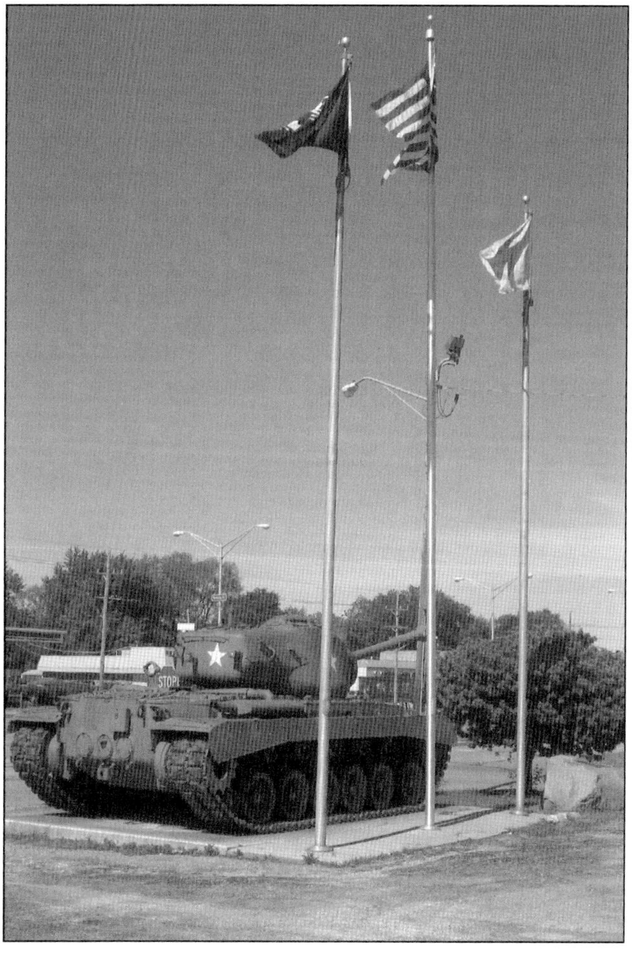

Veterans' Flag Burning. Many traditions remain from decades past. Here, veterans outside the American Legion Howard H. Rohde Post 888 on North Avenue hold a flag burning ceremony to properly dispose of old American flags. (Courtesy of Northlake City Hall.)

Northlake Landmark Tank. One of the most recognizable Northlake landmarks is this tank, which is surrounded by the American flag, the POW flag, and the City of Northlake flag. (Author's collection.)

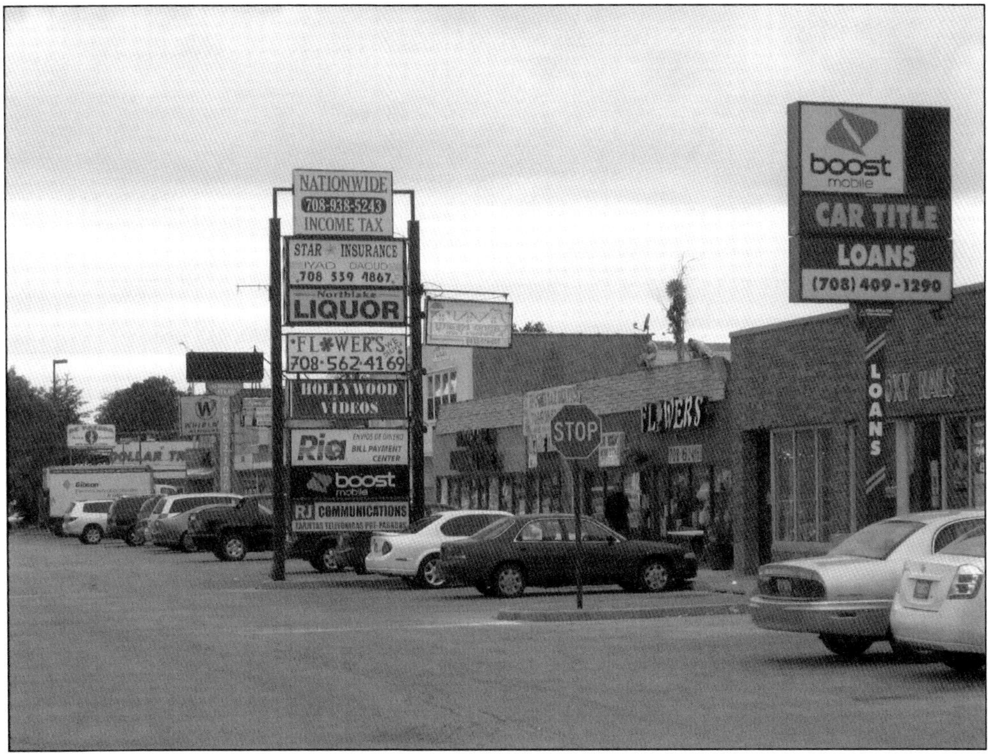

Northlake Shopping Center and Burny Brothers Bakery. The original Northlake Shopping Center, built in 1968, remains the same today in many ways. While the taxi service business that was founded under Mayor Neri is no longer there, small businesses such as a flower shop, a cell phone store, and a video store continue today. Unfortunately, smells no longer emanate from Burny Brothers Bakery (below). (Above, author's collection; below, courtesy of Mary Black.)

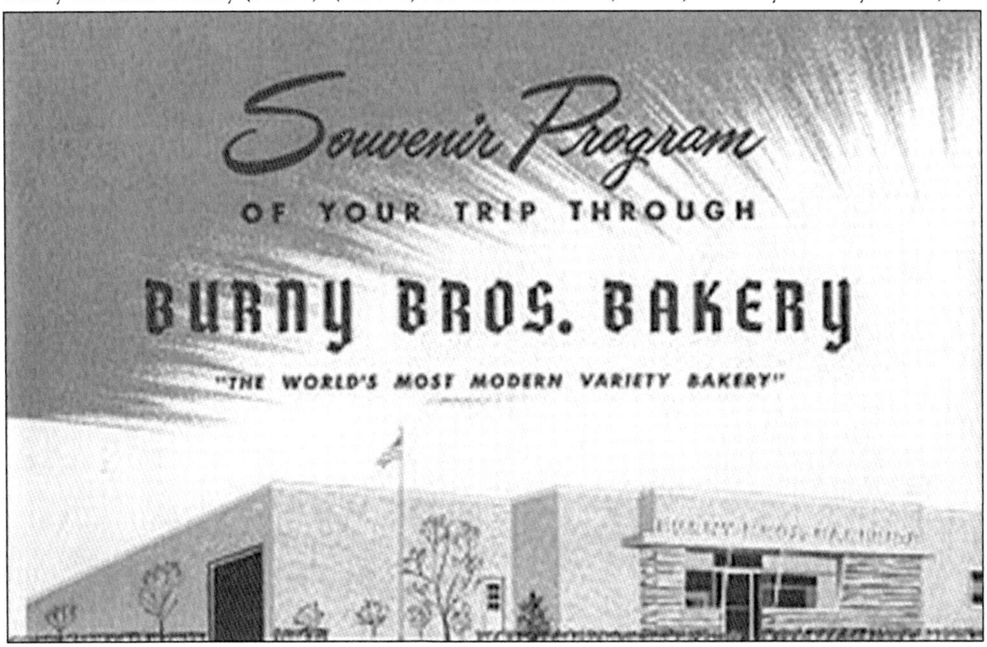

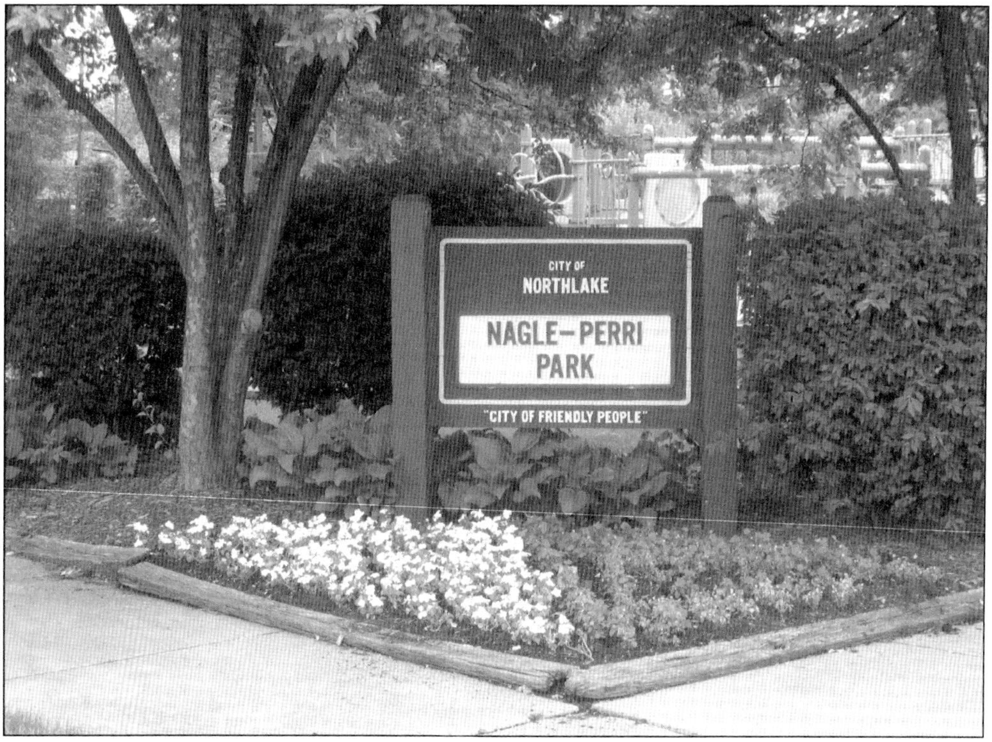

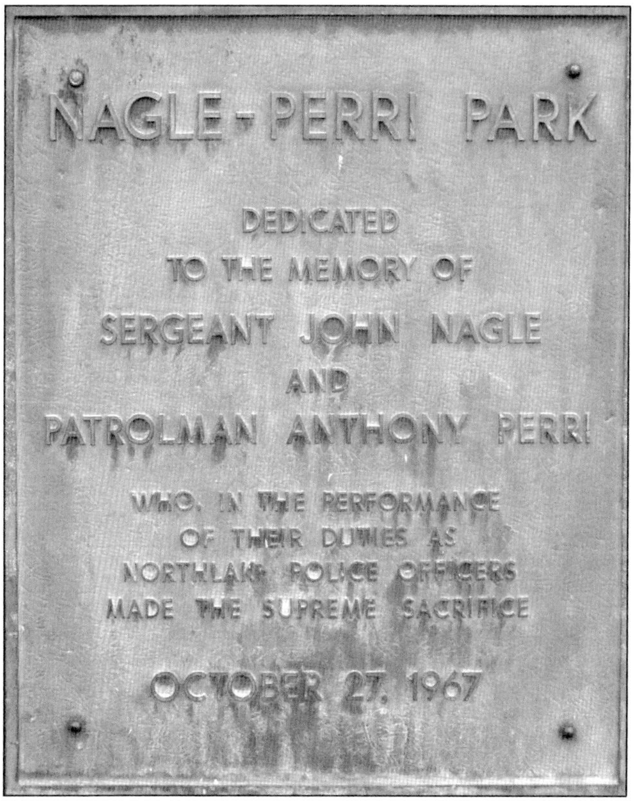

NAGLE-PERRI PARK. The park that was the site of a special ceremony in the early 1970s commemorating the deaths of police officers John Nagle and Anthony Perri continues to be a place of respite and entertainment for children. It is not uncommon to see kids frolicking on the grounds, walking up to the plaque to read it, and learning the history behind the park's name. (Both, author's collection.)

HERE ARE SOME FIGURES

Let us estimate the assessed valuation of the new city at one million dollars. As more homes are built, it will increase....but one million is not too high a base on which to figure. If the tax rate is 67¢ on each $100 of assessed valuation, the income therefrom would be $6,666.00. But experience in other cities shows that a full collection might not be made. Based on an 80% tax collection the total income would be $5,332.80. Additional license and permit fees would bring up the total, judged on experience in neighboring villages. The following tabulation shows the break-down for the various sources and the grand total:

General taxes..(the 67¢ we'd all pay)	$5332.80
Vehicle tags (@ $2.50 per auto for 500 autos)	1250.00
Dog licenses @ $1.25 per dog for 150 dogs	187.50
Building permits @ $25 per permit for 200 homes per year for the next 4 to 5 years	5000.00
Fines for traffic violation and violation of other village ordinances	400.00
Business licenses:	
Grocery, meat market, garages, filling stations, peddlers, restaurants, drug stores, signs, etc.	200.00
Cigarette licenses	100.00
Tavern licenses @ $250 each (now being paid to the County)	1250.00
State Motor Fuel Tax to be used for streets	3600.00
	$17320.30

Remember, these figures are only estimates based on charges now being made in neighboring communities. Likewise, the following expenditures are typical of what might be expected, adapted to a city the size of Northlake.

Salaries of Mayor and six aldermen (may be waived)	$ 300.00
Salary of City Clerk (may be waived)	120.00
(Mayor, aldermen and clerk are elected by us)	
Salary of City treasurer	1200.00
City Hall - Office Rent	250.00
Telephone service	75.00
Light and power	150.00
Postage	40.00
Annual audit	100.00
Gas and oil	35.00
Surety bonds and insurance premiums	200.00
Stationery and office supplies	125.00
Legal service and expense	1200.00
Collection and disposal of garbage	3500.00
Elections	100.00
Truck hire	350.00
Street and Alley maintenance (labor, materials, etc.)	4500.00
Salary of Police Chief (serving also as Building Comm.)	1800.00
Gas and oil for police	500.00
Police supplies	25.00
	$ 14570.00
This leaves us a balance for miscellaneous expenses of	2750.30
	$ 17320.30

Many of these items could be reduced or even eliminated and others might merit an increase. But as a budget for a new city, the above outlay is typical. No pavement? No sewers? No sidewalks? No street-lights? Not now. But an organized government adequate for our needs and laying the groundwork for the future improvements to come.

Financial Situation. Under the leadership of current mayor Jeff Sherwin, financial health has been a priority. This sheet, from the time of Northlake's founding, demonstrates the expenses the city faced with government salaries, licenses, taxes, and other expenses. Now, with large businesses, a strong educational system, and high athletic participation, Northlake has come a long way in the past 72 years. This community, which many labeled a "kick-the-can" community in decades past, continues today as a thriving suburb. (Courtesy of Northlake Public Library.)

DISCOVER THOUSANDS OF LOCAL HISTORY BOOKS FEATURING MILLIONS OF VINTAGE IMAGES

Arcadia Publishing, the leading local history publisher in the United States, is committed to making history accessible and meaningful through publishing books that celebrate and preserve the heritage of America's people and places.

Find more books like this at
www.arcadiapublishing.com

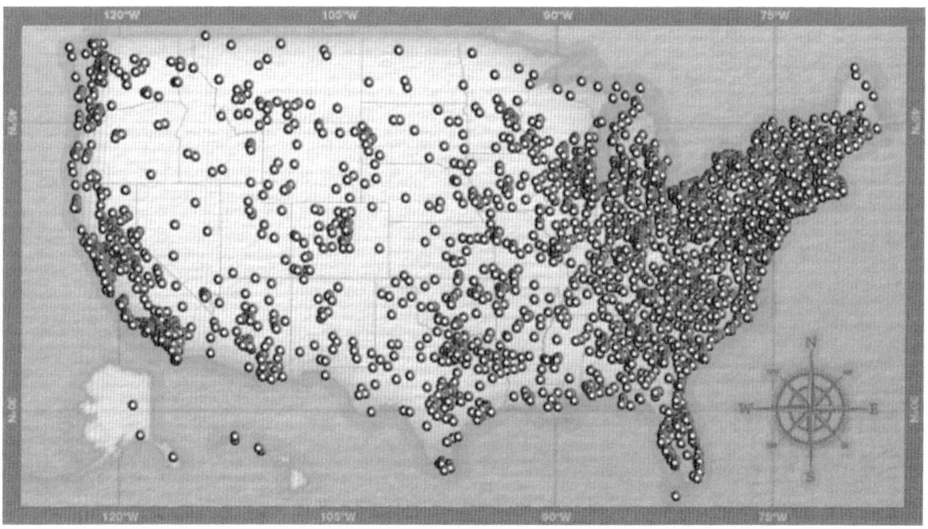

Search for your hometown history, your old stomping grounds, and even your favorite sports team.

Consistent with our mission to preserve history on a local level, this book was printed in South Carolina on American-made paper and manufactured entirely in the United States. Products carrying the accredited Forest Stewardship Council (FSC) label are printed on 100 percent FSC-certified paper.

MADE IN THE USA